THE HAMMARSKJÖLD FORUMS

Case Studies

on

The Role of Law

in the

Settlement of International Disputes

DS518.1
H35
1965

The Southeast Asia Crisis

BACKGROUND PAPERS AND PROCEEDINGS
of
THE EIGHTH HAMMARSKJÖLD FORUM

KENNETH T. YOUNG, JR.
Author of the Working Paper

LYMAN M. TONDEL, JR.
Editor

Published for

THE ASSOCIATION OF THE BAR OF THE CITY OF NEW YORK

by

OCEANA PUBLICATIONS, INC.

DOBBS FERRY, N.Y.

1966

JUL 19 1972

169046

(C) 1966 by

THE ASSOCIATION OF THE BAR OF THE CITY OF NEW YORK

All Rights Reserved

Library of Congress Catalog Card Number: 66-17536

PRINTED IN THE UNITED STATES OF AMERICA

TABLE OF CONTENTS

PART TWO

THE FORUM

APPENDICES

THE EIGHTH HAMMARSKJÖLD FORUM

October 18, 1965

Presiding

THE HONORABLE SAMUEL I. ROSENMAN

President of The Association of the Bar of the City of New York

Moderator

LYMAN M. TONDEL, JR.

*Chairman, Committee on the Lawyer's Role in the Search for Peace,
The Association of the Bar of the City of New York*

Participants

KENNETH T. YOUNG, JR.

Former United States Ambassador to Thailand (1961-1963)

LEONARD C. MEEKER

Legal Adviser to the Department of State

ARTHUR LARSON

*Professor of Law and Director of the World Rule of Law Center
at Duke University*

H.E. RADHAKRISHNA RAMANI

*Malaysian Ambassador and Permanent Representative to the
United Nations*

EDITOR'S FOREWORD

This is the eighth in the series of books based on the Hammar-skjöld Forums that are being conducted by The Association of the Bar of the City of New York as case studies on "The Role of Law in the Settlement of International Disputes". The first seven books were based on Forums on the Berlin-German crisis; the United Nations action in the Congo; the Cuban crisis of October, 1962; Disarmament; the international position of Communist China; the Panama Canal; and the *Sabbatino* case in the United States Supreme Court.

The Forum on "The Southeast Asia Crisis" on which this book is based was the second dealing with Asian problems. Since the Forum was held on October 18, 1965, at a time when emotions and frustrations were running high over the increasing involvement of the United States in Vietnam, there were those who would have preferred a presentation focused solely on that involvement and on the Vietnamese problem. The Committee decided, however, that the educational purposes of these Forums would be better served by trying to present the Southeast Asian problems, including that of Vietnam, in broader perspective.

As it developed, the discussion again brought out the degree to which Communist China is at the center of many of the world's major disputes, especially those in Asia. The Working Paper prepared by O. Edmund Clubb for Volume 5 of this series on "The International Position of Communist China" and the Working Paper prepared by former Ambassador Kenneth T. Young, Jr. for this volume, read together, provide an excellent basis for understanding the genesis of many of the current disputes in Asia. As any lawyer knows, the starting point in resolving disputes is to understand the facts and the motives.

What can the role of law be in settling the disputes in Vietnam and elsewhere in Asia? As stated in the forewords to the first four volumes in this series, when the Forums were inaugurated:

". . . It was deliberately decided to consider disputes of the first magnitude, involving political, military, economic and social, as well as legal, problems. It was understood that existing law might be found to play a minor role in these controversies. Yet it was felt that the role of law, whatever it might be, should be more fully appreciated because if there is to be meaningful progress towards international arms control or disarmament and the elimination of war as a means of settling international disputes, then means of settlement alternate to war—means under law—must be developed."

It was also emphasized that:

"If, as we must hope, fear of nuclear devastation is to drive the nations into finding means of peacefully solving controversies with each other, the search for such means can only be hastened by greater understanding of what actions, ambitions, needs or ideologies lead to critical disputes; of what procedures and devices have helped solve such disputes, and what have not; of what new law is evolving in connection with efforts to solve such disputes; of the extent to which rulers have had regard for at least the pretext of legality; and of what sanctions and obligations have restrained them the most."

At the Forum on Southeast Asia, Leonard C. Meeker, the Legal Adviser to the Department of State, emphasized the necessarily growing role of law in these words:

". . . Some will consider it remarkable that law has *any* relation to the politically-charged and grim military struggle for power in Southeast Asia. The element of law was not present much, if at all, in the two World Wars or in the armed conflicts of earlier centuries.

"Modern technology being what it is, international law has been transformed from a luxury to a necessity. Its role and influence will grow in the future. Progress will be recorded as more nations become convinced that law is better than force."

And Ambassador Ramani pithily put it this way:

". . . we lawyers as a class could be and indeed often are to an extent the cement that holds a new society together so that it is not dominated by emotionalism. . . ."

More specifically, Ambassador Young explained the role demanded of lawyers, and many other professionals, if the Mekong Community and the Mekong River Project are to become a reality—a vital force in stabilizing and developing the independent nations of Southeast Asia.

Such bar association programs as these Hammarskjöld Forums can do no more than add a jot to the knowledge of a *very* influential group—the American bar—regarding the background of major international disputes, with some suggestions as to the role law has played, and must play to an ever-increasing degree, if there is to be a generally peaceful world instead of, in due course, a nuclear war. Time is running out, and we lawyers, as well as others, must accelerate our knowledge, our understanding, our concern and our participation. To that end The Association of the Bar of the City of New York conducts these Forums.

In addition to distribution through usual channels, the volumes are being distributed by the Association, with the aid of a grant from the Ford Foundation and contributions from a large number of individuals in honor of the 90th birthday of James N. Rosenberg, Esq., one of those who helped most in instituting the Forums. The distribution of the volumes is to about 1,000 carefully selected leaders of the bar in the field of international law, teachers in related fields, and organizations interested in foreign affairs. Their reception has been excellent.

Without reporting all their names, our gratitude goes out again to all those who have helped in continuing the Hammarskjöld Forums —contributors, Officers and Executive Committee Members, Committee Members, Association Staff, and Participants. We acknowledge particularly, however, at this time the unique and irreplaceable contribution of the late Joseph L. Andrews, the distinguished, indefatigable, and learned Reference Librarian of the Association, to whom so much of the credit is due for the comprehensive bibliographies in all of the prior volumes in this series.

Lyman M. Tondel, Jr.

PART ONE

THE WORKING PAPER

The Southeast Asia Crisis *

KENNETH T. YOUNG, JR.

I. *INTRODUCTION: SOUTHEAST ASIA IN CONFLICT*

Turmoil and revolution, disunion and conflict, describe Southeast Asia. Yet, it has neither regional definition nor an interstate system in terms of politics and law.* What we call Southeast Asia is in fact a loose and disconnected collection of very independent nations, over 200 million people, numerous minorities, countless dialects, and such a diverse pattern of customs and peoples that anthropologists cannot decide whether unifying or divergent elements are predominant. From the point of view of politics and law, what we call Southeast Asia today and for the foreseeable future is far more centrifugal and divisive than it is cohesive or unitary. This is a so-called region without any feeling for community, without much sense of shared values and with few common institutions. If Southeast Asia were unimportant and non-strategic, these crosscurrents and differences would be of little account. However, Southeast Asia is now a crossroads of world power politics, the cold war, and many converging interests. As the news each day demonstrates, these conflicting and converging interests have brought about hostilities rather than peace, violence instead of order. Southeast Asia is a crossroads of chaos. It has no stop lights, no policemen and no rules of the road to control the congestion of all the internal and external traffic which is crowding this volatile and vulnerable intersection of peace and war in the twentieth century. Southeast Asia is an area of the world where there is power without law, and law with no power.

Inter-state and Internal Tensions

Each one of the nations of Southeast Asia is in opposition to at least one of its neighbors. The political and even military cross-

---

* The area now includes Burma, Cambodia, Laos, Thailand, the Republic of Vietnam (Saigon), the Democratic Republic of Vietnam (Hanoi), Malaysia, Singapore, the Philippines, and Indonesia.

5

fire among these nations has fractured whatever solidarity and cohesion might otherwise have developed. Burma has closed itself off in a kind of reverse "hermitage" and doesn't really want to have anything to do with anybody in the outside world. Cambodia has broken relations with Thailand and South Vietnam and carries on a kind of verbal warfare by radio and press with these two historical enemies. Malaysia and the Philippines have not established diplomatic relations since Malaysia's formation in 1963 because of their dispute over an issue of sovereignty in North Borneo. Laos does not have diplomatic relations with South Vietnam but does with North Vietnam. Communist China and Communist Vietnam are continuing to seek the overthrow of neighboring non-communist governments and to capture political control in Southeast Asia. From the southern part of the area, Sukarno, backed by the Indonesian Communist party, has left the United Nations and declared a campaign of "confrontation" against Malaysia and all countries supporting Malaysia.

Within each one of the Southeast Asian countries numerous minorities, most of them ethnic, either oppose their central governments in some fashion or are unabsorbed in the nation. The old and traditional societies of Southeast Asia are far less integrated as nations than appears on the surface. Nor are their boundaries as nation-states any more solidified than is the cohesion of their minorities. Internal crossfires tend to make some of the countries more like collections of competing groups than like stable nations. These observations apply less to Thailand and Cambodia than to their neighbors.

Unfortunately, Southeast Asia as an area lacks the processes and institutions for dealing with all of these crossfires, divergencies and disputes. A sense of community with a unifying theme and a set of shared values has been lacking to such an extent that Southeast Asia does not have regional structures for collective defense or mutual development. Nor is there any significant machinery or presence of the United Nations there for keeping the peace and resolving disputes on an international basis, although various permanent and *ad hoc* agencies of the United Nations have taken an active part in helping to deal with many political and economic problems in specific independent Southeast Asian countries since World War II.

Leaders in the governments of Southeast Asia have not had a great deal of experience in diplomacy and international relations for dealing with each other. They have had to learn by doing as they went along during the past twenty years. Under colonialism, these countries were shut off into watertight compartments linked exclusively to the metropolitan dominator which handled all foreign relations and kept the indigenous élite out of the affairs of war and peace. With the exception of Thailand which was never colonized, these independent countries began the post-war period with no modern experience in independent diplomacy and few, if any, people trained to handle international relations. Even today the best talent is sent outside of Southeast Asia to the United Nations or other diplomatic missions. Nationalist leaders, so intent on revolution, independence, and reconstruction at home, have remained ignorant of their immediate neighbors. The educational curriculum in most of these countries has focussed on European and American history rather than on national or Asian history.

A shift in leadership in these countries is making the task difficult. During the past twenty years, the international politics of Southeast Asia developed as the personal handiwork of the great leaders of national independence. They were the lawgivers of nationalism and independence. After throwing off the colonial yoke, they determined the initial decisions on foreign policy in the early years of independence. These nation-makers had world prestige and domestic command. As they leave the scene, one by one, lack of new authoritative leadership adds to the centrifugal and divisive forces at work in Southeast Asia. The viewpoint of the next generation of leaders there is one of the key variables. Some new leaders will be rooted more in their own culture and customs than were the Asian personalities of the past twenty years. Others will be internationally-oriented and cosmopolitan-styled. Leadership—old or young—will continue to pursue national transformation.

Southeast Asia is in revolution. Nationalism inspires the people. These old societies of Southeast Asia are changing themselves rapidly and radically. For twenty years each one of these countries has confronted revolution and created revolutionary groups. Modernization is social revolution. Revolutionary change rather than the *status quo* is the pattern in both rural and urban areas in Southeast Asia. Revolutionary groups, nationalist and communist, wish to move much faster than have conservative groups in clearing away old traditions and setting up new patterns. An increasing majority of the population is getting younger and attitudes towards respect for tradition and law are changing. Whatever its faults and excesses, communism captures some of the youth and commits them to work for the people and the nation—at least for a while. The key in this dangerous crossroads is the response of youth. Will the young people—especially the college students—become committed enough to sacrifice something for their own countries as the Chinese youth seem to do in Communist China?

Factors for Regional Cohesiveness

Offsetting some of these centrifugal and divisive forces discouraging the development of regional order in Southeast Asia are several positive and affirmative factors. It is first necessary to emphasize that the nations of Southeast Asia remain vehemently independent after nearly twenty years, even if they are not all convincingly viable or cohesive internally. Their nationalism may be abrasive but it is basic. And nationalism in many forms is the ideology of Southeast Asia. If a system of international law requires a group of independent states, that test is met. The people and leaders of Southeast Asia are passionately devoted to their own independence and sovereignty and to equality with Western and all other countries. A theory and strategy for stabilizing the area can begin with eight constituencies for foundation. But these countries now have highly synthesized, diversely-influenced societies and institutions with an aptitude for selective absorption complementing their pride and sensivity over independence.

Southeast Asia has never been an isolated corner in world history. It is the most internationalized section of the globe. The migrations of many different nations and cultures have converged

8

here for the past 2500 years of recorded history. Even Greeks, Romans, and Scythians left some imprint. Southeast Asia is called Indochina or Further India because India and China have both so influenced the kingdoms and cultures. For 2000 years one overlay of foreign influence after another has covered this area: The Indians of different kingdoms and empires with their Hinduism, Buddhism and commerce, the Mongols with force, the Chinese Empire since 200 B.C. with a "tributary system," the Arabs with Islam, the European powers with colonialism, the Japanese militarists, with occupation and war, the Americans with massive assistance and cosmopolitan customs, and the United Nations with technicians. Despite this cultural and political inundation of conquerors, missionaries, traders, adventurers, pirates, emperors, kings, presidents and prime ministers, the nations and societies of Southeast Asia have survived not only intact, but with their own style.

Perhaps that is the single most significant statement to make about Southeast Asia. It is the vital factor for community-building. The most characteristic attribute of these gifted if volatile and competitive peoples is their capacity to respond to outside stimulus, to absorb foreign influence, and to synthesize what they want into their own culture. Their synthesis of the principles and practices of many types of law demonstrates this remarkable faculty. Despite intense external pressure, Southeast Asians have resisted and avoided foreign conformity. Neither the comprehensiveness of Indian culture, the formidable power of Imperial China, or the technological impact of European colonialism obliterated them culturally or politically. This capacity for independent synthesis may well be the starting point for a new system of regional structure and cohesion.

Within the countries and cultures of Southeast Asia the tradition of law is ancient and professional, although it is today a combination of law quite different from what we know in the Americas or in Europe. Each country has its own customary law going back many centuries. The various traditional religions of Southeast Asia, Hinduism, Buddhism and Islam, emphasize the concepts of law and rules of social order. The concepts are universal, the rules intricate. The human being in Southeast Asia today has

9

to operate in a complex combination of customs and regulations handed down over the centuries. Most of ancient Southeast Asia adopted the Hindu scriptures and systems of legend and law so that the laws of Manu, the Ramayana and the Mahabharata with their precepts and norms were added to the traditional folklore and practices of the indigenous people to form the codes of law and jurisprudence under kingship. Buddhism then added the laws of Kharma and Dharma to Hinduism in Burma, Thailand, Laos, Cambodia, Vietnam and Indonesia for awhile. Then the law of the Koran became predominant in Malaya, Indonesia, and the southern Philippines. Out of this synthesis, justice and adjudication with respect for the law have formed part of the tradition as well as the foundation for independent Southeast Asia states for over 1000 years. Now they have added a considerable body of European and American law. The profession of the bar, the administration of justice, and the independence of the judiciary are not only the legacy of the past but the practice of the present.

New law grows in an atmosphere of common goals. Although Southeast Asia has not yet begun to develop a full sense of community or a systematic regional structure, the countries share the objectives of nation-building and a self-interest in world peace, while their policies and methods differ profoundly. Even though development is national and internal, the politicians, administrators and technicians in Southeast Asia find their preoccupation with social and economic development a common experience and a mutual urge. Notwithstanding their political and personal rivalries and feuds creating so many crossfires of political and even military hostilities, the wisest leaders, along with the educated people, and the population as a whole, want peace because they all know that war of any kind will destroy the revolution and prevent the creation of new societies out of old ones. The firing line will destroy the fruits of construction. The interest in peace and development is such a strong motive and incentive that it could facilitate an interest in and sacrifice for regional stability.

Fortunately, the peaceful development of Southeast Asia has a surplus of resources as well as a surfeit of turmoil. Food, space and natural endowment exist in relative abundance compared to the rest of Asia and much of the so-called developing world. They can feed themselves and export rice at least for another generation, unless their rapid population growth is not stabilized in time. There is land for the farmers and space for new towns or urban explosion. The internal resources in the land, in the oceans and under the seas are as diverse and complete as they are incalculable and extensive. The missing ingredient is management and a system for employing all this food, space and resources for their internal use and for trading with China, India and Japan.

A regional system for Southeast Asia would also take advantage of the similarity of life of the peoples in these countries. While there is much diversity in politics, religion and customs, 85% of the people live on the land or are connected with it. The rural way of life is much the same from Eastern Java to North Burma, from the Hanoi Delta to the tip of Sumatra. The village people share poverty, illness and ignorance. They also farm in much the same way, live in similar houses, organize their communities much alike, and seek identical goals today: health, education, justice, betterment and tranquillity.

The weakness in Southeast Asia is the lack of political leadership and organized incentive to put all of these positive factors to work for a revolutionary nationalism and peaceful progress. The traditional vacuum between autocratic ruler and suspicious population, between distant officials and neglected villagers, still typifies Southeast Asian politics. Paternalistic government operates from the top down. Law and order are compulsions of the privileged few to lord over the herded many. They obey from apathy, indifference and fear, not desire. But even if leadership were available to generate genuinely popular movements, there would be international complications and crosscurrents intensifying the internal intersection of interests and disputes. These international factors also add many centrifugal and divisive forces to the development and stability of Southeast Asia.

Much depends on whether or not the interests of external powers will permit freedom for new leadership and educated professional groups. Revolution can be an indiscriminate selector as well as a discriminating destroyer. The revolutionary crosscurrents which can change and destroy are so uncontrolled today in

11

Southeast Asia that the bargaining and mediating process which time requires for a true synthesis may not have time to produce a new combination of internal and external elements. In this respect, the contemporary crisis differs radically with the past. In the first place, China now menaces their independence in their view. During at least the past 1000 years, the kingdoms of Southeast Asia were relatively free to develop and synthesize as they saw fit. The international system, if one can call it that, was permissive and tolerant. The Indian kingdoms and empires did not seek to dominate Southeast Asia or establish colonies by conquest. Even the Mongols stopped from conquering Burma, Thailand, and all Vietnam. The Ming and Ch'ing emperors left the Southeast Asian countries, except for Vietnam, undisturbed militarily and exhorted them to accept the benefits of a sophisticated and complex international system of "overlords." The Chinese Empire never did conquer the Southeast Asian kingdoms or control them by force, except for Vietnam. Today a strong and militant China seeks to establish political hegemony in Southeast Asia. Secondly, the Southeast Asians now for the first time, apart from colonial rule, have a counterweight to Chinese ambitions. A Western power, the United States, is able to deter and contain Chinese power. In addition, there are the sanctions of the United Nations and international opinion to support the independence and survival of these countries.

This suggests that the future of the region either in war or peace cannot be divorced from the collective peace of the Atlantic as well as the Asian world as a whole. Regional equilibrium would be part of a "cluster" of countervailing, reciprocal associations of law, power, and policy. How a community in Southeast Asia might evolve would depend not only on the internal tensions within these states and their inter-regional relationships but also on the stability of relationships among the major powers and their ability to prevent the outbreak of disruptive and uncontrollable forces.

The Participants in the Conflict

Before going on to analyze some of the historical, political, sociological and legal factors substantially bearing on the conflict in what we loosely call Southeast Asia, it may be helpful to consider who are the parties, what are the terms of the conflict, and whether there can be negotiations in a bargaining situation. Clearly this area is not comparable to modern Europe nor even the Balkans. It is a complex collection of hostile participants, diverging interests and conflicting claims. And yet, like all human communities, some common values and prospects can probably be found. It is with these in mind that blueprints for some regional order, even of a minimal kind, can perhaps be devised by the parties in negotiations to resolve the basic terms of the conflict.

There are four sets of parties at interest: (1) the states of Southeast Asia; (2) non-regional and non-communist states including Canada, the United States, the United Kingdom, Australia, New Zealand, India, Pakistan, Japan and France; (3) the communist states of the People's Republic of China, the Soviet Union, Poland, and the Democratic Republic of Vietnam; and (4) several international organizations, including the principal organs of the United Nations in New York, its regional agencies in Southeast Asia and the Mekong Committee of four Southeast Asian countries in particular, the Southeast Asia Treaty Organization with its eight members, the Association of Southeast Asian States comprising Thailand, Malaysia and the Philippines, and the Geneva Conference of 14 members as a separate political institution with a distinct legal framework. This division into four sets of parties shows the complexity of the problem in Southeast Asia because a party in one set may also be involved in one or more of the others. The broad issue in the Southeast Asian conflict is to see whether any strategy can be devised for finding converging interests among the parties in these four sets, and whether there is a bargaining situation and negotiation process for them, in turn, to "litigate" some of their common disputes and some of their common stakes for a general settlement or a series of major and minor settlements.

One starts with this Southeast Asia grouping of ancient countries and states now undergoing violent social, economic and political change partly as a result of internal pressures, but mainly forced from outside. These states are objectives as well as participants in a struggle between outside powers not unlike many which have taken place in other parts of the world, except that here there is an unusual combination of geographic, political and demographic elements creating conflict. However, there are factors offering some prospects for an equilibrium based on legal institutions and a respect for a satisfactory social and legal order.

Apart from Indonesia and Vietnam, all of the states in this area are members of the United Nations. One of their leading citizens is its Secretary General. They have accepted the principles of the Charter, participate in its activities and benefit from U.N. technical assistance. They follow the principles and practices of current international law. The rising professional younger generations want an international way of life as a part of the existing order. Left alone, these peoples and states might weld together a regional community which could serve as a model for parts of Africa and even South America. Although now inhibited by the stresses and strains of the war in Vietnam and Laos, the policies of President Sukarno, and the persistent pressures of communist subversion, they are nevertheless participating actively in social and economic programs.

As we shall see, the Mekong River development offers prospects for sound community building, some security is provided by the SEATO structure based in Bangkok, legal disputes are settled by judicial means, and, above all, the United Nations, the United States, Australia, Great Britain, France, Germany, Japan and others afford impressive aid, both military and economic. Overshadowing all these factors, however, is the intense pressure from communist and allied forces to exploit every possible nationalist and other discontent to mold these countries into a new social order under the major hegemony of the People's Republic of China and the minor hegemonies of the Democratic Republic of Vietnam, and possibly, according to its authoritative statements, of the Republic of Indonesia.

Terms of the Conflict over Southeast Asia

The outcome will vitally affect the United States and the world. For all sets of parties the question is whether some accommodation between a stable system of international relations and a revolutionary system is feasible, or whether the terms are exclusive victory and annihilation of the position of the other side. Revolutionary policies and powers in the broad sense are probably more concentrated and diversified in Southeast Asia than in any other area of such critical mass in the world. The Soviet Union, the Chinese People's Republic, the Democratic Republic of Vietnam (Hanoi), the Republic of Indonesia, and numerous Communist parties are aiming their separate or combined activities at destroying what they consider to be the *status quo* and the legality of the current order of states. The revolutionary policies and movements in Southeast Asia tend to oppose international limits on permissible behavior, and foment instability or exploit discontent instead. They often seem to repudiate rules or agreements which restrict their freedom to do as they please to attain their objectives. Respect for treaties or sovereignty of others seems to be decreasing, and intervention growing. Subterfuges and indirect methods of intervention to circumvent international deterrents and restraints of law are systematically conceived and practiced in defiance of any sense of community, or need for reciprocity.

The history of Southeast Asia and of the contending parties, however, indicates that there are some limits and some interests which could contribute to a bargaining situation. It in turn could lead to constructing at least an elementary, if not a more developed, arrangement for a system of acceptable procedures and sanctions for starting an embryonic equilibrium of law and power.

Elements of a Bargaining Situation in Southeast Asia

In the perspective of the present conflict, it may seem idle to talk of a rule of law or to search for some order. Perhaps there is nothing which the parties can negotiate. However, various factors, as will be mentioned, would seem to indicate that the terms of the conflict in Southeast Asia can be negotiated. A potential bargaining situation is at hand for resolving the terms of conflict on a limited basis by all parties in convergence and not on an unlimited basis by one or another set of parties. While there are deep divergencies of interests and serious hostilities in Southeast Asia, there are also powerful common interests for reaching an outcome which will not be unacceptably destructive of the values

15

and stakes of all the parties. Their ability to gain some of their respective objectives is dependent to a large degree on the policies of the others in making their choices or decisions. Total and unlimited conflict as a deliberate policy on the part of any one participant would prevent its achievement of even limited policy objectives in Southeast Asia. Everyone's stakes and payoffs, therefore, are mutually interdependent and jointly determined by the strategic behavior of the principal units and members in a tacit or explicit bargaining process. The situation provides scope in a kind of precarious partnership and incomplete antagonism for general accommodation and common interest in avoiding mutual disaster and reaching stable if minimal agreements on the issues of principle and substance.

However, the institutional and structural requirements of the bargaining process and interdependent negotiations are clearly inadequate and incomplete for the parties in Southeast Asia at present. They lack regular and continuous communications, or satisfactory machinery for negotiations. The contestants do not recognize a geographical area or a political line as a joint limitation on threats and war. Furthermore, agreements among them are not yet enforceable because there is no outside authority with sufficient sanction and power to ensure compliance.

Consequently, one of the tasks of developing the role of law and a strategy of equilibrium for Southeast Asia is to create the matrix for bargaining and negotiation by bringing together the various interdependent elements and applying the strategy of mutual gains and losses, advantages and disadvantages, by commitments, threats and promises. Such a matrix must take account of several historical factors, the policies of the major contestants, existing precedents and institutions of a legal character, and such new concepts or rules of law as it may be possible to create.

II. *SOME HISTORICAL PERSPECTIVES*

During the past six or seven hundred years, many kingdoms of Southeast Asia were independent. In their own forms of diplomacy and interstate relations they were well-versed and highly-skilled. Not only India, China and Japan, but Thailand, Burma,

16

Cambodia, Vietnam, Malaya, Indonesia and others as well, had sophisticated, elaborate and formal concepts, systems and methods of interrelations, in many ways more subtle and involved than what Europe was then evolving or is developing even now. These systems and methods were mainly an intricate combination of Indian and Chinese concepts and practices. In both, relationships among rulers were always unequal in concept and practice. And they were constantly changing among the lesser states as strong monarchs and the practice of war and conquest built up or weakened various kingdoms.

Traditional Indian Concept of Concentric Circles

We do not know very much about the historical practice of an Asian interstate system in Southeast Asia for the period of 1250–1850, but it is sufficient for our purposes at this stage to note some aspects of "Indianization."[1] Hindu writings, known and practiced in premodern Southeast Asia, advised kings to follow the four methods of expedients of diplomacy called "Upaya."[2] They were the methods of diplomatic concilation, foreign aid, subversion and infiltration, and forceful coercion. There were at least three kinds of neutrality, so we should not be surprised at the varieties of neutralism in Asia since World War II.

The world view and strategic doctrine of kingship and court in Southeast Asia until very recently were guided by the Hindu codes of Manu, by the political thought in the Mahabharata and the famous Indian manual on politics called Arthasastra, particularly the classic work of Kautilya. These precepts and practices of statecraft assumed a political world of unequal beings and states in constant flux. As the Mahabharata advised:

"There is no separate species of creatures called foes or friends. Persons become friends or foes according to the force of circumstances."

These Hindu writings instructed the kings and ministers of Southeast Asia in the concept of "Mandala," the "circle of states." This constituted the theory and practice of Asian international relations until destroyed and replaced by the European state system of equal nations and modern diplomatic practices. Mandala did not provide a system of international law and organiza-

17

tion as we know it because it did not recognize "a family of sovereign nations." In Asia each state had to seek the extension or preservation of its own security and power by a combination of diplomacy and force among a conical hierarchy of stronger and weaker allies, neutrals and enemies. The "circle of states" was the basis for the diplomatic theory and practice of each state in the total series of hierarchies. Around any given state there was a concentric series of friendly, unfriendly or neutral powers whose foreign policies were predetermined by its geographic position and its given resources—in other words, by circumstances of power, not by precepts of law or justice. An adjoining state was assumed to be a natural enemy and the state beyond it was considered a natural friend. All together they made up these concentric circles of varying kinds of relationships for which detailed strategems and practices were written out and followed: As Kautilya's Arthasastra put it:

"By throwing a circumference of the circle of states beyond his friends' territory and making the kings of those states as the spokes of that circle, the conqueror shall make himself as the nave (or hub) of that circle."

Traditional Chinese System of Overlordship

To these Hindu precepts of statecraft the kingdoms of Southeast Asia borrowed the Chinese-type system of regulated "tributary" relations and ritualistic embassies between superior states and "vassal" states for the organization and procedures of hierarchical diplomacy. This might be called the system of "overlordship" centered on the Imperial Court of China at the top. The Chinese Court considered itself the superior of any state known to it, including Rome and, when they later appeared, the European powers. The system of hierarchy, or what is known as the "tributary system" of the Chinese, developed an elaborate and reciprocal ritual for observing the ranks of states in their proper relationship of superiors and inferiors. The Chinese concept and practice of overlordship was intended to create a "Confucian world order."[3]

This system embraced all aspects of interstate relations: the exchange of envoys and the conduct of diplomatic relations, repatriation and extradition of persons, regulation of trade and commercial interests of the state, and special efforts to secure the defense of China by intimidating, cajoling or subsidizing foreign rulers around the Chinese borders. The underlying assumption basic to an understanding of the Chinese system of overlordship was acceptance of the superiority of the Son of Heaven and his representation symbolically of all mankind. This system fitted the foreign rulers who accepted the system and desired benefits from Imperial China into a hierarchy of superior and inferior rulers —not states or nations as such. Elaborate ritual observances were developed as mandatory expressions of this unequal relationship.[4] But the relation was reciprocal if not equal. The "vassal" or "tributary" king received an official patent of appointment, a seal to use on his memorials to other rulers dated by the Chinese Imperial calendar and not by the foreign kings or date of reign. The Son of Heaven, or the Chinese Emperor in this world order of stability, showed interest in the orderly government of a tributary state and confirmed and sanctioned the succession of rule from one king to the next without which a new ruler was not considered legitimate by other states in Southeast Asia, or even in some cases by his own people.

China conferred the advantage of trade and commerce which it carefully regulated. The Emperor also sent moral exhortations to the rulers in Southeast Asia on many occasions. When strong enough, Imperial China offered military protection and arbitrated disputes. Several times the navy or army of China intervened in various parts of Southeast Asia, particularly in Vietnam, to maintain this Confucian stability, play one ruler off against another, and even punish some kings who did not obey the laws of the system. However, leaving aside the special case of North Vietnam for the moment, Chinese power did not intervene in Burma, Thailand, Cambodia, Malaya and Indonesia for purposes of conquest, trade or military hegemony.

Instead, the system of overlordship was based on a kind of cultural hegemony and reciprocal hierarchy. It was a defensive expression of Chinese superiority in Asia. All the kings of Asia, from India to Japan, apparently accepted this preeminent position of the Chinese Court during the 2,000 years ending about the middle of the 19th century. But other kings could also pursue their own forms of "overlordship" if they had the power and if they acknowledged China's suzerainty.

The historical records give some instances of the actual workings of this system.[5] In the 15th century, for instance, the Kingdom of Malacca (what is now Malaya) sent tribute for trade and sanction to both the Court of old Siam and to the Court of the Ming Emperors in Peking. The ruler of Malacca wanted the protection of China against the extension of Siam's suzerainty and overlordship. The Javanese kingdom also brought in the power of China to extend its hegemony and empire in the southern part of Southeast Asia. The naval fleets of the Ming Empire acted both as a deterrent to the extension of the powers of the Siamese and Javanese kingdoms and as a protector to the smaller princes. Vietnamese rebels frequently defeated Chinese armies but always applied to the Emperor for the recognition of legitimate succession, sent embassies to China, and accepted the tributary status of vassal in the hierarchy.[6] Siamese kings had a far-flung set of dependencies, while sending embassies to Peking until 1853. It was the practice of the Chinese apparently not to allow any one kingdom to become too overpowering in the hierarchy of the southern area, but to encourage at least the kingdoms of Siam and Java to have enough power to maintain a certain stability in the community of kingdoms. At all times, however, the Chinese Courts apparently sought to keep the more powerful rulers under control.

An example of 1404 shows the system at work according to Chinese official chronicles.[7] The Thais had arrested shipwrecked tribute envoys from the nearby Kingdom of Champa and had sent troops to take away the Imperial seal and patent from Sumatra and Malacca whose kings also, like that of Champa, complained to the Chinese Court. The Emperor sent a decree of reprimand to the Thais asking how they could "presume on power, seize their tribute envoys and rob their letter patent and seals. . . . You will have to return the Champa envoys and restore the seals and letter patents to Sumatra and Malacca. From now on obey the law, follow the right principles, keep your boundary, and be honest to your neighbors, that you may enjoy eternally the blessings of the great peace."

The Aftermath of Ancient History

Traditional Asian regulation of these interstate relations has left several legacies for our purposes today. First, it was based on a system of independent states comparable to the early independent states of Europe on which modern international law is based. The Asian states were dependent on power and custom but not on formal law or organization. It was the policy of a strong or weak king which determined the expansion or contraction of these states within the overall system of suzerainty. Second, the "old order" produced a semblance of equilibrium but not often a peaceful one. Neither the Indian concept of Mandala nor the Chinese system of overlordship was based on the maintenance of peace, any international organization or any system for the regulation of peaceful settlements and the avoidance of war. The pre-modern history of these states is full of savage wars of conquest and revenge. Buddhist states went to war against each other with as much vengeance and suffering as did the Christian states of Europe. There was no system of power or law for maintaining an internal equilibrium without dynastic wars. The people suffered from constant raids, depredations, and wars in what we would call today aggression, direct and indirect. War was a natural order of society; peace was the exception. To fight was the accepted mandate and expected duty of the king. Conquest of land and people was the normal way to expand the resources of the state and inflate the gross national product. By the same token, the Kingdoms had no defined or well-marked boundaries. The extent of a state's territory was a factor of policy and power—not law. Other than the Chinese Emperor, there was no court of appeal or "congress of kings." As far as is known, they never assembled together for common purposes on any equal standing. They had none. They came together only to render homage to a superior suzerain, as many did for the kings of Siam.

This pre-modern system did, however, leave the legacy of a form of community of custom in the "great peace"; a sort of reciprocity in diplomatic usage of Upaya, tributary regulations, state policies of "mandala," and general norms and precepts for intervention and non-intervention. The legacy of this system has also affected contemporary attitudes. Communist China is projecting memories of its overlordship, tributary system and commercial relations with the southern area into a new design of "great peace and grand unity." Cambodia, for example, is reacting against the traditional "overlordship" of Thailand and Vietnam for several hundred years over the Khmer Kingdom. Cambodian officials also take Peking's assurances and guarantees at nearly full value today because Imperial China never invaded or used overt force against the Khmer Kingdom. The myths and records of Javanese pretensions northward as far as present Vietnam, Cambodia, and Thailand apparently led President Sukarno of Indonesia to envisage a new Javanese "overlordship."

Legacies of Colonialism

One after the other, the Indians generated Southeast Asia's culture, the Chinese managed its politics, and the Europeans internationalized its economy. For less than 100 years, from about 1850 to 1942, the conquest, commerce and culture of Western colonialism dominated the life and changed the order of Southeast Asia. This was the European century of global power. The kingdoms of Asia, except for Thailand and Japan, were turned into Western provinces. All of Asia, and particularly Southeast Asia, became dependent on the world market and Western technology. Traditional subsistence farming for village home or feudal lord in the lowlands of Burma, Thailand, Cambodia, Vietnam, Malaya, Indonesia and the Philippines gave way to large-scale organized production of rice, rubber, pepper and other products for export. Colonial exploitation also developed mines and forests for export. During their century of mastery, the Europeans introduced Chinese and Indian workmen as settlers apparently for the first time in the history of this area. Its economy not only became internationalized: it was also integrated with the colonial powers and the Western system. Southeast Asia became dependent for the first time in its long history on the outside world.[8]

Colonialism also generated nationalism and spread the ideals of the Declaration of Independence and the Bill of Rights. Western-educated leaders and the general populace in these countries turned nationalism against the Westerners to throw off the colonial yoke and reassert their traditional independence in new forms of modern nationhood. The desires for political equality with the West and resentment against alien control are strong, intense emotions and motivations in Southeast Asia today. Most people there fear or suspect Westerners and the West. The fight for independence in Vietnam has been longer and more bitter than anywhere else since 1945. But most of the people in Southeast Asia, including the Thais, who were never colonized, remain sensitive to the West because of the psychological hang-over of colonialistic discrimination and subordination by the white men.

But neither colonialism nor nationalist independence has established either a democratic or an effective system of government and administration for these countries as a whole. Colonialism left the villagers and rural Southeast Asia alone to govern themselves as they had for centuries with government by neglect rather than concern. Colonialism continued the highly centralized and despotic divide between the governors and the governed, the rulers and the ruled. The modern nations of Southeast Asia, including communist regimes, have not yet overcome this legacy of the past. The gap of government is the most serious deficiency in Southeast Asia today. Communist forces are exploiting this political vacuum in the rural countryside by infiltrating among the people and capturing them away from their national leaders.

III. *CHINESE POLICY AND POWER*

China's World Blueprint—Old and New

An image of the past and a design for the future determine Chinese policy in Southeast Asia. The concepts and practices of the past are merging with the concepts and practices of Maoist China modified by contemporary circumstances and policies. One of the continuing concepts in the Chinese world view is the "great peace," about which the Emperor reminded the King of Siam early in the 15th century. Mao's concept seems to have evolved naturally and logically from tradition.

The idea of the great peace, or grand unity, is as old as pre-Confucian times and as enduring as China.[9] The ancient concept of a "world shared by all people" can be seen today on the tomb of Sun Yat-sen, the founder of modern China. In the Chinese concept there were two fundamental elements: the "empire," or everything under heaven in the literal translation of the Chinese term, on the one hand; and the country, or what we call today the nation, on the other.[10] This "world" was an abstract notion of a cultural and moral civilization for all peoples where morality and law played the major role and China was the preeminent civilizing instrument, the "Middle Kingdom," in a universal system of states of political inequality in power and status. The "nation" of China was the source of power and policy for establishing and maintaining the "great peace" in Asia. This utopian concept and political practice continued during 2,000 years of Chinese history into the last days of the Manchu Dynasty, when a conservative intellectual leader wrote a treatise about the concept of universal "grand unity" which caused considerable discussion more than fifty years ago and apparently impressed the young Mao:[11]

"Everything through the earth, large or small, far or near, will be like one. There will be no more nations and conditions will be the same everywhere. With this uniformity will come the age of the Great Peace."

Traditionalism and Leninism have logically combined to design a "great peace" and "grand unity" of Maoist proportions. The current thrust for a universal system of socialist Utopia is a natural outgrowth of the heritage and hangover of China's past. Today a new Son of Heaven sits on a Marxist throne in the Middle Kingdom. Mao's writings over the past forty years reflect a Maoist-Marxist version of the great peace, universalism and power. In 1919 Mao wrote of the "great union of the popular masses" which would rule over the whole world and bring about a "golden age of brilliance and splendor." In 1938 Mao predicted that "once man has reached the age of permanent peace, he will never again desire war." In 1949 he wrote Nehru that China and India would some day emerge in the "socialist and people's democratic family." His aim has always been to build a socialist and communist society in the world. And during the last few years Mao has often called for "world peace" and the forcible elimination of "imperialism."[12] Mao is as famous a poet as

24

he is a revolutionary leader and military strategist. In 1935 he wrote a poem about the mountains in Central Asia which ended (in translation):

> "Thus would a great peace
> run through the world,
> For all the world would
> share your warmth and cold." [13]

The "Great Peace" will only come after violent struggle against any and all opposition. Nearly thirty years ago he wrote, "political power grows out of the barrel of a gun." Now his gun will have nuclear warheads. It would appear that

"The Chinese view of the world has not fundamentally changed: it has been adjusted to take account of the modern world, but only so far as to permit China to occupy, still, the central place in the picture." [14]

For Southeast Asia the implications are tremendous.

Mao and his colleagues have just recently eased our task of determining their policies and the extent to which they will use power and violence to achieve them. On September 3, 1965, Peking published [15] an extremely significant declaration of objectives and strategy for destroying the United States and winning the war by a "people's war" in the countryside. This is a militant policy of violence and war. It seeks to mobilize the rural people in Asia, Africa and Latin America somehow to conquer the industrialized "city" of Europe and North America. This is a universal projection to "world peace" and "perpetual peace and happiness" of Mao's strategy in defeating the Chinese Nationalists in China. Let us have the declaration speak for itself:

"It must be emphasized that Comrade Mao Tse-tung's theory of the establishment of rural revolutionary base areas and the encirclement of cities from the countryside is of outstanding and universal practical importance for the present revolutionary struggles of the oppressed nations and peoples in Asia, Africa and Latin America against imperialism and its lackeys. . . . The peasants constitute the main force of the national democratic revolution against the imperialists and their lackeys . . . The countryside, and the countryside alone, can provide the broad areas in which the revolutionaries can maneuver freely . . . The countryside, and the countryside alone, can provide the revolutionary bases from which the revolutionaries can go forward to final victory . . . Taking the entire globe, if North America and Western Europe can be called 'the cities of the world,' then

Asia, Africa and Latin America constitute 'the rural areas of the world.' . . . In a sense, the contemporary world revolution also presents a picture of the encirclement of cities by the rural areas."

Such is Mao's new blueprint for the "great peace" and "grand unity." The declaration leaves no doubt that the Chinese Communist regime will follow the policy of providing more support and aid for "people's wars" and "revolutionary struggles" all over the world. It is in this sense that Mao's strategy stresses "the spiritual atom bomb of the revolutionary people" as a far more powerful and useful weapon than the physical atom bomb. It is just a question of time: victory is inevitable. The enemy "will be swept like dust from the stage of history by the mighty broom of the revolutionary people." According to Peking, their base areas in the war have grown to unprecedented proportions.

The significant assertion for us in this declaration concerns the importance ascribed to Vietnam in Southeast Asia. The statement declares that the struggle in Vietnam "is now the focus of the struggle of the people of the world against United States aggression." Peking's declaration states very bluntly that the Chinese People's Republic and the Chinese people "will do everything in their power to support the Vietnamese people until every single one of the United States aggressors is driven out of Vietnam." Nothing in the terms or phraseology of Peking's declaration would suggest that Mao and his colleagues now have an inclination towards compromise and accommodation or interest in a mutual system of law or equilibrium in Vietnam or Southeast Asia. Their statement could well be described as a declaration of war against law and order of any other kind in Southeast Asia or the whole world.

In view of this explicit declaration of policy and power, the consequences for the United States and other like-minded governments in seeking the rule of reason rather than resort to force in Southeast Asia would seem clear. The implications were well put in 1964 by Professor Tang Tsou of the University of Chicago:

"In South Vietnam, Washington has failed so far to devise a political-military program which can defeat the armed struggle waged by the Viet Cong, who have adopted Mao's political and military strategy. If the United States and South Vietnam can win the war against the Viet Cong, they will

26

have demonstrated to Mao that his strategy can be countered. Repeated success in coping with Mao's strategy will induce second thoughts in Peking—if not in the mind of Mao, then in the minds of other Chinese leaders. Mao's strategic concepts, a vital part of Mao's thought and prestige, will in time be eroded . . . If the Chinese are forced to abandon or modify Mao's strategic doctrine, some form of peaceful coexistence as we understand it in the West may eventually become the basis of relations between the United States and Communist China, and between the communists and the West." [16]

The Importance of Vietnam and Southeast Asia to Peking

The old area to the south—the Nan Yang where Chinese power and system have exercised influence for 2000 years—is the keystone in Mao's blueprint for victory of the "world countryside." Political capture and consolidation of rural Southeast Asia will begin the march to Mao's "great peace." The objectives of Peking's policy in Southeast Asia seem apparent to most students of Communist China, although much of the literature is unclear on this subject and there has been debate on the range of strategy and use of power.[17] Of course, Peking does not divulge its precise targets. Yet it now seems certain that it will continue to be Peking's objective and policy (1) to secure and maintain what the Chinese Communist leadership consider to be China's rightful and proper boundaries; (2) to assure and protect the well-being and survival of any Asian communist state and particularly North Korea and North Vietnam; (3) to avert a humiliating public defeat; and (4) to resist any assault on Chinese territory.

Most observers agree that Communist China has a series of objectives in Southeast Asia. The first is protection of the southern frontiers and boundaries of China from the sea all the way into the Himalayan Mountains. This is the sensitive "underbelly" of China. To understand its vital importance for any Chinese Government, one can think of China as a triangle. The security and integrity of all three sides are mutually vital and interdependent. On two of the three sides, China faces the two major nuclear powers in our bipolar world: the United States along the ocean frontier of the West Pacific, and the Soviet Union along the steppes of Central Asia. On the third side of the triangle, the south flank, China faces India, and a series of relatively small and independent states, some neutral and some not. But

27

Peking's first requirement in foreign policy is obvious, the maintenance and protection of its triangular territory.

Its second objective is to restore the old boundaries of the Chinese Empire, as Mao suggested some thirty years ago. In 1939 he referred in one of his essays to the "imperialist countries" which "forcibly took" from China a large number of "states tributary to China" as well as part of China's own territory.[18] He listed Annam, Burma, Bhutan and Nepal in addition to Korea, Taiwan, Okinawa, Hong Kong and Macao. This suggests that Mao "must still consider Southeast Asia, which sent tribute missions to Peking in imperial times, as a legitimate and primary sphere of influence for China."[19] This concept of a Middle Kingdom surrounded by a hierarchy in concentric circles of "barbarians and vassals" may still determine the fundamental outlook of Chinese Communist leaders in Peking under Mao's supremacy, and probably after. Peking has remained vague about which new nations it considers still to be "states tributary to China" and about the southern boundaries of China's influence as distinct from the delimitation of its southern frontier. During the past fifteen years, Peking has been rectifying its territorial borders in its favor by marking them precisely across Southern Asia from the Hindu Kush to Tonkin. A map published in a Communist Chinese history textbook in 1954 extended Chinese Communist historical claims of paramount influence in Southeast Asia down to Singapore and the Sulu Islands between the Philippines and Indonesia, but not including either.[20]

The third objective of Peking, seemingly obvious from substantial evidence but never explicitly stated with official precision, is to regain paramount political influence and political control over the new states in this southern area. To cite a report by a Study Group of the Royal Institute of International Affairs in Great Britain, Chinese policy towards the countries of Southeast Asia appears to be inspired by at least four motives: "a nationalist impulse to extend Chinese influence generally; a missionary zeal to extend the influence of Communist ideology; a desire to control the rice and raw materials of the area; and a desire to ensure China's own security."[21] Peking seems to be probing everywhere for promoting the political objectives so characteristic of all militant and self-confident regimes. An important geopolitical factor facilitating China's policy towards the countries of Southeast Asia is the fact that the Chinese People's Republic is occupying and developing the high mountains and valleys dominating the principal river basins of the Ganges, Irrawaddy, Salwein and the Mekong.

The Chinese drive for predominance in eastern and southern Asia creates the confrontation with the United States and the crux of the problem of developing a combination of policies, power and law to bring about an equilibrium at present. The policy of seeking predominance, paramountcy or hegemony there puts the Chinese People's Republic outside any law in any definition except its own. It is a revolutionary drive in the total sense. China's policies and use of power begin by being totally negative and therefore beyond the law.

A major policy of Peking is to force the United States out of Asia, and particularly out of Southeast Asia. The American presence there is the major obstacle to their objectives and policies. Peking cannot expand its "aggression by seepage" as long as American-supported governments and America itself exist and expand in Southeast Asia. China's policy of exclusion is directed first and foremost at the United States. The elimination of alliances with Washington, a nebulous neutralization of Southeast Asia, and reduction or removal of American access to the mainland of Southeast Asia would signify the beginning of a renewed Chinese overlordship in modern terms.

Peking also extends its policy of exclusion towards the other two major potential powers in Asia, India and Japan. The aim will continue to be to block any development of a coalition or understanding for security and development between Japan and India. Economic and political relations will be undermined and subverted. One purpose or by-product of the Chinese attack on India in 1962 was the discrediting of India's standing in the eyes of the Southeast Asians. A purpose in Peking's present support for Pakistan is to divide, subvert, and rule both India and Pakistan. China's communist propaganda and political harassment of

29

Japan seeks to keep it from developing a relationship with Southeast Asia politically or economically.

China's policies in Southeast Asia have also attacked regional and international cooperation. Of course, Peking has constantly denounced SEATO because it has been an effective deterrent to Peking's ambitions. Chinese Communists have also attacked any of the efforts of Southeast Asia to promote regional association. Peking called the formation of the Association of Asian States a mouthpiece and masquerade for the imperialists when Thailand, Malaysia and the Philippines put that first regional organization together in 1961. They have also opposed the activities and participation of the United Nations and its various agencies in Southeast Asia, and particularly in Vietnam.

The Strategy of Mao's Aggression by Seepage

The Chinese Communist leadership is planning and working to get political control of Asia. But we must clearly understand and accept the communist distinction between political power and military control. We should not jump to the unwarranted conclusion that Peking intends to invade and conquer the rest of Asia by force of arms in a military or nuclear showdown. Instead, Peking has devised and begun a political strategy to gain paramount control over Asia by essentially political means to avoid a major collision with our overwhelming knock-out forces. "Aggression by seepage" consists of two interdependent parts: the methodical, planned establishment of privileged sanctuaries within Chinese control and the careful organization of proxy parties outside China.

This seepage begins with stealth and slips in every crack and opening in people's hearts and minds. The agents, propagandists, agitators, assassins, party men or guerrilla bands do not attack frontally; they seep around and underneath at night and under cover. They do not talk Communism or Marxism at first. They approach rural people skillfully on their terms and in their vocabulary, appealing to the sentiments of nationalism and the desires for social justice. Communists attack unpopular evils of landlords, usurers, policemen and "foreign lackeys." The agents respond to the authentic needs of the people such as medicine, cash, books, tools, farm animals, and trade. They supply pay, pills, paper, promises and even opium. They propose a "brotherhood of solidarity" and a "union of goodness." If inducements fail, terrorism completes the task.[22]

Communist agents go after young people in rural areas. A frustrated farmer, a disaffected local official, a fed-up teacher or a tolerant priest is the target of this seepage. The communists take on anyone who seems to have some flair for agitation, leadership, sabotage and terrorism in the villages. By the time victims fed up with real poverty and corruption have been cleverly and fully "seeped," they form proxy molecules in the local political nucleus for power of Peking and Hanoi.

Selected individuals then go to Laos, North Vietnam, and Tibet or China for special training. They return to their own countries to form small cadres of secret cells completely separate from each other in the classic manner of all conspiracies. These local cells in turn build the nucleus for the proxy party and the underground force. They in turn create the political movement which is supposed to get control of the population and eventually form the one-party regime. Thus, each proxy group—little or large—enjoys both the protection of indigenous invisibility within these countries and the inviolate sanctuary in outside contiguous borders to engineer alien seepage. The proxy apparatus across borders does the seeping and subverting with aid and inspiration from the privileged sanctuary in a contiguous area.

A network of specially-prepared sanctuaries is emerging across China's southern flank to cover Kashmir, Nepal, Bhutan, Sikkim, Northeast India, Burma, Laos, Thailand, Vietnam and Cambodia. A new sanctuary is developing in Indonesia for infiltration northward into the Philippines, Borneo, Singapore, and Malaya. In each case the privileged sanctuary arises adjacent to the area marked for seepage in order to provide logistic support of various kinds. The most significant and dangerous is air and ground transportation. A system of elaborate, well-engineered and costly roads, airfields, and supply centers is developing rapidly in southern Tibet and southeast China in some of the world's most difficult terrain. Some of the tunnel and bridgework in this system is difficult and expensive. The whole system is designed for heavy weights and lengthy use. A new highway from Tibet to Nepal can carry 60 ton tanks, as can the roads into northern Laos and Burma.

Thailand and the rice bowl of Southeast Asia are now linked to China by highways—logistic sanctuaries and proxy parties. The supply bases and training centers in this logistic system develop, equip, and harbor the political and military cadres of proxy parties for infiltration and operations in South Vietnam, Laos, Thailand, Burma, Nepal and India, the Philippines and Malaysia. Meanwhile radio broadcasts from the sanctuaries, as well as from Peking and Hanoi, are bombarding all the peoples of Southern Asia with a daily radio barrage of familiar dialects and favorable programs. A new "Thailand Independence Movement" and "Patriotic Front" join the latest proxy party and underground operating out of the same communist controlled areas of Laos as do the Viet Cong. And this political base for a "war of liberation" is much further advanced in Thailand than most people suspect. The Chinese Communists have openly declared a "war of national liberation" in Thailand. They have announced that guerrilla operations would start there in 1965. Thai leaders are taking this warning seriously.[23] Chinese formation of a Tibetan-Nepalese proxy party is under way in Tibet to infiltrate and take over Nepal which, like Thailand, may well turn into another Vietnam or Laos if not prevented. Guerrillas, saboteurs, agitators and agents are seeping into Malaysia and the Philippines.

This 20th century system of proxy party and privileged sanctuary is all of one piece. It seeks to penetrate, subvert and capture its victims—a next door person and a neighboring nation—subtly, persistently, methodically, confidently, even if it takes years. Unless subject to exposure and attack, the proxy and the sanctuary are as sinister as they are effective because their points of supply, avenues of advance, and lines of escape remain intact and elusive. The network for seepage can go on opening and filling cracks until Southern Asia is neutralized and captured—without any major war at all unless stopped.

The Instruments of Communist Policy and Power
in Southeast Asia: Hanoi and Jakarta

Even though there may be disagreement as to the exact nature
of Peking's real objectives and intentions for Southeast Asia,
there does seem to be sufficient evidence to indicate that the
political and military instruments for the "war of national liberation" and aggression by seepage are expanding. Without any
question, the Communist party in each country of Southeast Asia
is the key instrument, whether it is legal and operating overtly,
or whether it is underground and operating as a clandestine
conspiracy.

In Burma, Thailand, Malaya, Cambodia and the Philippines,
the communist apparatus and strategies have not yet taken hold
on a broad basis since World War II. Communist parties remain
small, weak, clandestine, despite great efforts on the part of
Moscow, Peking and local communist leaders.[24] Nationalism of
different cultural varieties has held the initiative and maintained
some momentum in the development of these countries and in
nullifying the communist drive. Even with the Chinese minorities in these countries, Maoist or Asianized communism has not
taken hold—so far. However, the effort of Peking, Hanoi and
Jakarta to penetrate these countries by every possible means is
intensifying, as we can see in Thailand this year. The principal
instruments for carrying out the policies and objectives are the
Communist party in North Vietnam and the communist-backed
regime of President Sukarno in Jakarta.

The Communist party of the Democratic Republic of Vietnam
has been following the objective for at least two decades of subverting Vietnam, Laos, Cambodia and even Thailand. The Vietnamese version of hegemony, or neo-imperialism, is a revival of
traditional encroachments on western neighbors. As in the case
of Communist China, Communist Vietnam has now added a
militant ideology, a dynamic armed party and a logistic sanctuary
to its historical expansionism. For at least fifteen years, the Vietnamese communist leadership has envisaged a "revolutionary
movement" in which the Vietnamese party would "supervise the
activities of its brother parties in Cambodia and Laos."[25] In 1953

a Vietnamese communist broadcast declared "the Lao Dong Party and the people of Vietnam have the wills to make revolution in Cambodia and Laos. We, the Vietminh elements, have been sent to serve this revolution and to build the union of Vietnam, Cambodia and Laos." [26]

Since those revelations were made, the Vietnamese communists have moved well along the path towards this objective by virtue of the interlude provided by the Geneva Agreements of 1954 and 1962. The Lao communist movement, commonly called the Pathet Lao, has gained control of at least half of Laos, extending from the border of China along the entire Lao-Vietnamese frontier to the Lao-Cambodia border. And the Pathet Lao has become a constituent member of the government of the National Union in Laos, although the Lao communists have boycotted these arrangements. Communist Vietnam has used this communist half of Laos for infiltrating supplies and combat troops around the 17th parallel into South Vietnam and apparently even through Cambodia, contrary to the spirit and letter of the Geneva Agreements of 1954 and 1962. Judging by much of the circumstantial evidence, Hanoi would guide and direct these three communist states of Vietnam, Laos and Cambodia if the communist parties seized power. Inevitably, judging by all the circumstantial evidence, a communist Indochina backed by communist China would then focus on the infiltration of Thailand and seek to overthrow the nationalist government there and replace it with a Thai Communist party.

A new and developing instrument for organizing communist hegemony in Southeast Asia is what some observers see as the evolving entente between Peking and Jakarta. As one student of this trend has stated, "the Sino-Indonesian alliance is the most significant political development in Southeast Asia." [28] In the Asian way of doing things this is more informal than it is open and formalized. The Communist party of Indonesia is the strongest political organization in Java and probably in the islands as a whole. Aside from the personality of President Sukarno, it would appear that it will be the dominant political factor among the 100 million people of Indonesia for the immediate future. The expansionist policy of Sukarnoist-Indonesia goes well beyond the confrontation and destruction of Malaysia. It claims to seek a Jakarta-oriented and dominated region in the old southern part of Southeast Asia—a "greater Indonesia," according to several observers.[29]

Paralleling the objectives and policies of Peking and Hanoi, Sukarno seeks to force the United States and Great Britain totally out of Southeast Asia. And also paralleling Peking and Hanoi, Sukarno's concept finds some support from Indonesian history. During the past twenty years, Sukarno and a few other Indonesian leaders sharing these views have frequently referred to the Kingdom of Majapahit of 500 years ago. A map of that empire hangs on a wall in President Sukarno's office in Jakarta. Even though it did not encompass all of southern Southeast Asia, it was a Javanese hegemony, and Sukarno believes in or uses the Indonesian tradition that the empire included the Malay Peninsula, parts of the Philippines, all of Borneo, New Guinea, and all the intervening islands.

Some of the facts in this projection of the past into the future are on the record. In 1954, Sukarno revealed that he had dreamed of a "Pan-Indonesia" which would include Malaya, New Guinea and the Philippines. He then conceived of the islands situated between Asia and Australia and between the Pacific and Indian Oceans becoming a "single entity."[30] Recently, he has unilaterally renamed the Indian Ocean and the Straits of Malaya the Indonesian Ocean and the Straits of Sumatra. He has also claimed sovereignty over all the waters that divide the hundreds of Indonesian islands. And he has asserted that Indonesia should have "the right and primary responsibility to guard the security and peace in the region, together with its neighboring states, the Philippines and Malaya." The reasons for Indonesia's vehement denunciation of Malaysia and subversive infiltration of Malaysia are obvious.

Some observers conclude that Jakarta and Peking apparently reached some sort of an understanding in 1964–1965 on parallel or joint undertakings, since both governments have developed similar objectives with regard to policy, power and law in Southeast Asia. In his annual "state of the union message" to Indonesia on August 17, 1965, the occasion of Indonesia's independence,[31]

President Sukarno has referred to helping build an axis linking Indonesia, Communist China, North Vietnam, Cambodia and North Korea in a working alliance. Eviction of the United States and the United Kingdom from Southeast Asia appears to be one goal of the Jakarta-Peking understanding. Joint action in political, military and economic fields have apparently been discussed and agreed upon in meetings of leaders of both countries.

Indications of this parallel action with China are said to be seen in the fact that the Chinese Communist Press Agency has become the most influential disseminator of foreign news in Indonesia.[32] There are also indications that Soviet influence and activity in Indonesia are contracting, while Communist China's grows. Some speculate that Jakarta has asked Communist China for assistance not only in expelling the Americans and British from this region, but in helping the Indonesian Government to develop and explode nuclear devices. How far the actual partnership with Peking will extend is still secret, but all the available evidence indicates that the understandings may go much farther than is openly apparent at the moment.

Sukarno has recently stated that he wants to extend his original concept to Thailand, Cambodia, Singapore, Malaya and all of Borneo. The Indonesian Chief of Staff has stated that Indonesian defense "must cover all of Southeast Asia."[33] He recalled that Indonesian kingdoms in the past had maintained hegemony over Southeast Asia through control of the seas. He envisaged the days when an Indonesian navy would take over the role of the 7th Fleet and the British Fleet.

The prospects for any rule of law and the development of any internationally sanctioned community in Southeast Asia are clouded by the opposition of Peking, Hanoi and Jakarta to any form of "legalized stability other than their own." These three governments are not members of the United Nations and are deliberately promoting their policies and using their power in defiance of the Charter and outside of international institutions. Communist China and Communist Vietnam have repeatedly declared that they would brook no "interference" of the United Nations in any settlement regarding Indochina.

As a result, a combination of these three revolutionary hegemonic states is defying and subverting any development of international order and stability by the United Nations, by the Southeast Asian countries themselves, and by any mixture of Asian and non-Asian powers. The test for the communists will be success in capturing the rural populations in Vietnam, Thailand, Malaya proper, and the Philippines. Their strategy relies on coercion: threat, subversion and violence. They seek their own forms of regional equilibrium under their own exclusive control.

China's Nuclear Capability and the Rule of Law

The addition of a nuclear capability to this combination may well become a major problem in a regional equilibrium for Southeast Asia.[34] While it is doubtful that Hanoi or Jakarta will develop their own individual use of nuclear weapons and delivery systems in the next ten years under their own sovereign control, it is certain that Communist China will. It will have a nuclear capability for use in Asia, including ballistic missiles and nuclear-armed aircraft and submarines. This power and capability will bring to Peking the additional option of threatening to hold the capitals of Southeast Asia, South Asia and Japan in potential hostage. This is not to suggest that Mao and his intimate circle of old men or their successors in Peking would actually use nuclear weapons for tactical and strategic purposes in Southeast Asia if threatened with credible nuclear retaliation on a massive scale by the United States, but it is to suggest that atomic weapons will give Peking much greater leverage in Asian and world affairs in political and psychological terms. The Chinese communist leaders have not spent the last few years concentrating so much of their human and technical resources on the production of nuclear weapons just for an experiment in science or an exhibition of aptitude. Surrounded on two of its three long frontiers by the two major nuclear powers in the world and viewing the vulnerability of their southern flank, it is to be expected that Communist China will develop a series of nuclear weapons and delivery capabilities in its own defense and for its foreign policy. The United States tried to discuss the

Nuclear Test Ban Treaty with Peking in 1963 and 1964 but the Chinese Communist leadership rejected the effort and proceeded with its bomb.

For a law of peace and equilibrium to play a role in Southeast Asia there will have to be some control and deterrence of China's nuclear capability as a threat to Asian capitals and as an added component to the power of Communist Vietnam and expansionist Indonesia. From this point of view a regional system in Southeast Asia becomes even more essential. One question is whether the Soviet Union would participate in such a system for stabilizing Southeast Asia.

The Soviet Union in Southeast Asia

The Soviet role in questions of policy, power and law for Southeast Asia is much less distinct and even less consistent than that of the Chinese People's Republic or the United States.[35] Although it has been active in most of the countries of Southeast Asia and in much of the post-war politics of this tormented region, its diplomacy has blown hot and cold towards the independent states and its power has either been indifferent or incapable concerning the extension of communist revolution and power. The Sino-Soviet split has brought about a fundamental change in its role in Southeast Asia and in the triangular relationship of Moscow, Peking and Washington with respect to war and peace there.

As between the Soviet and Chinese Comunists considerably different approaches to socialism in Southeast Asia, to the use of violence there and to coexistence have been developed. As in the case of all other developing countries in Asia, Africa and Latin America, Moscow believes that it has a much better theory and practice for modelling a socialist state than do the Chinese.[36] The Sino-Soviet conflict erupted in good measure over this difference in ideology and practice. The differences have turned into rivalry and bitter competition for the allegiance of the communist parties of North Vietnam and Indonesia, the two key communist groups in Southeast Asia. To the extent that the Sino-Soviet conflict hardens and lasts, the communist policies and powers in Southeast Asia will become increasingly fractured, fragmented and diverse. This dichotomy between the Moscow and Peking models, plus the inherent nationalist tendency of most Southeast Asians, including the communists, have complicated the path of politics in the Southeast Asian countries compared to what it was in 1955. Then one could speak of a Moscow-Peking axis, a common front for the communist take-over of whatever was takeable. In 1954 Moscow and Peking worked together at the Geneva Conferences. At the Summit Conference in 1955 Moscow kept urging the communist line, but in the last few years Moscow and Peking have seemed to diverge on Southeast Asia. Soviet diplomacy there as a whole has not been active in recent years and now the Soviet Union seems to be losing face even in Indonesia. The Soviets are trying to develop an active relationship with Burma and Cambodia, but the neutrality of those two countries has somewhat inhibited the Soviet diplomacy of patronage and aid. The Thai Government has kept the Soviet diplomacy restricted and under wraps. Malaya and the Philippines do not have diplomatic relations with the Soviet Union. Both with the nationalist governments and with the internal communist parties, Moscow seems to have decreasing influence.

The question for any development of equilibrium in Southeast Asia insofar as the Soviet Union is concerned is whether or not it will seek to build back some of its influence and to promote some form of equilibrium, both to limit the danger of major hostilities and to restrain the policies and capabilities of Communist China. Until recently, the Soviet Union played an active role as Co-Chairman of the two Geneva Conferences. Since the American build-up in Vietnam and the military confrontation there, it has not been active as Co-Chairman either in seeking another Geneva Conference or in undertaking joint steps with the United Kingdom, the other Co-Chairman. No doubt it finds itself in an increasingly delicate and contradictory position. Whatever it does will help either the United States or the Chinese People's Republic and thereby hurt Soviet interests to some extent. In this situation it appears to be developing the role of a non-participant and spectator. Whether it would play a wider role in the establishment of an equilibrium remains to be seen. It is possible that the present leaders in Moscow will conclude that the national interests of the Soviet Union as a world nuclear power and as a modern society require their seeking to restrain the uncontrollable tendencies of Peking and Jakarta, aided and abetted by Hanoi and their taking part in an international effort to establish economic and political institutions in Southeast Asia.

The Issue of Unlimited or Limited Policy and Power

Whatever Moscow does, the basic question for Southeast Asia is whether China can become a "normal member of the community of nations," as Robert Elegant so correctly put it.[37] The combination of policy, power and law on Chinese terms suggests a dangerous inclination to seek ultimate ends by maximum means. The outlook of Chinese Communist leadership on policy and the propensity of the Chinese Communist State towards power could lead to catastrophe. The challenge for law and equilibrium there is to find ways by which the nations of Southeast Asia can help the community of nations persuade the Chinese to come to terms with the world and evolve a normal and rational relationship in the international family of nations. It may take a generation of 25 years or more before a succession of Chinese leaders in Peking—Marxian or post-Marxian—will give up an unlimited compulsion to dominate a "grand unity" of a merged world city and countryside and join a limited order of peace and security in Asia. However, we should not assume that there are no qualifications or limitations on Chinese Communist policy and power. There are several which can facilitate, even slightly, the difficult task of working out some rational order in Southeast Asia.

First, the Chinese are disinclined to use their military forces outside of China for conquest and control if others can succeed for them by proxy. The principal reason for this restraint is the actual deterrence and expected retaliation of American power in Asia. But the Chinese are also sensitive to Asian and world opposition, particularly among what they consider to be revolutionary groups, to the use of Chinese force for political control. The Chinese have not forgotten the sensitivities of their neighbors to historical Chinese overlordship. Peking knows that the Chinese communities in Southeast Asia are social liabilities as well as subversive assets because of the intense ethnic antagonism which they create. In any event, a search for regional equilibrium in Southeast Asia can probably assume that Chinese military force will not be sent madly, romantically, or irrationally to seize Bangkok or overrun Singapore—as long as the consequences of such rash action would be so devastatingly painful for China itself.

The second restraint on Chinese policies of exclusion and expansion comes from the element of caution and prudence which the aging Chinese Communist leadership has shown on some occasions during the past fifteen years, if not all. China's use of force and diplomacy has been versatile and skillful. When the odds seemed favorable, the Chinese forces have attacked, as in Korea, Tibet and India. When the opposition seemed too strong, as in Taiwan in 1958 and Vietnam in 1965, China has held back. While the Chinese communists have demonstrated rashness as well as boldness, they have shown restraint and prudence in making threats and warnings towards the United States and other countries, as well as in making commitments to other communist countries. It would seem from this record that Mao and his inner circle appreciate the power of the United States and comprehend the principles of managing conflict. Peking seems to understand the limits of its capabilities, the potentials of the other side's power, and the essentiality of maintaining China intact. The calculus of benefits and losses, disadvantages and gains, in a strategy of conflict is a determining factor in Peking's execution of foreign policy.

A third limitation is the recognition that revolution in Southeast Asia and the world countryside must be home-grown under a local brand. As the Declaration of September 3, 1965, reiterated: "Revolution cannot be imported." Only the people of a country can "overthrow reactionary rule" for "their role cannot be replaced or taken over by any people from outside." The outcome of a war will be decided by ground forces fighting at close quarters on battlefields and by the political conscience, courage and spirit of men. However one views or favors modernization, revolution and change in Southeast Asia, there is a basic truth in that statement for all concerned. The limiting and controlling factor for the role of law, power and policy is the attitude and choice of the decision-makers in Southeast Asia and their following—war or peace, freedom or communism will be theirs to decide in whatever pattern they select or accept in a complex interaction of external forces and internal trends, whether it be the pattern of some collective security, a regional community, the auspices of the United Nations, or something new.

Another limitation on the scope of Chinese power and the freedom of Chinese communist policy is the nationalistic tendencies within Asian communism. Nationalism in North Vietnam, Indonesia and all other countries in Asia is probably a stronger political force making a deeper emotional and psychological appeal than Leninism or Maoism. The North Vietnamese as Vietnamese have all the marked characteristics of Vietnamese nationalism which have distinguished Vietnamese resistance to Chinese encroachments for 2,000 years. Despite the parallel direction of policy and power in Hanoi and Peking, it would be a mistake to assume that there would be a constant relationship or a convergence and submergence of Vietnamese Communists to Chinese Communist domination. The experience of the past fifteen years in North Vietnam and in conferences with the Democratic Republic of Vietnam demonstrate that Hanoi prizes its independence within the communist movement and guards its independence with respect to its neighbors and the rest of the world. In fact, nationalism may be on the way to capture communism in Southeast Asia. There, as perhaps elsewhere, "polycentrism" is at work. Communist parties and the communist movement may be fractionating into separate competitive and even divergent parts. Despite its mass, nuclearized power and weight of leadership, Peking will confront limits to its assertion of influence and control in its own interest or for its grand design for the world countryside and eventual victory insofar as Vietnamese communism and Vietnamese communist leaders are concerned. Circumstances may persuade them to take differing attitudes towards patterns of collective security, against other strong nationalist states in Southeast Asia, successful regional development in the Mekong area, and even participation eventually in United Nations activities for the benefit of North Vietnam.

IV. *UNITED STATES INTERESTS*

Strategic Policy

Since World War II the United States Government has sought to deny the "South Sea area" to any foreign military conquest. At the same time it has sought no territory or had other designs in Southeast Asia for itself. Although it preferred neutralization to military intervention there in 1941, Japanese expansion into the Philippines, Thailand, Malaya and Indonesia was considered a threat to the United States and to the West. Even if there had not been a Pearl Harbor, the Allies probably would have eventually been forced to take joint military action against Japan because of its encroachments upon this area.

In the postwar period four Presidents of the United States and their Secretaries of State have developed this strategic concept of United States interests in Southeast Asia. Immediately upon the communist victory in China in 1949–1950, American Ambassadors in Asia and officials in Washington began to develop economic and military assistance programs for Southeast Asia. In 1950 the sudden outbreak of war in Korea led President Truman to aid French forces fighting the Viet Minh in Indochina and to seek a single comprehensive security system for the Far East including Australia, New Zealand, Indonesia, the Philippines, Thailand and Japan. Only separate alliances were feasible with some, and none with Indonesia. The United States has a bilateral Mutual Defense Treaty with the Philippines, and a bilateral Treaty with Australia and New Zealand, the former in force in 1951, the latter in 1952. After the armistice in Korea in 1953, the Administration in Washington became extremely sensitive to a possible shift of Communist aggression to Southeast Asia. President Eisenhower and Secretary Dulles sought united action, convinced that the defense of Southeast Asia was indivisible. Capture of any one of the countries there would endanger all others.

This last concept has become known as the "domino theory." At a press conference on April 7, 1954, President Eisenhower said that the possible consequences of the loss of Southeast Asia would be incalculable to the Free World. The tumble of one piece, or one domino, he suggested, would necessarily be followed by the fall of a whole series of neighboring "dominoes." If Indochina were to fall, it would be followed probably by the fall of Thailand. Then Burma would go in turn, succeeded by Malaya and then Indonesia. Such a sequence of losses would create vital strategic problems for the United States, he believed. Under the domino theory the defensive island chain of Japan, Taiwan, the Philippines, Australia and New Zealand would be greatly endangered. India would be outflanked and cut off from communications with East Asia and the Pacific. The strategic importance of Indochina thus became obvious. "If Indochina fell, not only Thailand but Burma and Malaya would be threatened, with added risks to East Pakistan and South Asia as well as to all Indonesia." [38]

Such was the strategic policy which led to the formation of SEATO and United States ratification of the Southeast Asia Collective Defense Treaty in 1955. This strategic policy also determined the decision of the United States Government to do everything possible to deter aggression in Southeast Asia, to back the State of Vietnam in 1954, to provide military and economic assistance unilaterally to Cambodia and Laos, and to join in a public pledge of the SEATO countries to support those three states under the Protocol of the SEATO Treaty. In the fall of 1954 and the first part of 1955, when Vietnam seemed to be disintegrating and the rest of Southeast Asia ready to fall in some fashion, either like dominoes or bowling pins, it was the decision of the United States Government, taken through the National Security Council to the President, that the Southern flanks of Asia as well as the vital strategic position of the Western Pacific would be progressively impaired if the United States did not make every effort with its Allies to strengthen the Nationalist movements of Vietnam, Cambodia, and Laos as well as all the other countries of Southeast Asia including Burma, Indonesia, and, of course, the Philippines. The policies in 1954, based on the strategic concept of Southeast Asia, were the ones that involved the United States in this area following the Geneva Conference. It was this strategic concept which underlay the now

44

famous letter of President Eisenhower to Prime Minister Diem of October 23, 1954.

In 1959 President Eisenhower changed his metaphor somewhat to say that the capture of South Vietnam by the Communists would menace the rest of Southeast Asia "by a great flanking movement." Such a loss of South Vietnam would "set in motion a crumbling process that could as it progressed have grave consequences for us and for freedom."

President Kennedy adopted this same strategic policy. About two months before he was assassinated, President Kennedy was asked if he had any reason to doubt the "so-called" domino theory, that if South Vietnam fell the rest of Southeast Asia will go behind it. He answered

"No, I believe it. I believe it. I think that the struggle is close enough. China is so large, looms so high just beyond the frontiers, that if South Vietnam went it would not only give them an improved geographic position for a guerrilla assault on Malaya, but would also give the impression that the wave of the future in Southeast Asia was China and the Communists. So I believe it."[39]

He too saw the indivisibility of the Asian countries and the regional requirement of counter-measures. President Johnson has established this continuity of policy in Vietnam and Southeast Asia on the basis that the issue "is the future of Southeast Asia as a whole."

Looking back, this strategic policy was based on the assumption that the United States could work with and assist all these countries of Southeast Asia on a mutual basis of friendship and cooperation. It has been and remains the policy of the United States to do everything possible and feasible to encourage and sustain the independence, survival, and growth of these states. Assistance in many forms has been extended to and welcomed by all of them in the first part of the past decade. Washington tried to encourage regional association in various forms, supported involvement of the United Nations in Southeast Asia, and endorsed Asian solutions to national and even regional issues. However, during the past ten years it is my view that these policies have not been pursued with sufficient vigor or imagination. The basic assumption

45

has now become invalid. Leaving aside the special and extreme case of Vietnam, we can deal freely and comprehensively only with the Philippines and Thailand compared to the widespread access and open welcome we had in Southeast Asia in 1955. As times have changed, so must policies, whatever the many complex reasons for this shift. In theory the strategic policy of regional indivisibility is still true, but in fact Thailand is the only area in the region—excluding the offshore islands of the Philippines—where full mutuality and reciprocity of partnership can still be positively undertaken without being subject to hostilities, the total breakdown of internal order, or the inhibitions of international agreements.

The Legal Basis for U.S. Interests and Involvements in Southeast Asia

A succession of executive commitments, treaties and laws forms the legal basis for the United States position with respect to Vietnam and all Southeast Asia. We can begin with the statement of July 21, 1954 regarding the Geneva agreements, when the United States declared that it would view any renewal of aggression in violation of those agreements as a serious threat to international peace and security. By this statement the Executive Branch of the United States Government indicated that it would feel free to take whatever action it then considered necessary to meet such aggressive violation.

The fundamental legal basis for United States action in mainland Southeast Asia, aside from executive acts, is the Southeast Asia Collective Defense Treaty which was signed at Manila on September 8, 1954. The Senate gave its advice and consent to its ratification on February 1, 1955 by a vote of 82–1. The President ratified the treaty on February 4, 1955. The instruments of ratification were deposited with the Government of the Philippines on February 19, the day on which the treaty came into force for all eight members. The Treaty basically provides that each party will act to meet the common danger of aggression by means of armed attack in the treaty area in accordance with the constitutional processes of each party.* The area includes South Vietnam.

---

* See Part V for the details on the Treaty and on SEATO.

The policy of the United States Government of assisting free Vietnam, Laos and Cambodia was undertaken not only in line with a strategic concept but also under the aegis of this Treaty. The massive program of assistance and the indirect military commitment have always been complementary. It would have made no sense to become so heavily involved without either a strategic concept or a legal basis. By the same token a bilateral treaty for the protection of South Vietnam alone would have been, and nearly became, meaningless without the substance of internal morale and political strength. That was the underlying essence of the letter of President Eisenhower to Prime Minister Diem of October 23, 1954. It began the long series of Presidential determinations for increasing and expanding assistance on behalf of the efforts of the free Vietnamese to resist aggression, subversion and other situations endangering the peace of the area.

While that letter began the unilateral involvement of the United States in Vietnam, it was highly conditional. First, it was predicated on the ratification of the SEATO Treaty so as to provide a constitutional mandate for whatever military intervention might be required to safeguard post-Geneva Southeast Asia. Secondly, the letter was conditioned on assurances from the Government of Vietnam of standards of performance in applying new reforms and in using United States aid. The letter stated that the Government of the United States expected that its aid would "be met by performance on the part of the Government of Vietnam in undertaking needed reforms." The purpose of such aid was to contribute "effectively" toward an independent Vietnam "endowed with a strong government." And the crucial sentence of this significant letter established the basis and the purpose of American policy in Vietnam:

"Such a government would . . . be so responsive to the nationalist aspirations of its people, so enlightened in purpose and effective in performance, that it will be respected both at home and abroad and discourage any who might wish to impose a foreign ideology on your free people."[40]

The United States proceeded to carry out its undertaking by a large program of social, economic and military assistance to encourage and promote a genuinely nationalist government and society in South Vietnam. The goals were good government,

47

rural reform, and effective security. The United States developed this policy with its French and British allies in a series of tripartite meetings in 1954 and 1955 at which several basic disagreements among them were reconciled by mid-1955. These understandings provided the diplomatic basis for United States policy. At that point all these countries were agreed on supporting South Vietnam as an independent state under international law, assisting the legal government of Ngo Dinh Diem and encouraging the consultations of the government in Saigon with the government in Hanoi regarding all-Vietnamese elections. Laos and Cambodia also received American assistance directly in much the same context in 1955.

With respect to Vietnam, the policy of assistance has continued under Presidents Kennedy and Johnson. The Joint Communique of Vice President Johnson and President Diem of May 1961, approved by President Kennedy, established a series of programs for strengthening Vietnam. On December 14, 1961 President Kennedy wrote President Diem that the Government of the United States continued to view any renewal of aggression in violation of the Geneva Accords with grave concern and as seriously threatening international peace and security. In accordance with that unilateral statement of 1954, reaffirmed in this letter of 1961, and in response to President Diem's request, President Kennedy assured him that the United States was prepared to help the Republic of Vietnam to protect its people and to preserve its independence.[41]

In 1962 the United States Government took executive actions which did not require ratification or advice and consent by the Senate but which did broaden the base for U.S. policy and law in Southeast Asia. In March 1962 the United States and Thailand agreed upon a unilateral interpretation of the SEATO Treaty that the United States could take action under the Treaty for the defense of Thailand, and by implication for any other member of the Treaty or designated territory, before other members had acted or even in spite of their non-action or veto.

In July 1962 the United States became a signatory with thirteen other governments to a Declaration on the neutrality of Laos. This Declaration removed Laos from the protection of

SEATO and obligated the United States and all other signatories to refrain from taking a number of actions with regard to that country. By the same token the United States was involved in these reciprocal obligations on the understanding that all signatories would adhere to this international contract.

A broad grant of authority to act in Southeast Asia was given President Johnson by the Joint Resolution of Congress of August 10, 1964.[42] For the second time since World War II, an act of Congress validated and reinforced the strategic policy of the United States in the area of Southeast Asia. The first act was the Senate's advice and consent to the Southeast Asia Treaty. The Joint Resolution of 1964 seems to have extended the intent of the Congress in this regard. Section 2 of the Resolution states that "The United States regards as vital to its national interest and to world peace the maintenance of international peace and security in southeast Asia." Never before had the Congress, or the Executive for that matter, asserted the vital strategic interest of the United States in Southeast Asia so categorically and clearly, although such interest was implied in ratification of the SEATO Treaty and in the hearings on it. This section of the Resolution went on, after referring to the obligations of the United States under that Treaty, to state that the United States "is prepared, as the President determines, to take all necessary steps, including the use of armed force, to assist any member or protocol state of the Southeast Asia Collective Defense Treaty requesting assistance in defense of its freedom." This Resolution was approved by a total vote of 502, with only 2 opposed. The Resolution, undertaken in Congress at the time of North Vietnamese Communist attacks on U.S. ships in international waters, declared that the United States had no territorial, military or political ambitions in Southeast Asia, but only desired that the people there should be left in peace "to work out their own destinies in their own way." The Joint Resolution provided that it would expire when the President determined that the peace and security of Southeast Asia were reasonably assured "by international conditions created by action of the United Nations or otherwise."

Finally, the United States is taking military and other actions in Vietnam and elsewhere in Southeast Asia on the basis of both international law and the United Nations Charter. Regarding the right of self-defense in the event of aggression, the United States takes the position that the Government of North Vietnam has ignored and violated the solemn commitments by which it is bound and which it undertook in the 1954 Geneva Agreements and the 1962 Geneva Agreements. These violations constitute aggression in the judgment of the United States. Accordingly it invokes the long-standing principle of international law— "that a material breach of a treaty by one party entitles other parties at least to withhold compliance with an equivalent, corresponding or related provision until the other party is prepared to observe its obligations"[43] According to the United States Government, South Vietnam is justified in withholding compliance with those provisions of the 1954 Agreements which limit its ability to protect its very existence. Those provisions would be the prohibitions against reinforcements of troops, foreign military personnel, arms, munitions and other military equipment, all over and beyond replacement requirements, and prohibitions against granting or establishing military bases in South Vietnam or entering into a military alliance.

In addition, the United States relies upon the provisions for self-defense in Article 51 of the United Nations Charter. Its actions, being defensive in character and designed to resist armed aggression as the United States determines and defines it, are consistent with the purposes and principles of the Charter in the absence of or pending action by the United Nations to maintain an effective peace in the area.[43]

All these legal bases for United States policies and actions in Southeast Asia derive additional Congressional and statutory authorization from the intent of Congress in providing authorization and funds for carrying them out.

The Commitment and Use of United States Power in Southeast Asia

Despite the strategic policy and legal bases for the United States view of its law and policy in Southeast Asia, there has been uncertainty and imprecision as to the desirable extent of military intervention by combat forces of the United States in Southeast

Asia during the past fifteen years. The United States has never clearly and unequivocally stated that it would intervene with its forces in Vietnam, Laos or Cambodia in the event of aggression and a request from those states for such assistance. Thailand is the only country or area in mainland Southeast Asia where such a deployment would flow from an advance commitment. Even today there is continuing doubt and uncertainty, as well as controversy, over the extent to which the United States should commit, deploy and use its military power in Southeast Asia subject to the wishes of the government or governments concerned. The question is of the greatest importance because the use of force by the United States can stabilize the security of the area. Uncertainty regarding its intentions will continue to weaken such stability.

In 1954 the Eisenhower Administration was conditionally prepared to commit and use U.S. military power in Southeast Asia and particularly in Indochina. When the situation in Vietnam was approaching a military catastrophe for the French in June of 1954, President Eisenhower told his principal advisers that he would approve American military action but only on certain conditions: (1) the United States should not undertake to counter Chinese Communist aggression unilaterally; (2) if the nations of the Southeast Asian area were completely indifferent to the fate of Indochina, the United States should undertake a reappraisal of its basic security policy in the region; (3) the Southeast Asian nations could not disclaim responsibility for their own safety and expect the United States alone to carry all the burdens of Free World security; and (4) if the President found it necessary to ask Congress for authority to intervene militarily in Indochina he wanted to assure the Congress that the United States had allies such as Thailand, Australia, New Zealand, the Philippines and the bulk of the Vietnamese people ready to join the United States in resisting Chinese Communist aggression.[44] This willingness to contemplate military intervention was geared to invasion by Communist China which was uppermost in the minds of the Administration as the dominant threat in 1954.

Secretary Dulles at the same time spoke on the conditions for American military intervention where there was no open invasion by Communist China but where the peace and tranquility of the area were being disturbed in part by that country. These conditions then were: an invitation from lawful authorities; clear assurance of complete independence of Laos, Cambodia and Vietnam; evidence of concern by the United Nations; a joining in the collective effort of some of the other nations of the area; and assurance that France would not itself withdraw from the battle until it had won.[45] Secretary Dulles stated in this public speech that only such conditions would justify the President and the Congress in asking the American people to make the sacrifices necessary for committing the United States with others to using force to help restore peace in the area. Eleven years later only a few of those conditions can be fulfilled. We have an invitation from the lawful authorities of the Republic of Vietnam. There is a collective effort—but not strictly speaking a SEATO action— of some of the other nations in the area, including Thailand, Korea, the Philippines, Australia, New Zealand, Malaysia, the United Kingdom, the Republic of China and others. Except for the military assistance provided by Thailand, Korea, the Philippines and Australia, this collective effort is more economic and moral than military. France has long since withdrawn its military forces from Indochina and seeks to negotiate an international treaty of neutrality for the area in opposition, and one might say defiance, of the United States at this particular time. As for the United Nations, no formulation has been taken, although the Secretary General, the Security Council, and many members of the General Assembly have registered interest and concern in various aspects.

Going back to 1954 again, the United States did not intervene with its forces then nor did it enter into an international agreement at Geneva to guarantee the enforcement of those agreements for the security and peace of the area. The question of military commitment was residual and contingent for several years, although the possibility remained real and likely. In 1955 Senator Mansfield's report on Vietnam warned that the Viet Minh might once again resort to force "to achieve their aim of domination of the entire country." Such a resumption of hostilities could have taken the forms of an uprising of the Viet Minh underground in South Vietnam or of an invasion of Viet

Minh forces from the north with or without support from the Chinese Communists. The Senator's report stated that hostilities by the Communists there would be a serious threat to world peace and would produce the gravest international repercussions. Since the U.S. policies respecting Vietnam were then serving the interests of the United States, the Senator believed that such policy "may well have reduced the danger of the direct and costly involvement of our military forces in Southeast Asia." [46]

In 1961 the issue of military intervention again confronted the United States Government at the beginning of a new Administration. This time the issue was the use of force to hold Laos if diplomacy could not maintain and neutralize it as an independent, neutral, non-Communist state. The outgoing Administration of President Eisenhower was prepared to commit U.S. forces but it had no further responsibility and went out of office with that recommendation to President Kennedy.

He faced a difficult dilemma with such a thin electoral mandate, and with Laos so difficult to explain or understand when it came to asking American troops to risk their lives in such a faraway, unknown country. In order to indicate certain limits beyond which the Communists should not go, he used a show of force by the Seventh Fleet off Southeast Asia. But his Administration recoiled from the decision in 1961 to deploy U.S. forces in Thailand and Laos under SEATO plans to hold the Mekong Valley, insure the cease-fire, and maintain lateral communications in the panhandle of Laos from Thailand across to Vietnam. Instead the Administration resorted to diplomacy at the Geneva Conference to obtain an agreement on neutrality. There was at that time no inclination among Congressional leadership, and certainly no pressure from public opinion, to commit and use military force to strengthen our bargaining position for negotiating the most satisfactory agreement possible.

In the spring of 1962 the Communists undertook military operations when it appeared that an agreement might not be forthcoming at Geneva. President Kennedy responded rapidly and effectively by deploying American combat forces to Thailand in May of 1962. The air and ground units were equipped, assigned and located for the defense of Thailand, but also for operations in Laos if need be. The signal of power came over loudly in Peking and Moscow. The Geneva Agreement was concluded six weeks later. Most of the American combat forces returned then to their regular battle stations. But the United States, in agreement with the Government of Thailand, made arrangements to leave all the necessary combat and logistic equipment ready in Thailand for another deployment. Fixed stationing of equipment was found to be a much more effective formula for translating static power into real power than an indefinite stationing of American troops. The locus and logistics for the commitment and use of American power in Thailand, for deployment there or elsewhere in Southeast Asia, remain an effective extension of U.S. power in that area.

In 1965 the United States Government began using its own military forces in Vietnam, North and South, and in Laos, for operations against the North Vietnamese Communist forces and military installations, to counter aggression. This commitment and use of power are tied to assistance for the Republic of Vietnam, at its invitation, and to a restoration of the "essence" of the Geneva Accords. In addition, such power is legally conditioned on action by the United Nations or some other international body to restore peace and security to the area. When any of those conditions have been fulfilled or changed, U.S. power will be withdrawn from Vietnam. No statement or implication by any United States authority would indicate that the commitment and use of U.S. power in Vietnam alone is anything but a conditional and temporary act taken by virtue of the legal bases underlying U.S. interests in Southeast Asia. However, there can be no doubt that the United States has finally decided to commit military forces to mainland Southeast Asia. This is a controversial act of policy even though it falls within the law as interpreted by the United States.

V. *SEATO AND COLLECTIVE SECURITY IN SOUTHEAST ASIA*

Apart from the U.N., the only forum for collective security in this area that is likely to remain is the Southeast Asia Treaty Organization. Yet, only two of its eight members are countries within the area: Thailand and the Philippines. The other six members are Australia, New Zealand (which are in the area of Southeast Asia but are not Asian countries as such), Pakistan, France, the United Kingdom and the United States.

SEATO was formed in the summer and fall of 1954 under the leadership of John Foster Dulles and the aegis of the United States and put into operation after ratification of the Treaty in early 1955.[47] It was conceived in a period of serious tension and great strain after the French fiasco in Vietnam and when the leaders of the eight SEATO members by common consent feared a continuation of communist aggression by invasion across frontiers or by major infiltration underneath them into South Vietnam, Laos, Cambodia, Thailand, and Malaya. An understanding of SEATO has to be based on an appreciation of the temper of its origins. It was designed to deter that aggression, particularly a military attack by conventional armies and air-forces against the states of Southeast Asia.[48]

SEATO has established a group of permanent offices and operations. It has its headquarters in Bangkok with a Secretariat of less than 100. The Council of Ministers has met every year but one when the United States preferred to avoid a meeting because of the difficulties in Laos. The senior military officers of the eight countries confer frequently and submit joint papers or individual recommendations as the military advisers to the Foreign Ministers. In the military sphere, numerous joint plans have been developed to meet every conceivable contingency of aggression from communist sources over the past ten years. To make these plans realistic, the SEATO members—either all eight or some combination—have carried out many military maneuvers and exercises. These have unquestionably improved and tightened the capabilities of the combined military forces involved in these exercises to conduct a defense against armed attack by communist forces in the Treaty area. In addition, SEATO has organized various committees on economic and cultural cooperation, but these have not yet had much impact on the development of regional equilibrium or cooperation.

The Treaty area covers the "general area of Southeast Asia and the Southwest Pacific," meaning the territory of the members in

55

Southeast Asia, East and West Pakistan but not India or For-mosa. When the Treaty came into existence a Protocol signed by the Ministers in Manila in 1954 extended the terms of the Treaty to the so-called "Protocol States" of Laos, Cambodia and South Vietnam. The governments of these three states then de-sired and agreed to this protection, which meant that if any one of them requested assistance from SEATO, the members would consult as to what action should be taken. However, Cambodia has since officially rejected any such protection and receded from the SEATO Protocol. In 1962 Laos was removed from the so-called SEATO umbrella by the Geneva agreement on the neu-trality of Laos. Only South Vietnam remains technically and actually within the terms of the Protocol to the Treaty today.

Article I of this collective Treaty provides that the Parties will settle any international disputes by peaceful means and re-frain from the threat or use of force in any manner inconsistent with the purposes of the United Nations. Article II provides that the Parties will separately and jointly by means of continuous and effective self-help and mutual aid, maintain and develop their individual and collective capacity to resist armed attack and to prevent and counter subversive activities directed from without against their territorial integrity and political stability. In Article III the Parties undertook to strengthen "their free institutions" and to cooperate with one another in the further development of economic measures to promote economic prog-ress and social well-being.

Article IV is the heart of the Treaty. In view of the fact that it is the principal legal basis for United States policy in Southeast Asia, it is well to quote it in full:

"1. Each Party recognizes that aggression by means of armed attack in the treaty area against any of the Parties or against any State or territory which the Parties by unanimous agreement may hereafter designate, would endanger its own peace and safety, and agrees that it will in that event act to meet the common danger in accordance with its constitutional processes. Measures taken under this paragraph shall be immediately reported to the Security Council of the United Nations.

"2. If, in the opinion of any of the Parties, the inviolability or the integ-rity of the territory or the sovereignty or political independence of any Party in the treaty area or of any other State or territory to which the pro-visions of paragraph 1 of this Article from time to time apply is threatened in any way other than by armed attack or is affected or threatened by any fact or situation which might endanger the peace of the area, the Parties shall consult immediately in order to agree on the measures which should be taken for the common defense.

"3. It is understood that no action on the territory of any State designated by unanimous agreement under paragraph 1 of this Article or on any territory so designated shall be taken except at the invitation or with the consent of the government concerned." [49]

As noted above, Laos, Cambodia and South Vietnam have been designated for the purposes of the Article, but the first two have since been removed from this classification.

Article IV thus provides that each Party will act to meet the common danger of armed attack in the treaty area against any of the Parties or as otherwise defined. That action could be individual or collective. As regards collective action, it has become the understanding and the practice that the unanimous consent of all the Parties would be required. As regards individual action, the United States and Thailand have interpreted the Article to mean that each Party is free to take such action without waiting for a unanimous or collective decision.

The second paragraph of Article IV only provides for consultation, and not for any collective or individual action, as Secretary Dulles pointed out in the Senate hearings on its advice and consent to this Treaty. However, the intent of this paragraph was, he said, to encourage and provide for common measures to emerge from such consultations. In its application to the Protocol States any threat other than of armed attack would require consultation, but there was no obligation, he said, to take action collectively.

The remaining Articles of this Treaty established a Council to meet at any time and to provide for military and other planning as necessary in the treaty area. Any other country could accede to the Treaty by unanimous agreement of the Parties. It remains in force indefinitely, but any Party may terminate its membership after one year's notice of denunciation.

In addition to the text of the Treaty itself, the United States introduced an understanding, which was recognized and validated by the other signatories, that paragraph 1 of Article IV applies only to "communist aggression," but that, in the event of other aggression or armed attack, the United States would consult under the provisions of paragraph 2.

Now all but forgotten, the signatories at the same time proclaimed a Pacific Charter for establishing common action to maintain peace and security in Southeast Asia and the Southwest Pacific. In this document the Parties declared that they: (1) upheld the principle of equal rights and self-determination of peoples and would earnestly strive by every peaceful means to promote self-government and to secure the independence of all countries whose people desire it and are able to undertake its responsibilities; (2) were each prepared to continue taking effective practical measures to ensure conditions favorable to the orderly achievement of the foregoing; (3) would continue to cooperate in economic, social and cultural fields in order to promote higher living standards, economic progress, and social well-being in this region; and (4) were determined, as declared in the Southeast Asia Collective Defense Treaty, "to prevent or counter by appropriate means any attempt in the treaty area to subvert their freedom or to destroy their sovereignty or territorial integrity." This Charter is still in effect.

For the United States, three aspects of the SEATO system on collective security are important insofar as seeking regional equilibrium are concerned. First, this country has consistently refused to ear-mark and deploy air, naval and ground forces to be stationed within the Treaty area in a manner similar to the deployment of U.S. forces to Europe under NATO. Thailand and the Philippines have often complained that this refusal weakened the Treaty, but the United States has maintained that flexibility of deployment of its strategic and tactical forces would serve as a much more effective deterrent to communist aggression than fixed bases or stationed forces in Southeast Asia. Insofar as the record shows, collective security by SEATO—which means, in effect, the Strategic Air Command, the 7th Fleet and U.S. ground forces—has succeeded in deterring any overt aggression in the conventional sense for the past decade. Presumably this deterrence has contributed to this kind of limited equilibrium in Southeast Asia and will continue to do so. Accordingly, SEATO contributes an element of stability within the laws of the member states and under Articles 51 and 52 of the United Nations Charter.

Until the crisis in Laos in 1961, the United States looked upon SEATO as a collective organization which would take military action, with all eight members participating in the actions as well as the decision. When that crisis occurred, however, it had to revise its interpretation as a result of the refusal of France to participate. The obstructive attitudes of the French so alarmed the Government of Thailand, much more threatened in Southeast Asia than France, that it considered it had either to persuade all its colleagues to amend the Treaty to eliminate from SEATO the principle of unanimity of decision, or to decide whether to remain a member of the organization. As a result of a complicated series of diplomatic negotiations, the dilemma was solved when the United States in 1962 made a significant and unilateral interpretation of its obligations under Article IV. In the joint statement of March 6, 1962 issued by the Secretary of State and the Foreign Minister of Thailand, the United States declared that its obligation under the Treaty to assist Thailand in the event of "communist armed attack" was "individual as well as collective and not dependent upon prior agreement by all the other SEATO members." While this interpretation did not change the underlying assumption made when the Treaty was drafted that the United States would do just that, Thailand had reaffirmation by the Secretary and approval by President Kennedy and could thus ignore the French "veto." The Treaty has thus become primarily a bilateral undertaking between Thailand and the United States but with the participation of other flags and forces in the operation. Without this interpretation, SEATO probably would have collapsed.

In the future, collective security under SEATO may become less secure as it becomes less significant. In effect, it today represents an assumption primarily and perhaps even uniquely for Thailand only. Not only is France a disinterested and negative partner whose exit from SEATO would have been more gracefully received than its continued obstruction, but Pakistan has also become disinterested if not totally disenchanted because the Treaty is not an instrument it can use against India. That is

59

what Pakistan wanted when it joined SEATO in the first place. Apparently, Pakistan does not consider itself a country in Southeast Asia even though East Pakistan is vulnerably connected with that area. Pakistan's policy of friendship with Communist China muddles its participation for some in the only collective security organization in Southeast Asia designed to deter and defend its members against communist aggression. The Philippines, too, does not need SEATO because it is allied with the United States in a bilateral Treaty of Mutual Defense.[50] And Australia and New Zealand, members of the British Commonwealth, are also similarly allied with the United States.[51] Thailand is thus the only one of the eight nations that is concerned from the standpoint of its own protection with the SEATO system of collective security.

However, from the point of view of the United States, the continued membership of at least six nations in SEATO is a considerable advantage in the absence of any other system for maintaining a minimum of stability and equilibrium against conventional or regular warfare. In the first place, the SEATO Treaty and the bilateral treaty with the Philippines give the United States the legal and constitutional basis for military operations in the area where the interests of Thailand and the Philippines are affected. Without the Treaty, American forces might not be able to operate out of bases in the Philippines for the broader purposes of regional security. In the second place, the Treaty and the Protocol provide some legal framework for United States military assistance and military cooperation on behalf of the Government of the Republic of Vietnam. At their very first meeting, the SEATO Ministers in 1955 issued a unanimous communique which specifically applied that Protocol to Vietnam as follows:

"Realizing the importance to the security of Southeast Asia and the Southwest Pacific of the States of Cambodia, Laos, and of the free territory under the jurisdiction of the State of Viet Nam, the Council reaffirmed the determination of the member governments to support these three States in maintaining their freedom and independence as set forth in the Protocol of the Treaty. The Council was informed of assistance which had been extended to the three States and expressed the hope that member governments would offer further assistance."[52]

In 1957 President Eisenhower and President Diem reaffirmed that relationship. The United States has not rescinded it since. In fact, this connection by virtue of SEATO has been reaffirmed.

What has SEATO otherwise accomplished? And should it be continued, expanded or disbanded? It is hard to draw up a balance sheet because the history of SEATO is full of complications. It certainly has not been an outstanding success as a "community-sanctioning process." At the same time it has not been a failure. It is not a well known, let alone a popular, organization even among its member states. It is, of course, disliked by neutrals in Asia and detested by the communists. There are many who criticize it on the ground that it has caused more disunity and violence than it has prevented. It probably has sharpened the division between the so-called aligned and non-aligned in Southeast Asia. It has not been effective in coping with aggression by seepage in Vietnam, Laos or Thailand. And it does not cover Malaysia. It has not attracted any new members since it was formed ten years ago. The only possibility was Malaya when it became independent in 1957, but the new Government then decided that its domestic problem of relations between Chinese and Malays made it impossible for political reasons to join SEATO. Moreover, Malaysia had a defense agreement with the United Kingdom and became a member of the Commonwealth. Even the United States has often been reserved and inconsistent in its attitude toward SEATO. For example, it landed forces in Thailand, began a program of air attacks in Vietnam and appealed for other countries to assist Saigon.

However, no signatory has suffered a direct military attack, whereas India and Malaysia have. The commitment and deployment of American forces in Southeast Asia has become an unchallenged fact as well as a vital factor. Even the neutrals during the past ten years have, privately or secretly, expressed gratification in having the insurance of SEATO's indirect protection without having to pay any premiums.[53]

The crux of the matter is that SEATO lacks constructive potentiality because of its very deterrent capability. It contradicts any law of convergence for Southeast Asia. It cannot respond to the requirements for a law of community. It cannot, by definition, provide any law of reciprocity with the communists in peace-keeping. It perhaps does connote the limits of warfare and contribute to the law of limited belligerency. But it is not producing a regional community or political stability.[54]

For these purposes it is doubtful whether SEATO as an organization can be useful, relevant, or practical. To be invoked for Vietnam, moreover, all eight votes would be required under Article IV. France and Pakistan would probably either object or abstain, nullifying the *total* collective action. However, the other members of SEATO are aiding the Republic of Vietnam—Australia, New Zealand, the Philippines, Thailand, as well as the United States. Nevertheless, if major forces of North Vietnam or Communist China invaded South Vietnam, or any other part of the Treaty area for that matter, it is probable that SEATO would react instantly, vigorously, and effectively. In any event, the United States would not be prevented from taking immediate unilateral action according to its interpretation of the Treaty.

VI. *PROSPECTS FOR REGIONALISM*

Forms of regional association including some or all of the Southeast Asian states would, of course, provide the foundation and the framework for a community-based equilibrium in the area. Some observers have regarded regionalism as the panacea to Southeast Asian problems. Others have considered any form of regionalism impractical if not impossible. Whether the force of diversity or the force of unity will win out if external powers were to leave Southeast Asia alone is a controversial but important issue.

The Record

The area lacks any historical precedent for regionalism that is not imperialistic. The pre-modern period of Southeast Asia's history contains no evidence of any grouping together of the kingdoms and principalities for some common interest—protection, trade or power. The hierarchical system of overlordship under China's benevolent sanction was area-wide, but the "Great Peace" of the emperors was more a wish than a reality. Colonialism was the highly-segregated antithesis of regional community.

Independence since 1945 has not yet demonstrated any deep roots or strong tendencies to encourage the growth of regional cooperation and association within the area.

The original leaders of the independence movements—the law-givers of nationalism and freedom in Southeast Asia—put forward proposals for political collaboration in the first few years after World War II. But in their later careers they have veered away from regionality, as have their successors. The great Burmese leader, Aung San, suggested an Asian "Potsdam Conference" and the formation of an Asian Commonwealth with India as one entity, China another, and Southeast Asia another. He also proposed a Southeast Asia Economic Union of Burma, Indonesia, Thailand, Indochina and Malaya. His assassination apparently ended Burmese initiative along these lines.[55] In 1947 the Thai Government announced that Thailand and France would sponsor a Pan Southeast Asian Union to include Cambodia, Laos, Thailand, Vietnam and later Burma, Indonesia, Borneo and India. The objective of this union would have been the joint development of water resources, fisheries and communications in the Mekong Valley. This idea never took hold. In 1949 another Thai Prime Minister took the initiative of inviting Burma, the Philippines and India to Bangkok to discuss political and economic problems in Southeast Asia. That conference was never held because the invited states declined. In 1950, on the initiative of President Quirino of the Philippines, a regional conference did take place in Baguio, Philippines, with Indonesia, Thailand, the Philippines from Southeast Asia, and India, Pakistan, Ceylon and Australia. Social, economic and cultural questions were discussed. However, no organization resulted from this conference. In 1954 a Thai official proposed a union or association of the Buddhist countries of Laos, Cambodia, Burma and Thailand, but nothing came of this effort either. Later on in 1954 the Southeast Asia Treaty Organization was formed, but it combined with non-Asian powers and should not be considered a truly Southeast Asian form of regionalism.

Two more recent efforts to regionalize relationships in Southeast Asia at the political level have also been tried and have not succeeded.[56] One of these was the "Asociation of Southeast Asia"

formed by Malaysia, the Philippines and Thailand in 1961 for
mutual economic, cultural, educational and other non-military
purposes.[57]ASA did begin to put together the first indigenous organization for carrying out joint or regional projects. The other
was Maphilindo formed by Malaya (not Malaysia), the Philippines and Indonesia in 1963.[58]

Prospects for Some Regionalism

It is doubtful that political regionalism or area-wide defense
will emerge to play a part in encouraging regional equilibrium
or regional institutions for political collaboration or collective
defense. Centrifugal and divisive tendencies are too strong.
Leaders will be more interested in relations with outside countries than among themselves, and more inclined to participate
in Pan-Asian or international conferences and organizations than
in exclusively Southeast Asian formations. They know that real
power and needed resources, which the Southeast Asian countries
do not possess, will continue to come from outside the region.
Even the common fear of Communist China and the threat of
Chinese minorities will not develop any sense of solidarity or
serve to coordinate the divergent policies of neutrality and align-
ment. One political dilemma in Southeast Asia is that these
new governments are trying desperately to become viable nation-
states in an area where the individual state may, despite internal
nationalism and good leadership, be turning obsolescent for the
security and development of the area, and where at the same time
a sense of regional community and purpose is lacking to comple-
ment and reinforce the nation-state.

On the other hand, the prospects for limited and specific forms
of interstate cooperation on a functional basis within Southeast
Asia are more promising than political or military regionalism.
Some form of functional federalism appears to be emerging. It
can even bridge the differences between neutralist and aligned
countries to bring them together in technical, social and economic collaboration. Organizations such as the United Nations
Economic Commission for Asia and the Far East (ECAFE), the
Asian Productivity Organization, the Eastern Regional Organisation for Special Administration, the Association of Southeast

Asian States, and even the non-military activities of SEATO, indicate that there has been a growth and that there are prospects of functional federalism and specific cooperation on a regional basis.[59] There are several practical considerations underlying these prospects. Personal conflicts among some of the prestigious personalities in Southeast Asia will decline as they disappear from the scene. The younger generation of professionally trained men and women will be studying, visiting or working in neighboring countries in increasing numbers. They already seem more concerned with cooperation than confrontation, and prefer conciliation to conflict in their own area. Academically, regional studies are just beginning. Nevertheless, these tentative and fragile prospects for technical cooperation and functional federalism need tactful encouragement and incentive from the outside.

The study and profession of law and the administration of justice probably could utilize many more direct contacts with their opposite numbers in Southeast Asia as well as with other like-minded countries. A program of international cooperation for providing law libraries, case studies for strengthening the teaching of law, and for exchanging views within the profession could be extensively promoted as a new and needed form of international technical assistance for nation building and regional equilibrium. Furthermore, new generations and younger leaders will require increasing assistance from international agencies to deal with the growing stresses and strains of modernization in conflict in both internal and external affairs in Southeast Asia. The more that individual governments and international agencies can strengthen the capacity of the new leaders to provide responsible and effective government at the national level and in the countryside and to meet the rising demands of modernization, the more these individual nations will be stabilized. Such stability will, in turn, contribute to the role of law and a workable order in this area.

In view of the fact that the individual states of Southeast Asia have so far had little economic interest in trading with their immediate neighbors or in their individual development, encouragement of economic reciprocity and some form of common economic interests would also contribute to the stability and equilibrium of Southeast Asia. It would be helpful to balance the tendency of these countries to trade in exports and imports primarily with countries outside the region. The economic concept of common productive facilities to be established in one country to supply the market in several is beginning to be considered. Even a Common Market for Southeast Asia is under discussion. Despite the structural deficiencies in regional cooperation, potentialities for overcoming economic nationalism and exclusive interest in the world economy can be developed. The Mekong River Basin, which President Johnson has singled out for particular attention this year, offers great promise as a core area for building an economic and regional community for functional federalism. Thailand, Malaysia and the Philippines also may develop into another "core."

Such encouragement of regionalism and regional solidification against communist take-over would both be strengthened and accelerated if the two major non-communist countries in Asia, India and Japan, could play a wider and more acceptable role in Southeast Asia as counterweights to China and as contributors to order and stability in the region. While many difficulties inhibit the policies and capacities of both India and Japan to play such a role, they have been participating effectively and quietly in many ways. The Japanese Government and Japanese business enterprise have been expanding trade, investment and developmental assistance in many of the countries of Southeast Asia, including the Democratic Republic of Vietnam. Japan could participate beneficially in the search for political equilibrium in Southeast Asia. India has played an extremely important role as Chairman of the International Supervisory Commissions in Vietnam, Laos and Cambodia. While there are limitations on India's relations with the countries of Southeast Asia, India is particularly interested in the prospects for settlement and equilibrium under law and order in this vital area to India's east. Furthermore, Chinese and communist domination of Southeast Asia would threaten the security of both Japan and India, and perhaps impair India's independence.

In sum, regionalism for Southeast Asia will require considerable qualification and careful encouragement to help produce a sense of community and the basis for foundation of regional equilibrium. With all their disorder, disunion and divergence, will the leaders and peoples join to meet common challenges or continue opposing in centrifugal policies? The Foreign Minister of Thailand has stated the alternative for Southeast Asia in 1964:

". . .The solution is not to be found in submission, at present or in the future, but in gathering sufficient strength to meet the challenge and in joining with others who are imbued with the same faith in their future and are willing to ward off the danger and defend their patrimony. The problem is to arouse the conscience of as many Southeast Asian nations as possible to the necessity of combining their strength, or working closely together and presenting a solid front to anyone daring to entertain evil designs against them. If they succeed, not only will each and every one of them be spared from destruction, but the region as a whole will emerge as a strong and free community, capable of serving its own interests as well as those of the world at large. This, we hope, will be Southeast Asia's lasting call, and that it will be heard." [60]

VII. *THE ROLE OF THE UNITED NATIONS*

The noteworthy fact about the United Nations in Southeast Asia is not that it has been deprived of a role in the problems of Vietnam, although that is deplorable. The remarkable fact is that the United Nations organization and its many agencies have participated so extensively and continuously with the other independent countries there. U.N. technical assistance, nation-building, and pacific settlement of disputes have brought a new kind of relations to the area.

Allegiance to the United Nations has been a focal point and first priority in the foreign policies of the non-communist states of Southeast Asia, including Indonesia until it withdrew from the United Nations early in 1965. The organization played a key role in establishing the sovereignty and independence of all of these nations. Their membership in the U.N. sanctioned their return to independence and their rightful association in the family of nations. Even the Republic of Vietnam would have been voted a member of the United Nations during 1954–1958 by a considerable majority of the General Assembly and the Security Council if it had not been for the veto of the Soviet Union.

The neutral countries and even the aligned nations of Southeast Asia have looked to the United Nations for general protection in the event of war and for assistance in modernization and development. Three distinguished men from Southeast Asia have held the highest positions in the organization: Prince Wan of Thailand and General Romulo of the Philippines as Presidents of the General Assembly, and U Thant of Burma as the current Secretary General. The specialized agencies of the United Nations and the United Nations Economic Commission for Asia and the Far East (ECAFE) are active in Southeast Asia where Bangkok, Thailand, is their headquarters.

ECAFE, the specialized agencies, and the World Bank have contributed immensely to the modernization and development of each of the independent states of Southeast Asia. The list of activities in the field of technical assistance and other kinds of development is voluminous in scope and substantial in amount. All of this effort has contributed to the internal strengthening of these states in economic, social and administrative capabilities. This aspect of the role of the United Nations is helping to build the groundwork for order and equilibrium, country by country. In an area where nationalism is intense and revolution pervasive, the United Nations provides facilities for these sensitive sovereign states which make it easier sometimes for them to accept external assistance and to abide by external decisions.

In the field of peacekeeping and settlement of disputes, the United Nations has been more active in Southeast Asia over the past twenty years than might be remembered or suspected. In this capacity it has been extending the role of law for community-building and reciprocal undertakings. Let us take the countries and the cases one by one.

Vietnam

It is unfortunate that the major institutions of the United Nations have not been able to make any contribution as yet to the cessation of hostilities and to an effective peace in Vietnam. Despite some tentative approaches and the desires of some members of the United Nations, it has not been able to exert much influence there.

Both the United States and the Soviet Union have acted in the

Security Council with regard to Vietnam during the past year either to make complaints or file information. When an American destroyer was attacked in the area outside territorial waters on August 2, 1964, by torpedo boats of the Democratic Republic of Vietnam (Hanoi), the United States Government declared that this was an act of aggression and requested the Security Council to meet immediately.[61] Both the Soviet Union and the United States agreed that the Democratic Republic of Vietnam should attend these sessions, and it was invited to do so by the Soviet Government. However, Hanoi rejected the invitation on the ground that it was not a member of the United Nations, that that body had no jurisdiction, and that the United States was the party guilty of aggression. Consideration by the Security Council of the United States' complaint was *ad hoc* and did not lead to any decision or to the establishment of any commission.

During 1965 the United States has communicated information regarding its policies on Vietnam to the members of the Security Council several times.[62] The United States has taken note of the failure of the Security Council to act in this crisis. Nevertheless, the U.S. Government has urged the non-permanent members of the Security Council and the Secretary General to do all they can to bring about peaceful negotiations. The Soviet Union has also complained in the Security Council of some of the military actions of the United States, Australia and New Zealand in Vietnam.[63]

In 1963 the United Nations General Assembly considered the question of the violation of human rights in the Republic of Vietnam as the result of the complaints and requests of sixteen member nations.[64] The Government in Saigon invited members of the United Nations to come to Vietnam to study the situation. Pursuant to a resolution of the General Assembly on October 4, 1963, the President of the General Assembly appointed a U.N. Fact Finding Mission consisting of Afghanistan, Brazil, Ceylon, Costa Rica, Dahomey, Morocco and Nepal. The Mission went to South Vietnam, held hearings with many witnesses, and submitted a report of the facts to the General Assembly.[65] The Mission reached no conclusions, the General Assembly took no action.

Several reasons possibly explain the inability of the United Nations to play a role in the Vietnamese part of the crisis and conflict in Southeast Asia. The principal one is that the Chinese People's Republic and the Democratic Republic of Vietnam are not members of the United Nations. Each has rejected and denounced any suggestion or effort on the part of the U.N. or any member to involve it in Vietnam. As we have seen, when the Soviet Union invited Hanoi to attend the Security Council in August 1964, the authorities in Hanoi denounced this action and the United Nations.

It is difficult to envisage any action by the General Assembly or the Security Council which would circumvent a Soviet veto and contribute to peacekeeping in Vietnam. It is as unlikely as it appears unfeasible that any of the provisions of the U.N. Charter or any of the organs of the U.N.—the Secretary General, the Security Council or the General Assembly—will be applied unless Soviet obstruction changes to cooperation. Even then, the resistance of Communist China will remain. Until the U.S.S.R. cooperates, it is unlikely that the General Assembly would provide support for a peacekeeping force to be established along the 17th parallel and the borders of Laos to observe, deter or prevent infiltration into the Republic of Vietnam or otherwise maintain peace in the area. It is equally unlikely that any agency of the United Nations could be established to replace the International Supervisory Commission established by the Geneva Agreements of 1954 for the cessation of hostilities in Vietnam, although that Commission is virtually inoperative in both North and South Vietnam. It is equally doubtful that the Secretary General or some United Nations body could undertake mediation, good offices, or some more direct involvement looking toward negotiations and a political settlement with the communist and non-communist governments involved as long as the authorities in Hanoi and Peking continue to reject any such involvement by the United Nations.

However, the United Nations might, if a sufficient majority in the General Assembly so voted, undertake a program of internal reconstruction similar to actions in the Congo and in South Korea. But here again the willingness of a large majority of the members of the United Nations to undertake and finance any such large-scale operation looks doubtful.

Security Council Mission to the Kingdom of Cambodia and the Republic of Vietnam in 1964

This action by the Security Council, of which it is still seized, and the Mission of Inquiry which it set up to deal with the continuing, serious problem of the Cambodian-Vietnamese border deserve some notice and study, even though this effort has not yet produced completely satisfactory results. Procedures for the regulation and settlement of disputes over this frontier would contribute substantially to a regional equilibrium in Southeast Asia.

Diplomatic relations have been severed between Cambodia and Vietnam since 1963. In April and May of 1964, Cambodia communicated to the Security Council its charges concerning aggression by the United States and Vietnam.[66] The Council met to discuss the situation from May 19 to June 4. A resolution was adopted to establish a Mission of Inquiry to consider measures to prevent incidents.[67] That resolution, among other things, called on all states and the members of the Geneva Conference to recognize and respect Cambodia's neutrality and territorial integrity. The President of the Security Council appointed Brazil, the Ivory Coast, and Morocco to make the inquiry.

The report of this mission of July 27, 1964, stated that Cambodia suggested that the Security Council send unarmed observers in civilian attire to be organized in teams and set up in fixed posts to supervise the frontier, but only from the Cambodian side of it. Nor would such observers supersede the International Supervisory Commission or Cambodia's desire for a Geneva Conference to guarantee its territorial integrity and widen the powers of that Commission. The Republic of Vietnam proposed an "international police force" or a sufficiently-organized and manned group of observers to keep the frontier under surveillance. Saigon also informed the Mission that it would respect Cambodia's neutrality and would accept any impartial measures to improve relations. The Mission recommended to the Security Council that it (1) establish and send a United Nations Observer Group to Cambodia under the implementation of the Secretary General; (2) recommend to both countries that they resume political relations; (3) appoint a Representative approved by both parties to facilitate relations and discussions between the two countries; and (4) note the statements of Vietnam that it recognizes and respects the neutrality and territorial integrity of the Kingdom of Cambodia.[68] Subsequently, the United States proposed in the Security Council an impartial international investigation of the situation, as well as a number of formulae for establishing a United Nations presence along the volatile and ambiguous frontier of Cambodia and Vietnam.[69] Naturally the Republic of Vietnam and the United States denied any intent of aggression.

On September 9, 1964, Cambodia described the Mission's recommendation to resume political relations as a flagrant interference in its internal affairs, and protested formally against the Mission's Report in so far as it concerned the dispute between Cambodia and South Vietnam.[70] Exchanges between Cambodia and South Vietnam concerning alleged aggressions continued throughout 1964, and Cambodia has continued up to the present time to complain to the Security Council about attacks by the United States and the Republic of Vietnam. On November 30, 1964, Cambodia rejected Vietnam's proposal for an international police force or group of observers, and expressed regret that Vietnam did not support its own proposal that Cambodia be internationally supervised by the International Commission for Supervision and Control in Cambodia.[71] That Commission had, on June 15, 1964, issued a report to the Co-Chairmen of the Geneva Conference, concerning certain border incidents, in which the majority stated that the Commission had found "conclusive evidence that the armed forces of South Vietnam were responsible for the violations" and was "convinced that none of these incidents were the result of any provocation from the Cambodian side." The Canadian delegation, in its minority report, refused to concur in the investigation reports and findings being submitted, on the ground that they did not take account of the views of the Republic of Vietnam and that the Commission was not empowered to investigate the particular type of border incidents in question.[72] On August 18, 1965, Cambodia rejected a suggestion made by the United States that a United Nations Mission of observers be sent to the frontier between Cambodia and Vietnam.[73] The Cambodian complaint remains officially on file with the Security Council.

United Nations Committee of Inquiry on Laos in 1959

In September 1959 the Government of Laos requested the assistance of the United Nations and the dispatch of an emergency force to halt aggression from the outside and to prevent it from spreading.[74] The Secretary General of the United Nations, on receiving this letter from Laos, requested the President of the Security Council to convene a meeting urgently. Despite the objections of the Soviet representative, France, the United Kingdom and the United States introduced a joint resolution approved by a 10-1 procedural vote in the Security Council appointing a subcommittee of Argentina, Italy, Japan and Tunisia to examine the case, receive further statements and documents and conduct such inquiries as might be necessary, and to report back to the Security Council as soon as possible.[75]

After visiting Laos, the Committee submitted its report on November 3, 1959, to the Security Council.[76] The Committee found that varying degrees and kinds of support had been accorded to "hostile" elements in Laos from sources on the North Vietnamese side of the border. During and after the Committee's inquiry, the activities of North Vietnamese and Lao Communist forces noticeably declined in Laos.

Subsequently, in November, 1959, the Secretary General visited Laos, recommended that it follow a policy of neutrality, and stationed a personal representative there to make a survey on how the United Nations might further assist Laos in its economic and social development. A report was submitted recommending that a number of coordinated actions be undertaken by the United Nations.[77]

This initial involvement of the United Nations in Laos was not followed up in 1960 and 1961, when the internal situation deteriorated into civil war and foreign military intervention from communist forces increased. However, many statements have been made in the 15th-18th Sessions of the General Assembly regarding the situation in Laos, but no action was taken. The U.N. is still theoretically "seized" of the Laos problem.

United Nations Good Offices for Thailand and Cambodia

In 1958–1965 Thailand and Cambodia have each complained of alleged violations on the part of the other regarding sovereignty and territorial integrity. Both have, from time to time, sought the good offices of the United Nations. As a result of their joint request in late 1958, the Secretary General appointed a Special Representative whose good offices with representatives of each country helped to improve relations and mutual understanding.[78] Both Thailand and Cambodia expressed their appreciation to the Seceretary General and the Security Council in 1959.[79]

Nevertheless, relations deteriorated over the next few years and Cambodia severed diplomatic connections with Thailand in 1961. Again in 1962 both governments requested the Secretary General to appoint a personal representative to inquire into the respective accusations and denials of both parties and to help in moderating the conflict between them. The Secretary General appointed Mr. Nils Gussing,[80] of Sweden, who commuted between Bangkok and Phnom Penh for nearly two years making various inquiries, working with each government, and extending his good offices to both, which shared the costs of the so-called "Gussing Mission" and its small staff. However, relations between the two countries could not be reestablished. The Mission was withdrawn in November of 1964.[81] Cambodia has continued to inform the Security Council of alleged violations by Thailand of the Cambodian frontier and territorial waters, which Thailand has denied. The Secretary General and the Security Council are thus still involved in disputes between these two countries.

United Nations Malaysia Mission

The United Nations has had a lot to do with sanctioning the formation and sovereignty of Malaysia as a legally constituted entity and as a member of the United Nations, although the U.N. has not been able to deal effectively with the confrontation between Indonesia and Malaysia.

74

In 1963, President Sukarno of Indonesia, President Macapagal of the Philippines, and Prime Minister Tengku Abdul Rahman of Malaya agreed that the Secretary General, or his representative, should ascertain the wishes of the people of North Borneo and Sarawak "by a fresh approach to ensure complete compliance with the principle of self-determination." The three heads of government suggested working teams under the Secretary General's representative, decided to send observers themselves to witness the carrying out of the U.N. Mission, and agreed to share its costs. The Secretary General concurred, as did the British Government, with this tri-partite proposal.

The Malaysia Mission was immediately formed and spent several weeks in Borneo hearing many witnesses from many groups. In its report it found that the participation of two territories in the proposed Federation of Malaysia had been duly approved by legitimate legislative bodies, as well as by a large majority of the people through free and impartially conducted elections in which the question of Malaysia was a major issue. On the basis of the Mission's report, the Secretary General of the United Nations issued his findings that a sizeable majority of the peoples of North Borneo and Sarawak wished to join the Federation in order to end their dependent status and realize their independence "through freely-chosen association with other peoples in their region with whom they feel ties of ethnic association, heritage, language, religion, culture, economic relationship, and ideals and objectives." [82] The report of the Mission and the findings of the Secretary General served to endorse the legality and authority of the participation of these two territories in the new Federation of Malaysia.

Before the Secretary General had published his findings on September 14, 1963, the Government of Malaya had already announced that Malaysia would come into being as a sovereign nation on September 16, 1963. The Secretary General regretted the timing of that decision.* Furthermore, the Philippines and Indonesia had difficulties in making arrangements for their observers to operate in the two territories. Partly as the result of this, they took strong exception to the report of the U.N. Malaysia Mission and to the substance of the Secretary General's find-

* See comment by Ambassador Ramani on page 135

75

ings. Both governments rejected the inclusion of North Borneo and Sarawak in the Federation on the ground that it had not taken place in accordance with the Manila Summit Agreement or the understanding with the Secretary General. The Philippines would not establish diplomatic relations with the new Federation. President Sukarno stated on September 25, 1963, that "Indonesia will crush Malaysia to the end because it is a form of neo-colonialism." [83]

Malaysia has had to face the hostile confrontation of Indonesia during the past two years and has informed the Security Council on several occasions of what it considered to be aggression by that country.[84] In September 1964 the Security Council met, during the period of September 9–17, to consider the situation. A proposed resolution to meet the situation was, however, vetoed by the Soviet Union.[85] Because of this veto the Security Council has not been able to act. Malaysia has continued to inform the Council of Indonesian threats and incidents in January, March and May of 1965. Thus, while the United Nations brought about the endorsement of Malaysia, it has not been able to undertake any role in conciliation or peacekeeping between Malaysia and Indonesia. And now Singapore has been separated from the Federation of Malaysia and has applied for membership in the United Nations.

Various United Nations Good Offices regarding Indonesia

Indonesia came into being partly as a result of a U.N. Commission for Indonesia of 1948. The United States was one of the three members of that body which had a great deal to do with helping Indonesia negotiate with the Netherlands to become a sovereign state and a member of the United Nations some fifteen years ago.

During the subsequent period Indonesia's principal non-economic experience with the United Nations was the effort to get control of the territory of West Irian, otherwise known outside of Indonesia as Western New Guinea. The General Assembly considered this issue many times from its 9th to its 18th Sessions. The dispute was settled in 1962 by both the Netherlands and Indonesia accepting the Secretary General's proposal that they discuss the possibilities of peaceful settlement with him and a mutually acceptable third party. U Thant selected Ambassador Ellsworth Bunker of the United States, who served as a moderator. After an agreement had been reached in the Security Council on August 15, 1962,[86] West Irian was transferred to a U.N. Temporary Executive Authority (UNTEA) until May 1, 1963. It was then replaced by an Indonesian administration. The agreement also provided for a cease-fire and financial arrangements. The UNTEA was established on October 1, 1962, and terminated as planned on May 1, 1963.[87] The United States supplied logistic support and asistance. This was the first time that the U.N. had directly administered a territory, even one so large and for such a short period.

Indonesia has agreed to invite the United Nations to assist in making arrangements for the exercise of the right of self-determination by the people in West Irian no later than 1969, but it is doubtful that this provision or other Indonesian compliance with U.N. mandates will occur. On January 20, 1965, Indonesia withdrew from membership in the United Nations on the grounds that Malaysia had become a member of the Security Council.[88] Further U.N. action on West Irian may thus be frustrated.

Burma

Going back to 1953 and 1954, the only direct experience of Burma, other than technical and economic, with the United Nations was the Burmese appeal regarding some thousands of Chinese Nationalist troops who had withdrawn into Burma. The Burmese Government made a complaint against the Republic of China in Taiwan in 1953.[89] A General Assembly resolution of April 23, 1953, established a Four Nations Joint Military Committee in Bangkok composed of Burma, the Republic of China, Thailand and the United States, to recommend measures for the repatriation and supervision of the evacuation of those forces.[90] Burma withdrew from the Committee in September of 1953. It reported in July 1954 that its regular program of evacuation had been completed with nearly 7,000 troops and dependents repatriated.[91] The remainder refused to leave Burma. In this case the United Nations was able to reduce the dimensions of, but not finally solve, a serious problem in a member state.

Aside from the extensive headquartering of United Nations agencies in Bangkok, and major assistance from them for Thailand's development, Thailand's experience with the United Nations in peacekeeping activities has been negligible and disappointing. The handling of the issues between it and Cambodia has not been satisfactory from the Thai viewpoint. Thai officials have welcomed and facilitated the good offices of the U.N., but that does not appear to have ameliorated the situation. The principal concern of Thailand for its security and independence has been the threat of Communist aggression and subversion from Laos, North Vietnam and the People's Republic of China and so far the U.N. have been unable to deal with this.

Thailand has had only one experience in trying to involve the United Nations in peacekeeping. After the fall of Dien Bien Phu in early May of 1954, the Government of Thailand requested the Security Council to consider the threatening situation in Indochina and to establish a Peace Observation Commission.[92] The Council met on June 3 and decided by a vote of 10 to 1, with the Soviet representative objecting, that the matter was procedural and the Thai appeal should be considered. Invited to take a seat at the Council table and explain his Government's position, the Thai delegate expressed his Government's concern over Communist Vietnamese propaganda in Thailand and the danger to Thailand of Vietnamese Communist activities in Laos and Cambodia. He proposed a resolution requesting that a commission under the General Assembly resolution of 1950 for such purposes be set up to send observers to Thailand and, if necessary, to visit Thailand itself. Thailand wanted the observers to report to the Commission and to the Security Council and to be able to request instructions from the Commission or the Council to visit states contiguous to Thailand. The Soviet representative opposed the resolution on the grounds that the interested parties, including Communist China, were considering the matter at the Geneva Conference and that action by the Security Council might impede a successful solution of this problem there. Nine members of the Security Council voted for the Thai resolution; the Soviet representative vetoed it. Thailand declared its intention to take the matter up at the next General Assembly or reconvene a special one.

However, Thailand took no further action within the United Nations in 1954 or subsequently regarding threats to its security. Instead, and perhaps because of its disappointment and frustration, it forsook its traditional policy of neutrality and joined in the preparation, ratification and implementation of the Southeast Asia Treaty for the collective security of its eight members.

The International Court of Justice Case of the Temple of Preah Vihear

Cambodia is the only country in Southeast Asia so far to have invoked the jurisdiction of the International Court of Justice. In this it was successful. It claimed sovereignty of a 1000 year old Temple, originally of Hindu construction and purpose, now resting somewhat in ruins and neglect at the very edge of a high escarpment which forms the physical but not specific boundary between Thailand and Cambodia. Built when the Khmer Empire extended over most of what is now central and eastern Thailand, it had subsequently at times been in Thai territory.

On May 26, 1961, the Court gave its judgment regarding preliminary objections in the case and upheld its jurisdiction.[93] On June 15, 1962, the Court, by a majority vote, handed down a judgment on the merits in favor of Cambodian sovereignty over the Temple.[94] The Government of Thailand decided that its obligations as a member of the United Nations required it to abide by the decision of the Court, despite strong feelings among the Thais that the decision was legally wrong and the matter insufficiently understood. Nevertheless the authorities in Bangkok took the necessary actions to permit Cambodia to enter and assume actual jurisdiction and sovereignty over this temple and a tiny triangular area on the edge of the escarpment.

Conclusion

Looking at the record of U.N. participation in Southeast Asia over the past twenty years from the point of view of establishing law and equilibrium there, the prospects for any enlarged role for it seem dim. The Soviet Union has consistently vetoed peacekeeping measures, no matter how mild, where its interests or the interests of Communist policy and power were adversely involved. In these circumstances, the U.N. *alone* cannot be expected to bring about a settlement in Vietnam or equilibrium in Southeast Asia. It *alone* cannot be a substitute for other means and efforts to develop some sense of community and some law of reciprocity among all the governments concerned with policy, power and law in the area.

It is mainly in the area of technical assistance, nation-building and regional development that the United Nations can contribute elements of stability and minimum public order. The functional federalism of the Mekong Committee, which is growing slowly under the auspices of the United Nations, may be the most promising contribution which the United Nations can make in the search for equilibrium there. In addition, the United Nations might establish a permanent panel or "conciliation mission" for disputes in Southeast Asia if the governments there agreed.

VIII. *THE MEKONG COMMUNITY*

In the Mekong River Valley, extending over much of Laos, northeast Thailand, Cambodia and the lower end of South Vietnam where the 2600-mile Mekong River empties into the South China Sea, the foundations and framework for a new and promising form of functional community are slowly and almost imperceptibly developing. While much has been written and analyzed *about* the physical resources of this large watershed and untamed giant of a river, it is the Mekong spirit and the institution of international cooperation for the development of this valley and the progress of each of these four riparian countries that particularly deserve attention and encouragement. This tentative and embryonic Mekong community may possess the makings for solidifying a structure of community purpose, facilitating reciprocal obligations and undertakings, overcoming national and sovereign antagonisms, and placing restraints on the threat of force or political intervention.

The initiative and auspices of various members of the United Nations and its Economic Commission for Asia and the Far East

(ECAFE) launched the beginnings of this Mekong project for research and investigation in early 1957. During the past eight and a half years, this unusual and even unique program for international cooperation has been steadily expanding and growing. Its core and its heart are the mandates of Laos, Thailand, Cambodia and South Vietnam to join together as sovereign states and take a series of actions by unanimous vote to organize and operate this Committee and develop the Basin together. Their endorsement, sanction and action are the key to realizing the potentialities of the mighty Mekong not only for the development of physical resources but also in the search for regional equilibrium.

These four riparian countries in September 1957 unanimously adopted the "Statute of the Committee for Co-ordination of Investigations of the Lower Mekong Basin." [95] This important document is the initial legal basis for the establishment and functioning of this four-nation instrumentality for action. It has clear powers for decision as a body as well as explicit duties and responsibilities to the four sovereign countries making up the Committee. Each national member of the Committee has "plenipotentiary authority." Chairmanship is rotated each year in the alphabetical order of the four member countries. The four governments authorized the Committee to cooperate with ECAFE in the performance of the Committee's functions. Article 4 of the Statute describes these functions as to promote, coordinate, supervise and control the planning and investigation of water resources development projects in the Lower Mekong Basin. The Committee is empowered to prepare and submit plans for research, study and investigation to participating governments. The Committee can make requests of them for financial and technical assistance and receive and administer such assistance. The Committee can also draft and recommend to the four participating governments criteria for the use of water of the Mekong River.

The meetings of the Committee have to be attended by all these four countries; its decisions have to be unanimous. The Statute provides, directly and indirectly, that the Committee and the development of the Basin shall proceed within the purview of ECAFE and within the auspices of the U.N. The Statute also provides, by inference, that other friendly governments and international organizations can be included within the terms of reference for the development of the Basin. In effect the Statute is the charter for joint development in the area, and the Committee constitutes the board of directors.

A year after its formation, the Committee decided that it needed an Executive Agent and staff stationed in Bangkok with authority to take decisions on a day-to-day basis.[96] Since 1959, the Executive Agent has carried out his duties of preparing requests for technical and other assistance; supervising the services of experts; arranging that field projects are undertaken by United Nations specialized agencies; developing bilateral programs for individual countries; and preparing programs of work. The Committee has itself endorsed a broad plan of work known as the "Development of Water Resources in the Lower Mekong Basin," the various technical and physical aspects of which have been developed and refined in subsequent years.

The 1957 plan of development for irrigation, hydro-electric power production, navigation, forests and fisheries, and mineral resources envisaged a 20-year program for the construction stage alone. The total cost of a complete program of development for the Mekong would run into billions of dollars over at least a 30-year period. This is the size of the program which these four countries have undertaken—a task larger and more monumental in the control and use of water resources than anything else in the world.

The Committee has been operating and cooperating effectively for eight years. This in itself is one of the several unique features of the evolving Mekong community. Diplomatic relations are broken and strained between Cambodia and Thailand and between Cambodia and Vietnam. Laos and Vietnam do not have formal diplomatic relations. Nevertheless the plenipotentiary representatives of these four sovereign countries have met nearly 30 times. Could Western governments be so flexible? The Committee not only has continued without interruption but is moving into new fields. The common bond—the common denominator —is the concern of each country with its rice cultivation, water flow, power output, and improvement of rural livelihood. Political leaders in Vientiane, Bangkok, Phnom Penh and Saigon have become increasingly enthusiastic about the Mekong Committee because sharing in the development of the Valley by international rather than unilateral action will help meet that concern.

Another unique feature of this emerging community of purpose is the fact that it is the one major international river in which the riparian countries are cooperating by a legal compact, with United Nations assistance, for a development program without any *prior* large-scale construction projects, individually or collectively, and without any conflict over water claims or any pressure to join together mainly for the resolution of contending claims. So far there have been no serious conflicts of interests in this eight-year period of investigation, research, preparation, and collection of funds for construction.

The Mekong Committee is also unique, or certainly unusual if not exceptional in regional cooperation, in its agreement to strengthen its executive and implementing capacities as the years have developed its plans and preparations. The four governments, by agreement, have developed training and education for village-level workers, pilot farm projects, and agricultural services so as to provide the people of the Valley with knowledge and skills to benefit from the development of the enormous resources and advanced technology which the Project will bring. Now the Committee is moving into the more difficult area of establishing priorities on construction projects, formulating additional agreements among the four participating governments for regionally sharing the benefits of development, and executing programs for the allocation of water and other resources among them.

For all these reasons the four governments have in turn strengthened their national ministries and planning agencies to improve their facilities and capabilities for dealing with the problems and opportunities of development on a regional basis in the River Valley.[97]

In the light of these developing requirements, the Committee held a significant session on May 10–11, 1965. In considering the rapidly growing work in water resources development on the Mekong River and its tributaries, in industrial and agricultural development activities, and in mineral surveys, the Committee recognized that it would have to devote increasing attention to road and rail transportation, public health, nutrition, education, and social affairs. Accordingly, the Committee felt that its terms of reference should be expanded to reflect these broader fields.

The Committee decided to alter its title to "Committee for the Development of the Lower Mekong Basin." This is now abbreviated as "Mekong Development Committee." It instructed its Secretariat to prepare an amended draft Statute for consideration at its next session and for submission to the four governments for ratification, but it decided to retain the essential features of its Charter, namely:

"concern with technical but not with political matters, no interest in assistance to which political conditions are attached, decision-making processes whereby no member of the Committee is ever asked to undertake or participate in any project not desired and approved by it, and determination to work for the benefit of all the people of the Lower Mekong Basin without distinction as to politics or nationality." [98]

In this way it has renewed and reinforced the pledge of a community of purpose or a kind of functional federalism in the Mekong area. This revised Statute, if approved, will move the Mekong community from investigation to development.

At this same May 1965 meeting, the Committee drew up a list of priority projects in water resources development and related fields which the four participating governments regard as vital to economic development. This list includes projects already accorded priority by the Committee to a total of $71.5 million; some major Mekong River projects, which hopefully will be at a stage in a few years where serious financial discussions can begin, in the amount of about $900 million; roadways for the proposed Asian Highway within the Lower Mekong Basin in an amount of about $70 million rising to about $300 million over several years; and numerous other smaller items of priority. Within this list the Committee reiterated its top priority for a tributary project in Laos which would provide electric power for the capital in Vientiane and for northeast Thailand, as well as irrigation and water for the Vientiane plain. This project, when completed, will become the first within the Committee's development program in which electric power will be an international commodity, moving across the international frontier of two of the Mekong countries—an incipient common market in power. The Committee also requested the Secretary General of the United Nations to assist it in the implementation and financing of its list of priority projects. The tentative estimate of cost of this list for comprehensive development of the Basin in the ten-year period 1965–75 would be approximately $2 billion.

On August 12, 1965, the first Mekong Power Exchange Convention was signed in Vientiane, Laos, to enable electric power to flow across the Laos-Thailand international border for the benefit of people on both sides of the Mekong River. All four participating governments and the United Nations adhered to the Convention as the parties directly concerned. The ceremony, which followed considerable negotiation of this Convention, took place after the opening of the 29th Special Session of the Committee by the Prime Minister of Laos, Prince Souvanna Phouma. Further changes in the Committee's terms of reference which are still under consideration at the governmental level, were also discussed at this session. Presumably this institution of Mekong cooperation will continue to evolve and grow to meet specific and actual needs.

This Mekong Project has involved more than the four participating governments and 12 United Nations agencies or units. Some 20 other governments are also participating in and contributing to it: Australia, Belgium, Canada, China, Denmark, Finland, France, India, Iran, Israel, Italy, Japan, the Netherlands, New Zealand, Norway, Pakistan, the Philippines, Sweden, the United Kingdom and the United States. By early 1965, international contributions to the project, which include substantial amounts from the United States, had reached the equivalent of nearly $68 million on hand and some additional resources pledged or offered. President Johnson reinforced and dramatized United States support and his own endorsement, by his address at Johns Hopkins on April 7, 1965 when he offered a billion dollars for regional development in Southeast Asia. Mr. Eugene Black has been working with Secretary General U Thant and the Committee. During the period of investigation and research, contributing governments have provided numerous types of technical personnel and highly skilled groups.

Is this a paper plan and an international facade or have the Mekong Development Committee, the contributing governments and the United Nations accomplished something real and potential? That they have can only be indicated in a short space. The technical data have been prepared in volumes. Engineering surveys have started. Two dams will be completed in 1965 in northeast Thailand. A dam in Cambodia and two in Laos are under construction on tributaries of the Mekong. Altogether the Committee is involved in work on 17 of the 34 principal tributaries of the Lower Mekong River. Investigations are well along on the three high-priority sites for major and massive dams across the Mekong, between Laos and Thailand at one site, and at two other sites in Cambodia. Navigation on parts of the River has been facilitated. Mineral surveys have disclosed large deposits of bauxite and rock salt, both obviously important to modern technology and industry. The Committee has held its first Economic and Social Seminar to study these aspects of the large mainstream dams and for comprehensive development of the entire Basin. The Committee's network of experimental and demonstration farms in the four riparian countries has continued to progress.

As an institution for building a community of purpose and a reciprocity of interests and obligations, the Mekong Development Committee shows promise. Some of Southeast Asia's most able and dynamic political leaders, administrators, economists, engineers and technicians are devoting their lives enthusiastically to this project. They are creating the skills not only of physical construction but of political cooperation against an enormous volume of water on one hand and a massive amount of suspicion on the other. And the Committee is demonstrating that political, economic and social cohesion and collaboration can be established in this part of Southeast Asia. National antagonisms and military hostilities do not necessarily bar regional administration of common resources. Some experience in Mekong development indicates that emerging issues and difficult controversies can be segregated and settled in some order of priority and solubility. The Mekong Development Committee is evolving a body of powers and experiences in the confrontation of such problems for solution by consultation, investigation, impartial conciliation and negotiation by sovereign independent states acting within the common bonds of the mutual interests of a single community.[99]

Traditional doctrines of international law regarding riparian rights, boundary waters and national priorities or prestige seem to be giving way to the development of more flexible and reciprocal doctrines of common interest and equitable apportionment for mutual benefit in the national interest of each participating government. Furthermore the decision-making process of the plenipotentiary authorities of the Mekong Committee is tending to some extent to become less national and more international in spirit and more technical, rather than political, in character.

Here the United Nations organizations and authorities have provided the vital ingredient of an impartial guide and promoter for some sense, as well as function, of symbiosis among these four countries. Their leaders and even some of their people are gradually coming to realize that they each need the others for their own development. Of enormous significance for the future is the catalytic effect of the process of international development in this region, for it strengthens the process of national development in each country and stimulates the notion that each country might increase its own well-being and prosperity by developing resources and commodities not only for its own use but for sale in a widening market of the Mekong region.

The questions for the future are organizational: whether new authority and a new structure for more than three dozen individual governmental and other units is necessary for efficiency, and whether financial resources will be forthcoming in sufficient volume from contributing governments to proceed with construction based on completed investigation and research.

Even if there is the will, the structure, and the money for the next ten years, the Mekong community and the development of the Basin will confront the critical challenge of security in a region torn by war and hostility where political power is law and law is a weakling. Could this evolving community lead to new arrangements for restraints on military hostilities and political intervention and to guarantees of national as well as regional integrity? Could the national self-determination of these four

Buddhist nations be translated into a regional mandate of international determination, to be protected and guaranteed by the major powers and by the United Nations? And ultimately, could the United Nations be persuaded to provide the security for those sites and sectors in the Mekong Basin which the Mekong Development Committee and the four governments so designated? Could the whole Mekong River from the shores of South Vietnam to near the borders of China be declared and guaranteed as an international community for peaceful development in its total watershed?

As Professor Gilbert White has so eloquently suggested, the substitution of a development goal and a regional area for an elusive firing line and indeterminate battlefield could provide the parties at interest in Southeast Asia, at least on the non-Communist side, with a dramatic and worthwhile peace aim.[100] A regional community of progress and development could be guaranteed and even safely neutralized because it would contain the will of the community, the specific reciprocity of mutual undertakings, and limitations on the use of any kind of force. Furthermore these four countries would have not only their own national determination but their own national capabilities, as well as international agencies and institutions, within the region to reinforce and safeguard their political integrity and internal security. All of this machinery, organization and personnel would make it increasingly difficult for aggression by seepage to nullify such a community.

IX. FRUSTRATED NEUTRALIZATION

Modern Southeast Asia has had several unhappy encounters with different forms of "neutralization" * This formula is now often suggested officially and privately for settling the problems of Vietnam and its neighbors in Southeast Asia. Yet neutralization has fared badly in this region. Many Southeast Asians suspect or reject it, although some believe in it despite the precedents of history. There have been seven attempts in recent years: the Anglo-

---

* The meaning is described in "Neutralism" by Peter Lyon on pages 91–93.

French neutralization of Thailand in 1896, President Roosevelt's proposal in 1941 for the neutralization of Indochina and Thailand, Thailand's own attempt to maintain neutrality in 1941, the abortive efforts of the Geneva Conference in 1954, the unsatisfactory neutralization of Laos in 1962, the unsuccessful efforts of Cambodia to obtain guarantees in 1960–65, and the controversial proposals of France and others in 1965 for a new conference to neutralize Vietnam and Southeast Asia.

Thailand's Experience in 1896

At the end of the 19th century France and England unilaterally "neutralized" Thailand as a buffer between them so that the former could complete its conquest of Indochina and the latter of Burma and Malaya.[101] For several years Paris had secretly tried to persuade London that both countries should declare Thailand a neutralized buffer state between their respective colonies in Indochina and Burma, and fix Thai boundaries unilaterally. In 1893 the French blockaded Thailand, sent gunboats to Bangkok with muzzles trained on the Palace, and demanded all territory on the left bank of the Mekong River in Laos. With mild support from London and Moscow, the Thai Foreign Minister refused some French demands, but conceded some Thai territory. To remove the "Siamese question" from the brink of war between them, Great Britain and France finally negotiated the Anglo-French Treaty of 1896 to guarantee the independence of the Menam Valley in central Thailand, seek no further unilateral and exclusive advantages from Thailand, and permit mutually-agreed upon spheres of influence in northeast Thailand and the Cambodian provinces under Thai sovereignty for France, and the Malayan Peninsula for Britain. Thailand lost territory but kept its independence. However, the King of Thailand, his Foreign Minister and advisers, were never consulted in this big power neutralization of their country. The memory is still sharp and bitter in Bangkok.

Roosevelt's Scheme for Indochina and "Siam"

In 1941 President Roosevelt secretly suggested neutralization of Indochina and Thailand to the Japanese and other interested governments but without informing the Thais. This scheme was part of his diplomacy to deter or delay a Japanese occupation of Southeast Asia. He envisaged an undertaking by Britain, China, the Netherlands, Japan and the United States jointly to neutralize and guarantee Indochina and Thailand by placing them in a status like Switzerland whereby Japan would have been able to obtain the raw materials of these areas on condition that it withdrew its armed forces in toto from Indochina and pledge no intervention in Thailand. He is reported to have made this proposal on Indochina and Thailand to the Japanese Ambassador in Washington in the following terms:

"The President stated that if the Japanese Government would refrain from occupying Indochina with its military and naval forces, or, had such steps actually been commenced, if the Japanese Government would withdraw such forces, the President could assure the Japanese Government that he would do everything within his power to obtain from the Governments of China, Great Britain, the Netherlands, and of course the United States itself, a binding and solemn declaration, provided Japan would undertake the same commitment, to regard Indochina as a neutralized country in the same way in which Switzerland had up to now been regarded by the powers as a neutralized country. He stated that this would imply that none of the powers concerned would undertake any military act of aggression against Indochina and would refrain from the exercise of any military control within or over Indochina. He would further endeavor to procure from Great Britain and the other pertinent powers a guarantee that so long as the present emergency continued, the local French authorities in Indochina would remain in control of the territory and would not be confronted with attempts to dislodge them on the part of de Gaullist or Free French agents or forces.

"If these steps were taken, the President said, Japan would be given solemn and binding proof that no other power had any hostile designs upon Indochina and that Japan would be afforded the fullest and freest opportunity of assuring herself of the source of food supplies and other raw materials in Indochina which she was seeking to secure.

"With regard to Thailand, in the judgment of the Government of the United States there was not the remotest threat of danger to Japan nor the slightest justification for Japan alleging that she desired to obtain such concessions from Thailand as a means of assuring a source of raw supplies or as a measure of military precaution. The President therefore desired the Japanese Government to know that the previous proposal which he had made to Japan with regard to Indochina be regarded as embracing Thailand as well, and that should the Government of Japan accede to the proposal of the President and abandon its present course with regard to Indochina, the President would request of the other powers which he had mentioned in connection with his proposal concerning Indochina the same guarantee and measure of security with regard to Thailand." [102]

Prime Minister Churchill considered this declaration "entirely good," and agreed to associate Great Britain and the Commonwealth formally with it.

The plan failed when the Japanese Government evaded and avoided the proposal altogether. As for the Thais, it appears from the record that they never learned of this unilateral attempt at neutralization until after the event.

Thailand's Neutrality in 1940–41

While the United States was secretly trying to neutralize Thailand and Indochina with Japanese agreement but without the knowledge of the Thais, the Thai Government was trying to get a guarantee for its neutrality from the Americans and British without the knowledge of the Japanese. As the pressure of Japan rapidly increased in Southeast Asia, the Thai Government sought guarantees of neutrality and assistance from the West as a counterweight to Japan. On June 12, 1940, Thailand signed treaties of non-aggression with Great Britain and France, but Japan would sign only a less binding treaty of friendship and cooperation. By the three treaties, Thailand took steps to establish its neutrality and to reinforce its position as an independent state.

Observing the build-up of Japanese forces in Cambodia and Cochinchina in the summer of 1941, the Thai Government spent intensive and urgent efforts to obtain American and British assistance and guarantees for Thailand's independence and neutrality. The Thai Prime Minister formally asked for American friendship and assistance in helping Thailand retain her complete independence, saying that Thailand looked to its "friends," the United States and Great Britain, in those difficult times.[103] This and many subsequent Thai appeals right up to the eve of Pearl Harbor netted only one vague commitment from the United States and no supplies or assurances of support from Great Britain. Washington did agree to a loan on December 6, but on the following day the Japanese launched attacks simultaneously on both Thailand and Hawaii. The Thai Government appealed for immediate military help from their treaty ally, Great Britain. As Japanese forces were approaching Bangkok a reply came to the effect: "Can spare only few howitzers. Good luck." This ex-

91

perience with neutrality still haunts the Thais and has largely determined Thailand's decision to join and stay in SEATO, and is a key to understanding Thai foreign policy today.[104]

Abortive Neutralization in 1954

The Geneva Conference of 1954 provided the occasion for several governments to propose the negotiation of an international guarantee for Cambodia, Laos and Vietnam. These efforts failed. The British Government proposed "an Asian Locarno Pact" among the participants in the Conference. The French Government suggested some form of guarantee of any agreements to be reached at the Conference. The Soviet and Chinese Communist Governments appeared to accept the idea in principle. On May 8, 1954, the French Foreign Minister made the following proposal as part of the French basis for settling the problems of Indochina:

"These agreements shall be guaranteed by the States participating in the Geneva Conference. In the event of any violation thereof, there should be an immediate consultation between the guarantor States for the purpose of taking appropriate measures either individually or collectively."[105]

He explained that agreements of the kind to be negotiated at that Conference were essentially fragile, "without solid guarantees," because they represented "only brief interludes or ill-respected armistices." To ensure their effectiveness he called for an International Control Commission which would observe and supervise the Agreements. But he pointed out that more was required if the new order was to be maintained:

"Unless the Commission has proper backing, there is a danger that its decisions remain a dead letter for lack of a court of appeal. Some body must be set up or selected to which the International Commission can appeal if circumstances so require. This body in turn would appeal to the guarantors. In our view, the guarantors should be the members of the Geneva Conference, that is, the signatories of the future agreements. The problem of guarantees has not yet been seriously studied by the Confrence. Only the principle has been accepted."[105]

While the Soviet Government could not agree entirely with the French proposal, it accepted the principle that the agreements reached at the Conference should be guaranteed by the participating states and that there should be consultations among the guarantor states in the event of any violation of the agreements. The purposes of such consultations, in the Soviet view, were to be the adoption of collective measures to implement the agreements. This, however, would mean a right of veto for any guarantor, including the Soviet Union.

The delegates of Cambodia, Laos, Vietnam, the United Kingdom and the United States all approved the principle of guarantees for the agreements along with their international supervision. The British Foreign Secretary, Sir Anthony Eden, said he wanted to examine the question of guarantees closely because he felt that they must be designed to ensure against any power having a veto over action considered necessary by the other guarantors to secure observance of the agreements. The Chinese Foreign Minister, Chou En-lai, put forward a six-point proposal which included a provision guaranteeing the implementation of an armistice agreement by the states participating in the Conference, and suggested that the question of the obligations to be undertaken by the guarantors should be examined separately at the Conference. He assumed that the principle of guarantee should be established and made "an initial agreement" of the Conference in view of the fact that none of the participants had objected to the principle. However, he supported the Soviet view that "the countries which are to provide the guarantee should carry on consultations and adopt collective instead of individual measures with regard to violations of the armistice agreement"— again the veto.

A fundamental, if inevitable, weakness of the Geneva Conference was the difference between the British and American governments over underwriting a big-power guarantee for Indochina and over associating with the final agreements to be produced at the Geneva Conference. At first it seemed as if Washington and London were together, but in the end they parted in complete disagreement at the conclusion of the Geneva Conference over these two major issues of policy. On June 29th, after consulting together the two governments agreed and jointly informed the French Government that they would respect and perhaps guarantee an armistice agreement on Indochina if, among other things, it preserved at least the southern half of Vietnam; did not impose on Laos, Cambodia, or this "retained" Vietnam any restrictions materially impairing their capacity to continue stable non-communist regimes, to maintain adequate forces for internal security, to import arms, or to employ foreign advisors; did not contain political provisions risking loss of the "retained area" to communist control; and provided effective machinery for international supervision of the agreement. These conditions partially defined the preliminary terms of neutralization or a "Locarno-type" agreement for Indochina.[106] President Eisenhower and Prime Minister Churchill apparently approved the principle and concept of a system of guarantees underlying these and others in the seven-point statement of June 29th which also included acceptance of Vietnamese partition at the 18th parallel.[107] As the President recalls, the interest of the United States in the Geneva negotiations arose out of the assumption that the U.S. would be expected to act as one of the guarantors of whatever agreement would be achieved.[108]

On July 12, 1954, Prime Minister Winston Churchill informed the House of Commons that his Government hoped that means might be found of "getting the countries which participated in the Conference to underwrite" an acceptable settlement of the Indochina problem and of getting other countries with interests in the area to subscribe to such an undertaking. Sir Anthony Eden tried hard for several weeks to persuade the Americans to agree to such guarantees and to associate with the final settlement. But they ultimately refused. His use of the word "Locarno" for a "defensive arrangement" in Southeast Asia had raised a "storm of outraged protest" in the United States. In his memoires Eden charitably ascribes this to American confusion and misunderstanding over what he really had in mind. After his talks with Dulles and other American officials, Eden was persuaded that the administration "not only understood what [Locarno] meant, but seemed to like the idea." Eden writes that the concept underlying the Locarno Pact of 1924 in Europe, that of a reciprocal defensive arrangement in which each member gives his guarantee of the agreement and action in case of violation, was "a

94

good one and might well be applied to our problems in Southeast Asia." [109]

But the big powers could not agree at Geneva on guarantees for the settlement. Five days before the Conference ended, the French Government published on July 16th its draft of a final declaration for the Conference without formal guarantees but with provision for joint signature by all the participants collectively, including the United States. As the Conference was reaching a climax, Dulles told Eden that, even if the settlement faithfully adhered to the agreed points of June 29th, the United States could and would not guarantee it. "American public opinion would not tolerate the guaranteeing of the subjection of millions of Vietnamese to communist rule," Eden writes.[110] Furthermore, Congressional opinion at the time opposed American adherence to any formal agreement which would also be signed by the Chinese Peoples Republic. There was also American objection to accepting the formal and binding partition of Vietnam against the wishes of the State of Vietnam, and the political provisions designed as an easement and conveyance for bringing about communist control of all Vietnam in 1956. The United States rejected proposals for an international guarantee or neutralization of the former states of Indochina in 1954. But the real reason why an international guarantee did not work out was that the Soviet, Chinese and Vietnamese Communist delegations all insisted that any guarantee be what they called "collective." By this they meant that it could only be put into effect by unanimous agreement. Any guarantor could thus veto any proposed action of all the others. As Sir Anthony pointed out, unanimous agreement was not a very probable contingency and any such arrangement was "completely unacceptable." [111]

A reciprocal guarantee was accordingly replaced by the Final Declaration of the Geneva Conference which consisted of an unsigned undertaking by Great Britain, France, Cambodia, Laos, the Soviet Union, the Chinese Peoples Republic, and the Democratic Republic of Vietnam to respect the sovereignty, independence, unity and territorial integrity of Cambodia, Laos and Vietnam and to refrain from any interference in their internal affairs. The Declaration also provided that the members of the Conference would agree to consult with one another on measures to ensure that the agreements for the cessation of hostilities in Cambodia, Laos and Vietnam would be respected.

As a result of these differences of views, the states of Indochina were never effectively neutralized. However, neutralizing provisions were contained in the agreements on the cessation of hostilities for Cambodia, Laos and Vietnam. They were enjoined from alliances, establishing military bases, or building up unqualified military defenses.

The 1962 Neutralization of Laos

The Geneva Conference of 1961–62 and its Agreements of July 23, 1962, established several international guarantees which would have neutralized Laos and eliminated foreign intervention in that country had they been faithfully observed. The Declaration and Protocol signed at Geneva on July 23, 1962, pledged the signatories not to impair the sovereignty, independence, neutrality, unity or territorial integrity of Laos.[112] They agreed to refrain from interfering in the internal affairs of Laos, or using its territory for interference in the internal affairs of other countries. They would not bring Laos into any military alliance, including SEATO, or establish military bases in Laos. They would withdraw foreign troops and military personnel and introduce none in the future. The Protocol to the Declaration established the machinery of the two Co-Chairmen of the Conference, the United Kingdom and the Soviet Union, and a new International Commission for Supervision and Control in Laos again composed of Canada, India and Poland to supervise and control the cease-fire and other aspects of the neutralization. The Commission was given more powers and a wider mandate than the Commission set up under the 1954 Agreement at Geneva. On the other hand, the Commission of 1962 had less facilities for observing and supervising the terms of the Geneva Agreements.[113]

However, it would appear from most accounts that this second Agreement on Laos was no more effective and has become even more disappointing than the 1954 Agreement,[114] particularly to the governments of Cambodia, Laos, Thailand and South Vietnam. In 1965 Hanoi and Peking officially called for the abolition of the International Supervisory Commission. They have used Laos to infiltrate Vietnam, and prevented the Commission from visiting that half of Laos under *de facto* Communist control. As officials of the United States Government have repeatedly pointed out, the experience with neutralization in Laos is a bad precedent and poor example.[115]

Unsuccessful Neutralization of Cambodia

For five years, the Government of Cambodia has unsuccessfully tried to obtain various forms of neutralization with guarantees for its territorial integrity and political sovereignty. Several times a new Geneva Conference of its 9 members has been proposed for Cambodia. Such an agreement would have guaranteed Cambodia's frontiers with Thailand on one side and the Republic of Vietnam on the other, if they could be delimited and agreed to. It also would have provided legal sanctions against interference in Cambodia by North Vietnam or Communist China. Such an agreement would have done more for Cambodia than the agreement of 1954 because the latter did not deal with Cambodia's frontiers precisely and because it was drawn up in general rather than specific terms. Furthermore, the Declaration of 1954 was not adhered to by the United States, the Republic of South Vietnam, or Thailand.

However, Cambodia has encountered many difficulties in trying to arrange for such a conference on its neutralization. Thailand and the Republic of Vietnam have not wished to participate in another Geneva Conference. Nor has the United States apparently wanted to expose itself to the incessant propaganda tirades from Peking and Hanoi which it endured in 1961–1962 during the Conference on Laos. Then in 1965, when the United States and other possible participants seemed willing to attempt such a conference on Cambodia, the communist states opposed it. Cambodia itself urged postponement on the ground that such a conference would be held primarily to discuss the situation in Vietnam and not Cambodia. Moreover, the 1954 and 1962 experiences of guaranteed neutralization have displeased all concerned in one way or another, especially the Cambodian Government.[116]

DeGaulle's Proposals for Neutralization of Vietnam and Southeast Asia

In 1963, 1964, and 1965, President de Gaulle has proposed that the Geneva participants conclude "a neutrality treaty concerning the states of Southeast Asia." Neither he nor other French officials have publicly described in any detail what the terms and conditions of such a neutralization would be. President de Gaulle has associated this proposal primarily with what he considers to be the need to bring the People's Republic of China into the question of Southeast Asia and its settlement. He believes that "there is no political reality concerning Cambodia, Laos, Vietnam, India, Pakistan, Afghanistan, Burma, Korea, Soviet Russia, or Japan, etc. which does not interest or concern China." In his view, no peace or war is possible without implicating China.[117] As in the previous cases of external attempts to neutralize parts of Southeast Asia in 1896 and 1941, the Government of France apparently has not consulted the Southeast Asian countries themselves with the possible exception of Cambodia. They have not consulted their nominal SEATO ally, Thailand, nor South Vietnam, the principal subject of the French proposal for a neutrality treaty.

The proposal is apparently patterned on the Declaration of Neutrality and the agreements on Laos of 1962, and on the abortive efforts of France and Great Britain to bring about a guaranteed agreement on the Locarno pattern at the Geneva Conference of 1954. In February 1965, President de Gaulle has called for the reconvening of the 1954 Geneva Conference to seek "an international accord excluding all foreign intervention in Vietnam, Laos and Cambodia." On September 9, 1965, he said:

"It is in very different conditions, but with similar thinking, that we believe that in Asia an end to the current fighting and a satisfactory development of peoples could only be achieved by the relations to be established, the negotiations to be opened and a modus vivendi to be accomplished between the powers that since World War II have committed their direct or indirect responsibilities to events of the southeast of that continent—that is, China, France, America, the Soviet Union and Britain.

"We also believe more firmly than ever that the essential condition for such a rapprochement and perhaps for such an association would be an effective end to all foreign intervention and consequently the full and controlled neutralization of the fighting area.

"This, by the way, is what France agreed to, as far as she was concerned, in 1954.

"She has rigorously respected that since, and believes this is necessary, since the United States intervened after French troops had left Indochina. But this is not at all the path being taken, and that is why all speculation about French mediation in this affair is only imagination.

"For the present, France has nothing to do but to conserve for the future, if the moment ever comes, the possibility of acting in Peking, Washington, Moscow and London to establish contacts for reaching a solution, the controls to guarantee it and the assistance to be given to these unhappy peoples whom France certainly has not forgotten." [117]

De Gaulle's conception of "controlled neutralization" focuses on the role of China, France, the United States, the Soviet Union and Britain. And this general formula does reflect the proposals which France actually made at the Geneva Conference in 1954 for guarantees which the United States rejected.

The United States has not been sympathetic to or enthusiastic about de Gaulle's proposals on neutralization. Official comment has emphasized their ambiguity as they have been echoed by repeated French statements as well as by Hanoi and others. It has viewed the proposal with considerable distaste, if not alarm, because of the danger that it would lead to a weakening rather than a strengthening of peace and security in Southeast Asia. On December 31, 1963, President Johnson wrote the new head of the Republic of Vietnam that "neutralization of South Vietnam would be unacceptable," because it "would only be another name for a Communist takeover" as long as the Communist regime in North Vietnam persisted in its aggressive policy.[118] The disappointing experience of the United States with the neutralization of Laos has convinced American officials that a similar neutralization of South Vietnam would lead to the result which the President predicted. In fact, the view of the United States Government seems to be that the honoring of the 1954 and 1962 Geneva Agreements would be preferable to any new treaty of neutrality.

Thailand as well as Vietnam has also rejected the French proposal for neutralization. To the Thai in particular, it is too uncomfortably reminiscent of 1896, 1941 and 1962. At the SEATO Council meeting on April 13, 1964 the Thai Government formally opposed the neutralization of South Vietnam and other states in Southeast Asia because (1) it would present many "grave dangers" to Vietnam and the whole of Southeast Asia; (2) application of the Laos formula would turn Vietnam "with hands and feet bound" over to aggressors; (3) decisions of national policy "belong to the people of the country and not to outsiders,"; and (4) "the time is long past when nations, especially the smaller ones, may be moved as pawns up and down the international chess board." [119] But far from letting suggestions of neutralization lapse, the French Government and some American commentators have continued to push them. So far Hanoi, Peking, and Moscow have shown no interest.

The tests for successful neutralization are (1) adequate communications between the major powers and effective machinery for negotiation and enforcement; (2) a tacit or explicit understanding by the major powers that they will not intervene *militarily* or *politically* inside the country or the area voluntarily and jointly neutralized; and (3) the desire and capacity of the countries or areas being neutralized to resist political encroachments and subversive infiltration which would otherwise subvert the government and take over all or part of the administration as well as control of the territory and people of the country or countries concerned.[120] The crux of the proposals for the neutralization of Vietnam or Indochina is the ability to prevent political intervention. It is not really a question of preventing or deterring major military interference: it is the difficult problem of neutralizing political interference and aggression by seepage. This is perhaps why the Geneva Agreements of 1954 and 1962 have been disappointing and controversial. The internal politics of Laos and South Vietnam have not been able to prevent encroachments. The purposes and conditions of President Eisenhower's letter of October 23, 1954, regarding Vietnam have been nullified.

X. *GENEVA REVISITED*

If there were to be another negotiation on Vietnam, what would it mean to return to the "essential purposes," "basic provisions" and "strict implementation" of the Geneva Agreements of 1954? What did they provide? What is their relevant status and worth eleven years later? What might they contribute, if anything, to a new equilibrium of respect for independent states, promotion of a community of purpose, establishment of reciprocal undertakings, enforcement of international obligations, and limitations on belligerent use of power?[121]

The Documents

The "Geneva Agreements" of 1954 consist of twelve documents. Three military Agreements on the Cessation of Hostilities in Cambodia, Laos and Vietnam were signed by the Vietminh Vice Minister of National Defense and a military representative of the Commander-in-Chief of the French Union Forces in Indochina insofar as the armistices for Laos and Vietnam were concerned, and by General Nhiek Tioulong for the Commander-in-Chief of the Khmer National Armed Forces, now Prince Sihanouk. Six unilateral declarations were made, two each by Cambodia, Laos and France. Then there was the "Final Declaration" of the Geneva Conference, which was not a signed instrument. The United States and the State of Vietnam each made a unilateral declaration. These twelve documents incorporate policy and law into what might be called the Geneva order for Indochina of 1954. If we assume that the Geneva Declaration of 1962 on the Neutrality of Laos amends and supplements the Agreements of 1954, then we have the total body of understandings and undertakings arising out of the Geneva settlements for Indochina.

The 1954 Agreements are now somewhat vague as to their signatories, binding provisions, and permanent effects. Only the three military agreements were and remain signed obligations. The eight national declarations were unilateral statements of policy. They do not constitute treaty or compact law. The Final Declaration was not signed by any government.* To get around the problem of American refusal to be associated with it, the two Co-Chairmen of the Conference, Eden and Molotov, agreed to eliminate signatures and provide the Declaration with a heading in which all the nine participating countries would be listed indi-

---

* Appendix B for text.

vidually or collectively. At the final plenary session seven delegates *orally* registered on the official record their approval, agreement, or non-objection. Eden nevertheless described it in that
final session in almost his last words there as "the Statement of
the Conference as a whole." A curious as well as ambiguous assertion. The Declaration has some legal effect only on the part of
those seven participants which "associated" with it at the final
plenary session on July 21, 1954.

It is generally felt that the United States declaration was not
such an association. It took note of the three agreements on the
the cessation of hostilities and the first twelve of the thirteen
paragraphs of the Final Declaration, declared concerning them
that it would not use force or the threat of force to disturb them,
called for unity through free elections in Vietnam supervised by
the United Nations, refused to join any arrangement hindering
self-determination in Vietnam, and hoped that the "agreement"
would permit Cambodia, Laos, and Vietnam to play their part in
"full independence and sovereignty" in the peaceful community
of nations. The State of Vietnam also did not associate itself with
the Final Declaration, but consented not to use force to resist the
cease-fire. The United States did not even take note of paragraph
13 of the Final Declaration which provided for consultation
among the members of the Conference to study measures to
ensure respect for the three Agreements on the Cessation of
Hostilities.

The Machinery

The Geneva order of 1954 and 1962 created an institutional
structure for implementation, supervision, and consultation.
First, there is the composition of the Geneva Conference as a
continuing but not corporate body. There were nine members
in 1954: Cambodia, the Democratic Republic of Vietnam, France,
Laos, the Chinese People's Republic, the State of Vietnam, the
Soviet Union, the United Kingdom, and the United States. The
Conference of 1962 added Burma, Canada, India, Poland and
Thailand. The Conference can meet only if all members agree
to attend.

Secondly, the Geneva structure has a presiding officer. Sessions of both conferences were chaired alternately by the British and Soviet Foreign Ministers. These two Co-Chairmen have served as the headpiece to receive and distribute the reports of the International Supervisory Commissions on Cambodia, Laos and Vietnam, and to maintain contact and consultation with the participants of the 1954 and 1962 Conferences. The 1962 Agreements on Laos specifically defined the Co-Chairmen as the Co-Chairmen of that Conference and then their successors in the offices of the Secretary of State for Foreign Affairs in the United Kingdom and Minister for Foreign Affairs in the Soviet Union. Article XIII of the Protocol to the Declaration on the Neutrality of Laos formalized the role of the Co-Chairmen as far as Laos was concerned. They were instructed to receive reports from the International Supervisory Commission, circulate these reports and other important information from the Commission to members of the Conference, exercise supervision of the observance of this Protocol and Declaration, keep the members of the Conference constantly informed and consult them when appropriate; and under Article XIX submit a report with recommendations to the members of the Conference on the question of the termination of the International Supervisory Commission within and not later than three years after the entry into force of this Agreement on July 23, 1962—a provision ignored since that date passed. The Co-Chairmen have consulted with each other, often disagreed, and distributed numerous reports during the past eleven years. They reactivated the Conference on Laos in 1961.

Thirdly, the International Supervisory Commissions for each of the Indochina states and Joint Commissions of equal numbers of the military commands of the two parties concerned in each of the three countries were to constitute the daily operating machinery. In each case, their function was to execute and implement the joint military decisions on the Agreements on the Cessation of Hostilities. The first three International Commissions, each consisting of representatives from Canada, India and Poland, with the Indian serving as Chairman, began functioning in 1954 in each country. While they have had seriously frustrating experiences, they are still intact as organizations in each country. However, their operations have been seriously curtailed. The Joint Commissions have long since disappeared.

Thus, the Conference members, the two Co-Chairmen and the Commissions make up an existing international corporate body for Laos, Cambodia and Vietnam outside any other international framework, including the United Nations, but established by virtue of the sovereign decisions of each one of the participants.

Collective Personality or Community

When we speak of the "essentials" of the Geneva Agreements, we are referring at least to this incomplete and unachieved organizational machinery. Yet we should be careful to remember that the Geneva order did not really foster any trend toward a law of community purpose. The failure of guaranteeing it prevented that, either by evasion of the basic divergencies between the communist and noncommunist powers, or inability to find a device for reconciling their differences. As we have seen, the negotiations of 1954 and 1962 were unable to secure a reliable arrangement to guarantee the independence and security of Cambodia, Laos and Vietnam and the enforcement of these agreements. In ten years the Conference reconvened only once, with expanded membership, when it spent an acrimonious year negotiating the second agreement on Laos. The communist attacks, particularly Peking's, on the United States and other members of the conference were violent and repetitive.

The common interest in 1954 and 1962 was to prevent war in Southeast Asia and world-wide hostilities. As far as 1954 is concerned, two of the participants have not been bound by the Final Declaration and have had no meaningful contacts with the People's Republic of China or the Democratic Republic of Vietnam. The Co-Chairmen have served primarily as a clearing house for communications and not for reflecting or generating any sort of "Geneva spirit of cooperation." The three Supervisory Commissions have operated independently. Each has had a checkered and different history compared to the others.

In brief, the machinery of the two Geneva Conferences neither projected nor promoted a community of purpose among the

104

members of the Conference. However, some building materials for creating a future community among the "Geneva countries" are at hand if there is a common will and mutual interest.

Substantive Military Essentials

There were five military objectives. The *first* was a simultaneous cease-fire in the three countries. The Agreements of 1954 were nine parts military and one part political. The sixth point of the Final Declaration recognized that "the essential purpose of the agreement relating to Vietnam is to settle military questions with a view to ending hostilities and that the military demarcation line is provisional and should not in any way be interpreted as constituting a political or territorial boundary." The Geneva Agreements and the subsidiary negotiations of the Conferences did bring about a military cease-fire in Vietnam, Laos and Cambodia in 1954, and again in 1961 in Laos. But the cease-fire has not continued in Vietnam or in Laos where it has been ruptured frequently and now constantly in both countries. But the minimum or primary essential of those Agreements, as well as the 1962 Agreements on Laos, was cessation of hostilities.

The *second* military essential was detailed provision for the disengagement and regroupment of combat forces in specified areas which was completed and then violated. The Vietnamese communist troops withdrew from Cambodia according to that Agreement. They have not returned to fight against Cambodian forces since 1954. However, there apparently is evidence that in recent years Vietnamese communist personnel and cadres have passed through Cambodia from Laos to Vietnam and have used Cambodia as a privileged logistic sanctuary for conducting guerrilla warfare against South Vietnam, although Cambodia challenges both counts. But that essential provision of the agreement on Cambodia was carried out. In Laos, the Vietnamese communist forces were also withdrawn and the Lao communist forces regrouped in two northern provinces. However, Vietnamese communist combat units and troops have returned in the thousands either to conduct hostilities in Laos as the International Commission and the United Nations Mission of Inquiry have found, or to use Laos for infiltrating South Vietnam. Thus the second essential for Laos and Cambodia has also been breached. It has been a much more complicated matter for Vietnam. The regular forces of North Vietnam and of France were regrouped into specified areas in South Vietnam and North Vietnam. After an agreed period of time French forces moved to the South and then entirely out of Vietnam, while Vietnamese communist troops moved back to North Vietnam. The total number of non-communist forces remaining in Vietnam by 1956 was substantially below their total final strength at the time of the Agreement on the Cessation of Hostilities. Yet not all Vietnamese communist forces went north. Many have returned south in violation of the Agreements.

The *third* essential military aspect of the agreement on Vietnam was the establishment of a "provisional military demarcation line and demilitarization zone" across Vietnam from the seacoast to the Lao frontier along the river at approximately the 17th parallel. The first nine articles of Chapter I of the Agreement on Vietnam provided for this line and zone which continue in being today. This strip separates the territory of North Vietnam from South Vietnam. While there apparently have been infiltrations on the ground across this line over the past few years, it is one provision which has been more honored than breached by both sides. However, the Vietnamese communist infiltration through Laos and by sea into South Vietnam has outflanked and nullified the essential purpose of the zone. American air operations into North Vietnam have also gone "beyond the parallel." The other agreements did not include any such zones, although the Lao communist forces were told to use a corridor along the Vietnamese frontier to reassemble in the regroupment provinces of North Laos.

A *fourth* military essential of the Geneva agreements of 1954 and 1962 was the prohibition against reinforcement of troops, foreign military personnel, arms, munitions and other war material, except for replacement purposes (as defined in the Agreements) through designated points of entry under the supervision of the International Commissions. The history of this prohibition remains one of the most controversial and difficult aspects of the Agreements. Although it levied equally binding and quantitative provisions on both sides, yet within a few months of the signing of the 1954 Agreement there were charges based on convincing evidence that the Vietnamese communist forces of the North were rapidly increasing in size. By 1956, the United Kingdom, as Co-Chairman, reported that this strength had increased from 7 divisions to 20.[122] That was in violation of Article 16. The International Supervisory Commission found that its mobile teams could not verify this expansion in the North and that its fixed teams were not able to ascertain the entry of military equipment which was moving into the North. On their side, the communists lodged numerous complaints with the Commission that South Vietnam and the United States were introducing more than replacement equipment and increasing the number of military personnel in Vietnam and in Laos under both Agreements. But the breakdown in these essential provisions of the Geneva agreements has led to a situation where the articles of prohibition and the provisions of reciprocity have become dead letters.

The *fifth* essential military provision of the Geneva Agreements precluded these three countries from establishing new military bases and from adhering to any military alliance. The two areas, or zones, of North and South Vietnam were not to be used for the resumption of hostilities or to further an aggressive policy. In the case of Vietnam, the armed forces of each party—meaning the Vietnamese communists and the French—were enjoined to respect the demilitarization zone and the territory under the military control of the other party and to commit no act and undertake no operation against the other party. In the case of Laos and Cambodia, an escape clause was added to the military prohibitions to the effect that the prohibitions would not apply if the security of Laos or Cambodia were threatened.

Political Provisions

The Geneva Agreement on Cambodia helped to establish that nation in unified independence. Except for what the Cambodian Government still considers to be threats to its integrity, it could be said that the Geneva Agreements were allowed to work and were not subverted in their political essentials for Cambodia.

The experience in Laos has been much less favorable. The 1954

Agreement provided that the Lao communist forces would be concentrated in the two northern provinces pending a political settlement and that each party to the Agreement would refrain from reprisals and discrimination against the other side. The Lao Government agreed to hold elections to integrate the Lao communist forces and armies into a united nation. Despite these agreements, the communist forces, with Vietnamese communist backing, continued military harassments for several years and used those two provinces as logistic sanctuaries adjacent to North Vietnam for "aggression by seepage." They accepted the principle of integration, yet communist military elements in fact did not demobilize but remained intact. Although the Lao communists were designated as one of the three parties of the Central Government under the 1962 agreement, they have expanded their monopoly of the *de facto* administration not only of those two northern provinces where they regrouped ten years ago, but also of at least the whole eastern half of Laos running from China to Cambodia. The Lao Government of National Union, including King Savang, and the International Supervisory Commission have been excluded completely from any part of this important corridor next to Vietnam. This clearly violates the spirit and letter of the Agreements of 1962. They contained a provision to prevent a corridor on the Vietnamese side of Laos from being used by communist forces from North Vietnam to infiltrate South Vietnam. Paragraph 2 (i) of the Declaration calls on the thirteen members of the Conference other than Laos to undertake that "they will not use the territory of Laos for interference in the internal affairs of other countries." Laos pledged a reciprocal undertaking that it would not allow any country to use Laos territory "for the purposes of interference in the internal affairs of other countries." The delegation of the Republic of Vietnam introduced this idea of a prohibitive corridor. Nevertheless, despite the binding character of the obligations and reciprocal undertakings in the 1962 Agreement on Laos, it has in fact become politically partitioned in half, the communists have boycotted the National Government, and the International Supervisory Commission cannot enter, let alone inspect, the very territory of Laos which is the source of conflict and cause of violation. The Agreements of 1954 and 1962 on Laos have led, for political reasons and because of the use of military power on the communist side, to a political settlement of actual division rather than to any unity or order of the country.[123]

The political provisions of the Geneva Agreement of 1954 on Vietnam have proved even more difficult and controversial to implement or even interpret. As we have noted, it was nine parts military and one part political, but that ten per cent was perhaps more significant for the insecurity and present crisis of Southeast Asia than all the other parts of all of the documents of 1954 put together. The negotiation regarding Vietnam in 1954 ended on the assumption that elections would be held in all of Vietnam in 1956 which would create a single government for the entire country. That was the bargain reached between French and Vietminh negotiators, despite the protest of the South Vietnamese and the rejection by Washington. It was also the assumption of many at Geneva and elsewhere that such a government in 1956 would in fact be the communist regime in Hanoi under the leadership of Ho Chi Minh. It is probable, although it cannot be definitely proved as yet, that such assumptions formed the basis for Hanoi's concessions and acceptance at Geneva on all the Agreements.[124] The communists agreed to the cease-fire and the provisional division of the country at the 17th parallel on the expectation that elections in 1956 would bring about a communist political victory and communist control of the entire Vietnamese country. They had bargained first for the 13th parallel and elections in 1955.

During the Geneva Conference, the communists pressed for far-reaching political settlements to their advantage in all three of the Indochina states. They had to settle for a totally independent Cambodia, indirect if potential but not certain control of two provinces or more in Laos, the temporary division of Vietnam, and the promise of elections to reunify Vietnam under their sole control. The delegation of South Vietnam fought such efforts. The French and British delegations also resisted the Vietminh ambitions. But most delegations resigned themselves to the probability that the provision for elections would result in a communist victory. That is why the delegations of the United

States and South Vietnam disassociated themselves from the Agreements on Vietnam and refused to guarantee the Agreements as a whole.

However, the provision for all-Vietnamese elections was contained not in what would be called a binding international treaty, but in the Final Declaration, even though there was probably a tacit or diplomatic understanding among the participants other than the Americans and the South Vietnamese that such elections should legally be held. An International Commission composed of representatives of Canada, India and Poland, like the International Supervisory Commission on the Military provisions, was to supervise such general elections. The full text of paragraph 7 of the Final Declaration reads as follows:

> "The Conference declares that, so far as Viet-Nam is concerned, the settlement of political problems, effected on the basis of respect for the principles of independence, unity and territorial integrity, shall *permit the Viet-Namese people to enjoy the fundamental freedoms, guaranteed by democratic institutions established as a result of free general elections by secret ballot.* In order to ensure that sufficient progress in the restoration of peace has been made, and that all the necessary conditions obtain for *free expression of the national will, general elections* shall be held in July 1956, under the supervision of an international commission composed of representatives of the Member States of the International Supervisory Commission, referred to in the agreement on the cessation of hostilities. Consultations will be held on this subject between the competent representative authorities of the two zones from 20 July 1955 onwards." (emphasis added)

The Agreement on the Cessation of Hostilities in Vietnam, signed by the French and Vietminh military authorities, did not contain any terms and conditions for elections but did use language clearly indicating for the two co-signers that the military demarcation line, the demilitarized zone, and the two "regrouping" zones on either side of the line were provisional until elections had unified the two parts of the country and the whole country was under a single government. Article 14 provided for provisional political and administrative measures in these two regrouping zones. It stated that, "pending the general elections which will bring the unification of Vietnam, the conduct of civil administration in each regrouping zone shall be in the hands of the party whose forces are to be regrouped there in virtue of the present agreement." At the time of the agreement in 1954, the "party" in the South was France, or the forces of the French Union, legally speaking. Article 14 also contained the political provision that each party undertook to refrain from any reprisals or discrimination against persons or organizations on account of their activities during the hostilities and to guarantee their democratic liberties. In addition, civilians living in one zone were to be permitted and helped to move to the other zone. While a question arises as to whether or not the Republic of Vietnam became the legal "party" as a successor state to France to carry out Paragraph 7 and Article 14, in view of the explicit refusal of the State of Vietnam to be bound by these accords, the government in Saigon in fact only became the implementing authority for such of the Agreements on Vietnam as it decided to comply with.

However, insofar as the assumptions regarding the Vietnamese elections were concerned, the State of Vietnam and the United States explicitly took a different position at the Geneva Conference. Before the Final Declaration was issued and before the Agreement on the Cessation of Hostilities was signed, both called for genuinely free elections to bring about the peaceful unification of Vietnam, and both advocated fair, effective supervision by the United Nations. The delegation of South Vietnam in fact proposed the institution of a provisional control by the United Nations over all Vietnam governing the reestablishment of peace and arrangements for free elections.

In 1955 and in 1956 when the time came under Paragraph 7 for consultations and elections, the Government of South Vietnam, despite its formal non-adherence to the Geneva Agreements and particularly the Final Declaration, was ready to discuss electoral procedures with the northern authorities provided they first complied with the Agreements, ended terror, and permitted political liberties comparable to those in the south.[125] Moreover, the Republic of Vietnam reiterated in 1955, 1956, 1958, and 1960 that it was prepared to undertake effectively supervised and generally free elections and to consult with northern authorities about them if they first complied with the intent of Paragraph 7 by creating the necessary conditions of fundamental freedoms, democratic institutions and free expression of the national will by secret ballot. But Saigon resisted all pressures to enter into unconditional consultations with Hanoi on paragraph 7. They insisted on reciprocity in fact. Such a stipulation literally would have required freedom of speech of parties and candidates in the north, the termination of totalitarian control and terroristic intimidation against the people, and the total transformation of the communist apparatus for a one party state into a multi-party system in the north. Obviously such a transformation never did and never could take place.

Whether or not this complicated and even nebulous suggestion for Vietnamese elections was in fact a binding obligation or just a political assumption, it called for the kind of elections which the communist authorities in Moscow, Peking and Hanoi did not then and would still not accept: free general elections by secret ballot under effective supervision. The former Foreign Minister of the Soviet Union, Molotov, told his Western colleagues on several occasions that there would never be free elections in the Western sense of the term in any of the communist-controlled countries, such as Germany, Korea and Vietnam. There only one party and a single slate of candidates would be offered to the general electorate for voting. Any other arrangement was out of the question. And this adamant rejection of any form of free elections and multiple choice remains the attitude of Moscow, Peking and Hanoi insofar as North Vietnam is concerned. Thus, from the very beginning of the Geneva Agreements there was in fact no possibility of any free general election by democratic institutions and parties in North Vietnam under effective supervision. This has been the real crux of the issue rather than the question of whether or not the United States and the Republic of Vietnam were bound legally in any way to comply with Paragraph 7 of the Final Declaration and Article 14 of the Agreement on the Cessation of Hostilities. There could be no genuinely reciprocal undertakings to implement the political provisions of the Geneva agreements of 1954 regarding Vietnam even if there had been legal obligations. Such implementation would have been one-sided, non-reciprocal and unequal.

There of course remains the question of policy rather than law as to whether or not it might have been wiser for Washington and Saigon to have begun consultations as a matter of sovereign choice rather than out of any assumed obligations. Both governments could have made it quite clear that they were not taking such actions to comply with or fulfill the Agreements to which they had not adhered and by which they were not bound to take any positive action. Nor would they have compromised their insistence on UN-supervised elections. The United States Government indeed did try to persuade President Diem and his colleagues in Saigon to conduct the discussions for as long as necessary and in elaborate detail with the communist authorities in a location which would have been provided for this purpose in the demilitarized zone. However, as a matter of policy, the government in Saigon decided that it should not and could not compromise its position by any such consultations. The governments of the United States, France and Great Britain agreed jointly to persuade the government in Saigon otherwise, but, despite their efforts, they were not in any position to force what they considered to be a sovereign government, recognized by many nations, to undertake action which was considered detrimental, possibly leading to vital harm, to the national interest and integrity of that *independent* state. At the Summit Conference in July 1955 the Soviet delegation was apprised of this situation but did not show particular concern. In 1956 the Western governments were of much the same opinion. The British and Soviet Co-Chairmen, anticipating that the elections under Paragraph 7 would not take place, advised the Vietnamese authorities in North Vietnam and in South Vietnam not to disturb the peace and to cooperate with the International Commission. Apparently the Soviet Government did not put any great pressure on its communist colleagues or on its Western adversaries to enforce these so-called election provisions of the Geneva Agreements.[126]

Another factor significantly affected these political provisions of the Geneva Agreements on Vietnam. That was the immediate and rapid expansion of communist military forces in 1954–56 and the increasing inability of the International Supervisory Commission to observe and supervise the essential military provisions in North Vietnam in that regard. In brief, the authorities in the north appeared instantly after the Geneva Conference to have begun to violate the military prohibitions of the agreement and to restrict and prevent the legitimate operations of the Commission. Under those conditions, elections in the north could not have been satisfactorily guaranteed and supervised by a comparable Commission. Meanwhile, the military build-up as well as the reprisals against individuals in the north would have made conditions for free elections even worse. In the spring of 1956 the Government of the United Kingdom, as Co-Chairman, took note of these developments contrary to the spirit and letter of the Geneva agreements on Vietnam.

As a further matter of policy and power on the part of the communists, their failure and disappointment to see the political assumptions of Geneva bring about their political control of all of Vietnam in July 1956 led to the decision to use force and terror rather than just non-violent political means to unify all of Vietnam under the control of the Vietnamese Communist Party. That decision was taken some time in 1956.[127] The communists began to implement it in 1957 with the assassination of village leaders in outlying remote districts of South Vietnam. Another war for the forcible unification of Vietnam under communist control had started imperceptibly but definitively. Aggression by seepage had begun in the outlying areas of Vietnam. The International Supervisory Commission, the Government of Vietnam and the United States with other allies and friends have been hard put to seal off this growing seepage and furtive war. For a long time the demarcation line at the 17th parallel and the corridor in Laos provided a protected sanctuary and a protected access for the communists into Vietnam despite the Geneva Agreements.

The Competence of Supervision

One of the most difficult questions of policy and law, and to some extent of power, has been to negotiate the authority and functions of international control and enforcement with the communists. In the 1954 Agreements, the International Commissions were given the responsibility to ensure that the control and supervision of the execution of the Agreements by the signatory parties, that is, the Vietminh military authorities, the French, and the Cambodians. The Commissions did not become involved to any great extent in the political processes. Their functions related primarily to the military terms of the Agreements. The principal difficulties in the terms of reference for the Commissions in the 1954 Agreements and in the 1962 Agreement on Laos had to do with the issues of the negative veto and the power of enforcement. The 1954 Agreements stipulated that decisions of the Commission had to be unanimous on questions concerning violations or threats of violations which might lead to a resumption of hostilities. Any recommendations of the Commission on this critical point had to be unanimous. In other words, one member could veto a recommendation or action by the Commission in the key matter of violations. Other recommendations were to be taken by a majority vote, including the Chairman's. In the event of a veto in case of violation, the Commission could submit a majority report and a minority report to the members of the Geneva Conference. The Conference was the only court of appeal to which the Commission could go for any enforcement of its decisions or for any recourse on hindrances to its activities. But the Conference never has functioned as a body. The Commissions were provided with fixed and mobile inspection teams in Vietnam, Laos and Cambodia, and with logistic support and staff to operate. However, the activities of these inspection teams were restricted or in many cases eliminated in communist-controlled areas. In South Vietnam the relations between the Vietnamese authorities and the Commission were never cordial and often difficult.

The Conference on Laos in 1961–1962 had to deal with these vital questions of veto and enforcement. The duties of the Co-Chairmen were spelled out for their supervision of the observance of the Agreement, but without giving either one a veto, as the Soviet Government had attempted to obtain. The Commission was directed to carry out investigations on violations on its own initiative or at the request of the Government of Laos. The important stipulation here was the provision that such investigations and decisions to undertake these investigations could be taken by a majority vote. This was a considerable improvement over the 1954 Agreements. Furthermore, the Commission could undertake an investigation regardless of the opposition of any

115

individual member if the Government of Laos requested it. The only difficulty there was that the avowed communists had been named part of the government and of course vetoed or opposed such investigations and therefore declared them illegal and not reflecting the request of the Government of Laos. However, decisions of the Commission on questions relating to violations of the cease-fire or of the withdrawal or introduction of foreign troops and the introduction of arms and military equipment had to be taken unanimously. This was a compromise between the original Soviet position that all questions except procedural ones had to be unanimous and the Western position that any decision should be taken only by majority vote. However, the Commission could send conclusions on major questions and all recommendations to the Co-Chairmen and the Conference by majority vote. Furthermore, decisions on the initiation and implementation of investigation were explicitly a matter for majority decision. In other words, the Commission could always report by two votes to the Co-Chairmen in the Conference, which has been its really significant function. However, the Commission on Laos has not been an enforcement agency and has no means beyond what the Conference would provide to enforce its inspection where it is now prevented Yet, even the provision in Article 19 of the 1962 Agreement calling on the Co-Chairmen within three years to report their recommendations to the Conference on the termination of the Commission has passed the deadline and become a dead letter. The communists have now officially called for the abolition of the Commission.

Violations and Aggression

The official documentation under all of these Geneva Agreements is full of charges and countercharges, findings and recommendations, regarding violations of the essential military provisions and the so-called political provisions. In the case of Vietnam, the significant document is the Special Report to the Co-Chairmen of the Geneva Conference on Indochina submitted on June 2, 1962 by the International Commission for Supervision and Control in Vietnam.[128] By a majority vote, with Poland dissenting, the Commission reported to the Co-Chairmen that the People's Army of Vietnam (Communist North Vietnam) had seriously violated Article 10 providing for a complete cessation of all hostilities, Article 19 not to use the regrouping zone for resumption of hostilities or to forward an aggressive policy, Article 24 not to violate the demilitarized zone and to respect the territory under the military control of the other party by committing no act or undertaking no operation against it, and Article 27 to ensure full compliance by all elements of military personnel under the command of the North Vietnamese authorities. The Canadian and Indian members of the Commission concluded that North Vietnam had sent arms, munitions and other supplies from the "zone in the north to the zone in the south" to support, organize and carry out hostile activities including armed attacks against the armed forces and the administration of the zone in the south. A majority of the Commission considered these acts in violation of Articles 10, 19, 24 and 27. The majority of the Commission also found that the North Vietnamese authorities had allowed the "zone in the north" to be used for inciting, encouraging and supporting hostile activities in the "zone in the south . . . aimed at the overthrow of the administration in the south." The majority of the Commission considered the use of the northern zone for such activities to be in violation of Articles 19, 24 and 27. At the same time, the whole Commission considered the charges of the North Vietnamese against South Vietnam and the United States for importing war material and introducing military personnel to be in violation of the agreement. The Commission concluded that the Republic of Vietnam had violated Articles 16 and 17 of the Geneva Agreement in receiving increased military aid from the United States of America which the Republic of Vietnam had not deducted from the credit it had received for military equipment which had been worn out or removed from Vietnam, in view of the fact that the Republic of Vietnam was not permitting the Commission to make proper inspections. The Commission reported that both parties had immobilized the activities of the Commission's teams and hampered the Commission's proper discharge of its obligations to supervise

117

the agreement. Needless to say, the Commission has not been able to improve the situation since 1962.

The United States Government has considered and declared the activities of communist elements in Vietnam—north and south—to be aggression against a legitimate and duly-constituted independent, sovereign, legal state—the Republic of Vietnam. SEATO has officially concurred. The American charge of aggression has been documented with much evidence. On February 7 and 27, 1965, the United States filed complaints of such agression with the United Nations in letters to the President of the Security Council and circulated a special report on "Aggression from the North."[129]

South Vietnam's Independence

With regard to the political provisions, the Geneva Agreements of 1954 neither established nor nullified the legal basis for the independence of South Vietnam. That had happened separately and concurrently. The State of Vietnam was a recognized member of the Geneva Conference and a state under international law. In June 1954, France concluded an agreement with it for its independent existence. France recognized its independence and transferred the functions and attributes of sovereignty completely to it. This took place during the negotiations at Geneva which were concluded several weeks later. Therefore, no provision or inference of the Geneva documentation could deny the sovereign independence of what was then called the State of Vietnam. The United States Government entered its intention on the official record of the Conference to treat South Vietnam not as a "provisional zone" but as an entity entitled to "full independence and sovereignty." It was also the policy of the British and French governments before and after the Conference. South Vietnam was independent prior to the conclusion of those Agreements and their binding effect on the signatories. Furthermore, the State of Vietnam declared its non-adherence to the Agreements in terms of a declaration not to use force to overthrow them. It could continue independent beyond 1956. It did not have to execute the political condition of Geneva 1954 which would have liquidated its life.[130]

118

Conclusions

The question now is whether or not a return to the essentials of the 1954 Agreements and the Geneva ensemble still contains anything valid for a renewed effort at a regional equilibrium in Southeast Asia—"a reliable arrangement to guarantee the independence and security of all in Southeast Asia," as President Johnson put it. One point of view holds that a return to a faithful honoring and implementation of the military provisions would bring peace and stability to Laos, Cambodia and Vietnam. Even genuinely free and effectively supervised elections according to Paragraph 7 could be a basis for political stability by resolving the issue of Vietnamese partition and unification. There are others who hold that such a return to the "basic essentials" of Geneva is really a semantic fallacy. The Agreements were so inept and confusing and they have been so completely violated or ignored for ten years that there is little or nothing to return to, in that view. Even if there were a will on the part of all parties to honor them, it is perhaps too complicated just to call for a resurrection of their tattered provisions. Yet, if we look at them for principles and not provisions, they might provide some guidelines for limitations on belligerency, some measure of specific reciprocity, and an elemental form of community guarantee of at least a minimum of purpose. In bare essentials the old Agreements can teach us what to avoid and perhaps how to avoid it.

The question for law, policy and power in Southeast Asia is whether some principles of the Geneva order could be reworked into a new set of agreements, recognizing the vital flaws in the 1954 and 1962 Conferences and Agreements in that they did not provide for any form of enforcement or any guarantee of joint measures in the event of violations. There is much machinery but no muscle. If we were to adopt something which might be called a policy of convergence in Southeast Asia designed to bring the various parties of interest together in a negotiating situation to bargain for a minimum public order in a limited community of purpose, then the principles of these Geneva Agreements might be refashioned with reciprocal guarantees in a kind of permanent conference as one important factor seeking to stabilize a formal and specific equilibrium in Southeast Asia. The issue is one of high policy, particularly for the United States, to answer the questions of cease-fire, military regroupment, military prohibitions, political relations between south and north, external guarantees and relationships for Vietnam, and the composition of any new conference.

XI. *APPROACHES TO RESOLUTION OF CONFLICT AND REGIONAL ORDER*

The challenges to United States and international diplomacy are so formidable and even overwhelming in Southeast Asia that the possibility of reducing or resolving conflicts may seem too remote for us even to consider new approaches. The apparent irreconcilability of communist expansion and nationalist aspirations may be unbridgeable. Yet the depth of the Southeast Asia crisis, with its danger of war compel us to find a possible and practical alternative.

Looking ahead, the basic factors in the situation are changing. New challenges require new solutions. We can no longer assume, as we could in 1955, that there is an "arc of free Asia", of independent countries following more or less similar policies towards the United States. For the future we may need a much more selective diplomacy in Asia. China's potential for nuclear "hostaging" will alter the political and strategic outlook for all Asia, and require an extensive commitment of United States land and missile forces together with an up-to-date system of cooperative security among several Asian states from Teheran to Tokyo. Asia, and particularly Southeast Asia, will soon reach a point in time when a "line of limit" of some geographical and political zone is needed to separate the two major sets of contending forces and stabilize the possibilities for negotiating conflicts.[131] The Sino-Soviet rivalry and the nationalistic fragmentation of communism will also radically alter the terms of the conflict and the possibilities for its settlement, if the Soviet and United States Governments can begin to develop parallel or even joint policies in support of regional order. And, in looking ahead, the Vietnamese leaders and people in both the north and the south may find a special role to play in preserving independent states in Southeast Asia and in promoting a sense of regional community, however unlikely that may seem in 1965. Moreover, the swift and substantial evolution of United States policies toward Southeast Asia this year has opened up possibilities for developing these potential changes not only for Vietnam but also for expanded participation of the United Nations and regional cooperation for stability. Much will depend in the immediate future and particularly in 1966 on how the new, emerging pattern evolves in Southeast Asia: the rejection of the United Nations by at least two states, with possibly one or more to follow; the threatened breakup of Malaysia; and the North-South squeeze play.

To reverse the trends, the independence and solidity of Vietnam and its neighbors in Southeast Asia form the primary need for any such regional stabilization. Only if these state-nations withstand the pressures and threats of communist take-over or social disintegration can international law influence that crossroads of conflict. The historic tenacity and traditional adaptiveness of Southeast Asians are vital for peace in the 20th century. The first priority for them and for us is to uphold and reinforce the contemporary principles of international law, in particular the injunctions not to intervene in the domestic affairs of other states, to refrain from the illegal use or threat of the use of force, and to settle disputes by peaceful means once transnational aggression is stopped.[132]

Transcending these states is a recognizable and operable region called "Southeast Asia" which does represent a tangible and objective community as well as convergence of diverse interests for the United States, many other governments, and international institutions. A combination of nationalism and internationalism is translating this community of interest into new social, economic and political forms. Legal-sanctioning and institutional-building elements for reconstructing a regional order are available, although they are elementary and inadequate, as we have seen. SEATO, ASA, the United Nations, the Mekong Community, and even the Geneva arrangements have something to contribute for a new synthesis which might evolve out of a broad-scale diplomacy and negotiation. It is significant that the United States has finally demonstrated that it is interested and involved in this region *per se* in terms of the needs of the people and the nations of the region itself, and not as a reaction to the policies of

Europe, Russia or China. Likewise the outcome in Vietnam is directly linked to the region as a whole and cannot be treated separately, even though Vietnam has become the arena of decision.

The resolution of conflict and new approaches to regional order will require a skillful meshing of political and military actions and the use of diplomacy and force in tandem. Military containment alone is not enough. Only a mixture of political, social, economic and defensive measures, particularly in Vietnam, can give us any hope for some stabilization.

Vietnam is the crux of this challenge and the keystone for peace or war. Political success in closing the "government gap" and in rallying the people, particularly the younger generation in the cities and farms of Vietnam, will decide the outcome, assuming that military operations on our part will create another opportunity for political reconstruction and social justice.[133] But we cannot afford to lose what may be the last chance politically speaking.

A new approach of international diplomacy for the conflict in Vietnam and in all Southeast Asia must first seek to find workable means of communication for the participants, so that they can establish limits on belligerency, stabilize the "area of intermediacy" between an armistice without peace, on the one hand, and war without declaration, on the other, and subscribe to reciprocal obligations and guarantees. They would have to agree on (1) demilitarized lines of limit and zones of insulation over which military and paramilitary forces and equipment could not legally pass, (2) impartial supervision and enforcement of their contractual obligations, and (3) pledges not to interfere with the natural development of a "law of community" among some or all of the states of Southeast Asia. If the major powers could agree on just these reciprocal undertakings, the states in Southeast Asia would then have time and tranquillity to work out common objectives and structures for cooperation and authority within the region.

The search for a law of community with positive goals and reciprocal undertakings is probably the challenge most needing a concentration of legal talent, political aptitude and technical resources for Southeast Asia. A law of community would require the enlightened self-interest of the regional participating states in looking inward "nationalistically" and outward "internationally" at the same time—not an easy thing for any government to do. They would reflect a sense of interdependence rather than just independence. Their law of community would go beyond that individual sovereignty which can lead to national suicide, and seek regional association which could bring national survival. Such a concept would seek to show that there are interests outside each state which would make a community of purpose more beneficial than would national isolation or non-involvement.

While nationalism is the integrating influence and is just holding its own, the task is to design appropriate and varied means for transnational communication and collaboration for the decision-makers in Southeast Asia. This means putting the role of the sovereign nation-state in its proper perspective in the world of the future, where the realities of population explosion, urban revolution, nuclear weaponry, international intermingling and rapid technological change will make the nation-state a weak instrument for social progress and national survival. Such communication and collaboration can demonstrate the superiority of modern science—social and physical—over the 'cold war and hot revolutions, over narrow nationalism and totalitarian communism.

The search for an equilibrium in Southeast Asia would seek the ultimate goal of a new law of regional organization and functional cooperation to synthesize concepts and practices of limited belligerency, specific reciprocity, and community purpose. The decentralization of responsibility into a Southeast Asian form of "functional federalism" could be the target for regional equilibrium. Authority in action would be undertaken and exercised by the collaboration and coordination of the constituent parts of such a functional order. It might begin with simple, elemental and specific targets with short commitments in time, small requirements for resources, and low risks of political impairment. This form of functional federalism could expand in a widening concentric "circle" with a sequence of targets as the confidence and experience of the decision-makers, technicians and people developed.

In addition to procedures for pacific settlement of disputes, new approaches should include new means for guaranteeing respect for human rights and social minorities, promoting self-determination of peoples within nations, and organizing new forms of international cooperation for human welfare. A new jural order in Southeast Asia would, of course, be accelerated and assisted by the evolution of an international jural order or a series of regional orders in different parts of the world on a similar basis and reflecting the new "law" of technical assistance and economic development.[134] This new type of "convergent law" and "functional federation" also might serve to create negotiating and bargaining situations among diverse players.

A proposal for a policy of convergence beyond containment might include the following five points:[135]

1. *International Insulation*: Before any political or economic development can be assured, some strip or zone in Southeast Asia must be demilitarized. An Indian proposal for an Asian force suggests a positive approach[131] which could be promoted and negotiated when the combat situation is stabilized.

2. *U.N. Commission for Southeast Asia*: To expand the role of the United Nations for peace-keeping as well as nation-building, a formal or informal organization of experts in various fields could be established by the General Assembly for the Secretary General and the governments of Southeast Asia to call upon. In addition, the role of the United Nations in Southeast Asia would be considerably strengthened if both the Republic of Vietnam and the Democratic Republic of Vietnam would each agree to become members, if approved by the Security Council and the General Assembly.

3. *Development of the Mekong Community*: Regional cooperation offers many possibilities for strengthening the spirit and structure of transnational institutions in Southeast Asia. Efforts should be continued to expand the role of both Vietnams in regional projects. There are many possible ways of developing the Mekong community as a unifying factor for regionalizing the economies of the riparian countries by a common strategy of development, and even defense, under the auspices of the United Nations.

4. *New Geneva Order*: Subject to military and political conditions, a new forum including additional participants in a conference or a series of conferences should be undertaken sometime within the next few years to negotiate a guaranteed settlement, continuing machinery for consultation and means of effective enforcement for military and political neutralization.

5. *Vietnamese Federal Co-Existence*: Regional order will come about to the extent that ways and means can be found to persuade the two Vietnams to live and let live and work within the framework of a Geneva order, a Mekong community, and the auspices of the United Nations.

1966 promises to be a year of crystallizing decisions for the governments of Southeast Asia, the United States, the U.S.S.R., the C.P.R., and the United Nations in Southeast Asia. Many of the issues underlying the conflict there will come to a head in either a convergence of critical deadlock or of possible resolution.

FOOTNOTES

(In the footnotes to Part VII, the symbol "A/ . . ." refers to the U.N. General Assembly document series, and the symbol "S/ . . ." refers to the U.N. Security Council document series.)

[1] Cady, John F. Southeast Asia: Its Historical Development. 1964. Chapter II, pp. 21–48;

Coedes, George. Les Etats Hindouises d'Indochine et d'Indonesie. 1948.

[2] Modelski, George. Kautilya: Foreign Policy and International System in the Ancient Hindu World. The American Political Science Review. Vol. LVIII, September 1964, pp. 549–560;

Spellman, John W. Political Theory of Ancient India. 1964. p. 157 contains a hypothetical illustration of the Mandala Theory.

[3] Reichauer, Edwin O. and Fairbank, John K. The East Asian Tradition.

[4] Fairbank, John K. and Teng, S. Y. On the Ch'ing Tributary System. Ch'ing Administration, Harvard-Yenching Institute Studies, 1961. pp. 107–246.

[5] Hall, D. G. E. A History of South-East Asia. 1964. pp. 76, 77, 96, 97, 134, 135, 147–154, 161–166, 183–189, 194–197. See also

Fisher, Charles A. South-East Asia, A Social, Economic and Political Geography, 1964. Chapter 4, Political Geography of the Pre-European Period. pp. 102–125.

[6] Huard, Pierre, and Durand, Maurice. Connaissance du Viêt-Nam. 1954. pp. 15–35;

Buttinger, Joseph. The Smaller Dragon, a Political History of Vietnam. 1958. Chapters 2 and 3 on Chinese Rule and Vietnamese Independence. pp. 67–197.

[7] "Thailand in the Light of Official Chinese Historiography—a Chapter in the History of the Ming Dynasty" by T. Grimm, The Journal of the Siam Society. Vol. XLIX Part I, July 1961. pp. 1–20.

[8] Fifield, Russell H. The Diplomacy of Southeast Asia: 1945–1958. 1958. pp. 1–42;

Cady. op. cit. Note 1 Parts 5 and 6;

Fisher, op. cit. Note 5 Chapter 6. The Legacies of the West. pp. 160–202.

[9] Clubb, O. Edmund. Twentieth Century China. 1964. pp. 303, 423.

Elegant, Robert S. The Center of the World, Communism and the Mind of China. 1964. pp. 85, 155–159, 171–172.

[10] Levenson, Joseph R. Modern China and Its Confucian Past. 1964. pp. 135–139.

[11] Elegant, op. cit. Note 9 and Sources of Chinese Tradition. p. 733.

Levenson, op. cit. Note 10.

[12] These references are from The Political Thought of Mao Tse-tung. Schram, Stuart R. 1963.

[13] Chen, Jerome. Mao and the Chinese Revolution. pp. 339 and 360.

[14] Fitzgerald, C. P., p. 71.

[15] New York Times, September 4, 1965, for complete text.

[16] Tsou, Tang. Mao Tse-tung and Peaceful Coexistence. Orbis Vol. VIII, Spring 1964, No. 1. pp. 36–51.

[17] For views on the expansionist element in Chinese Communist foreign policy see:

Barnett, A. Doak. Communist China and Asia. 1960;

Boyd, R. G. Communist China's Foreign Policy. 1962;

Dutt, Vidya Prakash. China's Foreign Policy: 1958–1962, for an Indian viewpoint;

Fisher, op. cit. Note 5.

Fifield, Russell A. Southeast Asia in the United States Policy. 1963. Chapter 3.

Friedman, Maurice. "The Chinese in South-East Asia: A Longer View." The

China Society, London 1965;

Wint, Guy. Communist China's Crusade. 1965;

Griffith, Samuel B. II. Communist China's Capacity to Make War, in Foreign Affairs. Vol. 43, No. 2, January 1965;

Crozier, Brian. Southeast Asia in Turmoil, 1965;

Butwell, Richard. Southeast Asia Today—and Tomorrow, a Political Analysis. 1961.

For a somewhat different treatment see:

"The Impact of China" by Philippe Devillers in *South Asia Pacific Crisis,* edited by Margaret Grant 1964, pp. 136–159 for a French View;

Harris, Richard. Communism and Asia, Illusions and Misconceptions. International Affairs Vol. 38, No. 1, January 1963. pp. 13–23;

Caldwell, Malcolm. Luddites and Lemmings in Southeast Asia. International Affairs Vol. 41, No. 3, July 1965. pp. 420–440;

Purcell, Victor. The Revolution in Southeast Asia. 1962.

[18] MacFarquhar, Roderick. China Goes It Alone. Atlantic Monthly, April 1965.

[19] Schram, *op. cit.* Note 12 p. 257–258.

[20] See the map on the inside cover of Southeast Asia: Problems of United States Policy. William Henderson. The M.I.T. Press, 1963.

[21] Collective Defence in Southeast Asia: The Manila Treaty and Its Implications . . . The Royal Institute of International Affairs. London 1956; also see:

Barnett, Prof. A. Doak. Communist China and Asia. 1960. p. 291.

[22] Warner, Denis. The Last Confucian, Vietnam, Southeast Asia and the West. 1964. See chapter entitled "Aggression by Seepage."

[23] Langguth, Jack. Smiling Through with Thanom of Thailand. New York Times Magazine, January 3, 1965. p. 13, 22, 23.

Peking Supports Thai Rebel Front. New York Times, February 5, 1965.

Beech, Keyes. Reds Preparing Another 'Viet Nam' in Booming, Bustling Thailand. The Daily Times, Mamaroneck, N.Y., April 1, 1965. p. 14.

Hughes, John. Articles from Christian Science Monitor:

Thailand feels Red pressure. April 21. 1965.

Thais ask: Is banditry a Red prelude? April 28. 1965.

Picturesque Thailand maintains grim vigil. April 29. 1965.

McGhee, Peter S. Thailand—Next Asian Domino? New Republic, July 10, 1965. p. 11.

Sanders, Sol W. Thailand: Next Vietnam?—An on-the-scene Report. U.S. News and World Report, July 26, 1965.

Keatley, Robert. Troubled Thailand—Asian Ally Begins Drive to Win Village Support, Block Inroads of Reds. Wall Street Journal, New York, August 27, 1965.

Darling, Frank. Thailand and the United States. 1965. pp. 216–228.

[24] Barnett, A. Doak, ed. Communist Strategies in Asia, A Comparative Analysis of Governments and Parties. 1963;

Brimmell, J. H. Communism in South-East Asia, A Political Analysis. 1959;

Trager, Frank N., ed. Marxism in Southeast Asia, A Study of Four Countries. 1959; also The Communist Challenge in Southeast Asia; Problems of United States Policy, pp. 157–158 for a balance sheet on communist influence in Southeast Asia.

[25] Crozier. *op. cit.* Note 17 p. 120.

Honey, P. J. Communism in North Vietnam. 1963.

[26] Crozier, *ibid.* p. 120.

[27] Fall, Bernard. The Two Vietnams. 1963. pp. 190–200.

[28] van der Kroef, Justus M. The Sino-Indonesian Partnership. Orbis Vol. VIII Summer 1964 No. 2.

[29] See Bernard Gordon's record of his conversations with Indonesians in his

Problems of Cooperation in Southeast Asia, World Politics, Vol. XVI, January 1964, pp. 237–240; also

Hyde, Douglas. Confrontation in the East.

30 Crozier, *op. cit.* Note 17 p. 113.

31 New York Times August 17, 1965, and August 22, 1965. p. E3.

32 New York Times, August 25, 1965. p. 1.

33 New York Times, August 22, 1965, and August 25, 1965, for the articles of Seymour Topping.

34 Halperin, Morton H. China and the Bomb. 1965.

Ralph L. Powell. China's Bomb: Exploitation and Reactions, Foreign Affairs Vol. 43, No. 4. July 1965. p. 625 on hostage theory.

35 Zagoria, Donald S. Some Comparisons between the Russian and Chinese Models in Communist Strategies in Asia, A Comparative Analysis of Governments and Parties, edited by A. Doak Barnett, 1963. pp. 11–33.

36 North, Robert C. Two Revolutionary Models: Russian and Chinese in Communist Strategies in Asia, *op. cit* Note 35 pp. 34–60.

37 Elegant, Robert S. The Center of the World.

38 Eisenhower, Dwight D. Mandate for Change. p. 333.

39 Public Papers of the President, John F. Kennedy, 1963. p. 659 of the transcript of broadcast on NBC Huntley-Brinkley Report of September 9, 1963.

40 Background Information relating to Southeast Asia and Vietnam (revised edition), Committee on Foreign Relations, U.S. Senate, June 16, 1965.

41 See documents in *ibid.*

42 Ibid. for Text p. 128.

43 Ibid. Document No. 66, Legal Basis for United States Actions Against North Vietnam: Department of State Memorandum, March 8, 1965. p. 194.

44 Eisenhower, *op. cit.* Note 38 p. 362.

45 Documents on American Foreign Relations, 1954. p. 277.

46 Mansfield, Senator Mike. Reports on Vietnam, Cambodia and Laos. October 6, 1955. 84th Congress.

47 Southeast Asia Collective Defense Treaty and Protocol, TIAS 3170. September 8, 1954.

48 Modelski, George, ed. SEATO, Six Studies. 1962.

49 TIAS 3170 *op. cit.* Note 47.

50 Treaty of Mutual Defense between The Philippines and the United States, TIAS 2529. August 27, 1952.

51 Treaty of Mutual Defense between Australia and New Zealand and the United States, TIAS 2493. September 1, 1951.

52 Conflict in Indo-China and International Repercussions, Cornell University Press, p. 231.

53 Fifield, *op. cit.* Note 17 See chapter on the Southeast Asia Treaty Organization, pp. 113–158.

54 Collective Defence in South East Asia, *op. cit.* Note 21.

55 Vandenbosch and Butwell, Southeast Asia Among the World Powers. 1964. p. 250.

56 Fifield, *op. cit.* Note 8. Chapter on Regionalism.

57 Fisher, *op. cit.* Note 5, Chapter on "ASA".

58 Fisher, *op. cit.* Note 5, Chapter on Maphilindo.

59 Gordon, Bernard K. Problems of Regional Cooperation in Southeast Asia. World Politics, Vol. XVI, January 1964, p. 2222.

60 Khoman, Thanat. Which Road for Southeast Asia. Foreign Affairs, Vol. 42, July 1964, p. 639.

61 Document S/5849.

62 S/6278, S/6575, and Corr. 1.

63 S/6260, S/6363, and S/6435.

64 A/5489, and Add. 1–3.

65 A/5630.

66 S/5666, and S/5697.

67 S/5741.

68 S/5832, and Corr. 1:

69 S/5894.

70 S/5952.

71 S/6092.

72 S/5996.

73 S/6640.

74 S/4212.

75 S/4214.

76 S/4236.

77 United Nations Security Council. Report of Special Representative of Secretary-General, December 17, 1959.

78 United Nations Security Council. Announcement of appointment of Secretary-General's Representative (Press Release, December 22, 1958).

79 S/4158, S/4161.

80 S/5220.

81 S/6040.

82 U.S. Participation in the UN, Report by the President to the Congress for the year 1963, Department of State Publication 7675, International Organization and Conference Series 51, Released August 1964. U.S. Government Printing Office, Washington, D. C., p. 99.

83 Ibid., p. 100.

84 S/5930, and S/5966.

85 S/5973.

86 S/5169.

87 A/5578.

88 A/5857 and Corr. 1.

89 A/2375.

90 A/PV. 428.

91 A/2740.

92 S/3220.

93 I.C.J. Reports 1961, p. 17.

94 Ibid., 1962, p. 6.

95 See Appendix for full text.

96 Schaaf, C. Hart, and Fifield, Russell H. The Lower Mekong: Challenge to Cooperation in Southeast Asia. D. Van Nostrand Company, Princeton, N.J. 1963. This booklet gives a concise description of the Committee, the Plan, and the Mekong Project; see also
Annual Report 1964, Committee for the Coordination of Investigations of the Lower Mekong Basin. This report describes the objectives, current construction and implementation, the management and organization, as well as participating countries and private organizations and the prospects for the future.

97 Economic and Social Aspects of Lower Mekong Development: A Report by Gilbert F. White, Egbert de Vries, Harold B. Dunkerley and John V. Krutilla to the Committee for Co-ordination of Investigations of the Lower Mekong Basin. January 1962.

98 Communique of the 28th Session of the Committee for Coordination of Investigations of the Lower Mekong Basin on May 10–11, 1965. (Document of the United Nations Economic and Social Council E/CN.11/WRD/MYG/L.149 Rev. 1).

99 Lepawsky, Albert. International Development of River Resources. International Affairs, Royal Institute of International Affairs. London. October 1963. pp. 545–550.

100 White, Gilbert F. Lower Mekong—A Proposal for a Peaceful and Honorable Resolution of the Conflict in South Vietnam. Bulletin of the Atomic Scientists. December 1964.

101 Young, Kenneth T., Jr. The Foreign Policies of Thailand. Prepared for the Asia Society and Association for Asian Studies Conference on the Foreign Policies of the Southeast Asian States, May 14, 15, 1965. Part 6: "The Scars of Neutrality and Neutralization." For the 1896 scheme see "The Menam Question" in "A History of Southeast Asia" by D. G. E. Hall, 591–611; also "Southeast Asia Its Historical Development" by John F. Cady. p. 427.

102 Foreign Relations of the United States, Japan 1931–41. Vol. II, pp. 529, 539, 540.

103 American Foreign Relations Treaty Series. 1941 Vol. V. p. 273.

104 Modelski, op. cit. Note 48 p. 90.

105 Command 9186. Documents Relating to the Discussion of Korea and Indo-China at the Geneva Conference, April 27–June 15, 1954. pp. 110, 127, 135, 140–141, 163.

106 Avon, Lord. Full Circle. p. 149.

107 Eisenhower, op. cit. Note 38 p. 368.

108 Ibid., p. 357.

109 Avon, op. cit. p. 150.

110 Ibid., p. 156. Also see "Vietnam A Diplomatic Tragedy" by Victor Bator pp. 109–111 and 113–119 for a version of Anglo-American differences in 1954 regarding guarantees.

111 Conflict in Indo-China and International Repercussions. p. 188.

112 Dommen, Arthur J. The Politics of Neutralization. 1964. p. 285–300, 303. This study also contains the texts of the 1962 agreements. pp. 311–319;

Modelski, George. International Conference on the Settlement of the Laotian Question 1961–62. Working Paper No. 2, Department of International Relations, The Australian National University. 1962. Describes the preliminaries, the organization and issues, the proceedings and the outcome of the second Geneva Conference.

113 Czyzak, John J., and Salans, Carl F. The International Conference on the Settlement of the Laotian Question and the Geneva Agreements of 1962. A.J.I.L., Vol. 57, 1963, pp. 300–317.

114 Trager, Frank N. Laos and the Defense of Southeast Asia. Orbis Vol. VII, Fall 1963, No. 3. pp. 550–582.

115 Department of State Bulletin. Vol. LIII, No. 1358, July 5, 1965. Secretary Rusk reviews efforts to reach peaceful settlement in Southeast Asia. pp. 5–12.

116 Armstrong, John P. Sihanouk Speaks. New York. Walker. 1964; see also Stebbins, Richard P. Section 29, Cambodia Reconsidered, The United States in World Affairs. pp. 195–197.
"The Scrutable East" by Robert Trumbull. 1964. pp. 189–193.

117 New York Times, February 1, 1964; Sept. 10, 1965.

118 Background Information op. cit. Note 40 pp. 106–107.

119 Foreign Affairs Bulletin of the Royal Thai Ministry of Foreign Affairs, Bangkok, Volume III, No. 5, April–May 1964. p. 461.

120 Lyon, Peter. Neutralism. 1963. pp. 91–93.

121 The texts used are in Cmd. 9239, Miscellaneous No. 20 (1954) Her Majesty's Stationery Office, on "Further Documents relating to the discussion of Indo-China at the Geneva Conference, June 10–July 21, 1954."

122 Lancaster, Donald. The Emancipation of French Indo-China. 1961. Contains a summary of the Geneva Conference, the documents and their aftermath.

123 Dommen, op. cit. Note 112.

124 Avon, op. cit. Note 106; Eisenhower, op. cit. Note 38; Bator, op. cit. Note 110.

125 "Elections in Vietnam" by Otto D. Tolischus in The New Leader, August

16, 1965, p. 9; "Vietnam Some Neglected Aspects of the Historical Record" by the Republican Conference, House of Representatives, August 25, 1965, pp. 8–10.

126 United States in World Affairs, 1956.

127 Fall, *op. cit.* Note 27, p. 316.

128 Cmd. 1755, June 1962.

129 Background Information. *op. cit.,* Note 40, pp. 149 and 190.

130 For an opposite American view, see "The United States in Vietnam" by George McT. Kahin and John W. Lewis in the Bulletin of Atomic Scientists, Vol. XXI, No. 6, June 1965.

131 For several versions of the idea of a line of limit see:

Maruyama. A Peace Corridor in Indo-China—a Proposal. 10 Japan Quarterly 166–74. 1963.

The proposal of President Radhakrishnan of India on April 24, 1965 for forming an Afro-Asian force to police the "boundary" between both Vietnams in the weekly India News of the Indian Embassy in Washington, D.C. for April 30, 1965, and the New York Times of April 25, 1965. The Government in Peking is reported in one Indian newspaper to have attacked this proposal (Hindu Review, April 29, 1965.)

Warner, Dennis. Drawing the Line in Southeast Asia. The Reporter, September 10, 1964, pp. 33–36.

Baldwin, Hanson W. Vietnam: New Policy in the Making. The Reporter, August 12, 1965. pp. 18–19, on the strategy of the "line of limit."

Trager, Frank N. Laos and the Defense of Southeast Asia. *Orbis,* Volume VII, Fall 1963, pp. 579–582.

132 Young, Kenneth T., Jr. The Challenge of Asia. State Department Bulletin, August 27, 1956, for a general treatment as of the mid-fifties; for a systematic approach to the law of states see the Documents of the Special Committee on Principles of International Law Concerning Friendly Relations and Cooperation among States of the United Nations General Assembly. A/AC 119/L.1, L.2 and L.34.

133 Shaplen, Robert. The Lost Revolution, Chap. XII.

Carver, G. A. The Real Revolution in South Vietnam. 43 Foreign Affairs 387–408.

Young, Kenneth T., Jr. New Policies in New States, Foreign Affairs, April 1961.

134 For new approaches in international law for Southeast Asia see:

Jenks, C. Wilfred. The Common Law of Mankind. Praeger 1958.

Fisher, Roger, ed. International Conflict and Behavioral Science, The Craigville Papers. Basic Books, Inc. 1964.

Hoffman, Stanley. International Systems and International Law. The International Systems edited by Klaus Knorr and Sidney Verba, 1961.

McDougal, Myres and Feliciano, Florentino P. Law and Minimum World Public Order. Yale University Press. 1961 Chapter 4. For a "functional" analysis.

Kaplan, Mortan A. and Katzenbach, Nicholas de B. The Political Foundations of International Law. 1961. Chapters 12 and 13 on functional or regional organizations.

Schelling, Thomas C. The Strategy of Conflict. 1963. Chapters 1–5.

135 See: Sohn, Professor Louis B. Letter to the New York Times of June 29, 1965, on a "Proposal for Vietnam" for similar ideas (New York Times July 4, 1965); and

Clubb, Oliver E., Jr. The United States and the Sino-Soviet Bloc in Southeast Asia, for a detailed discussion of many issues and options in his Chapter 5.

Larson, Don R. and Larson, Arthur. Vietnam and Beyond, A New American Foreign Policy and Program. 1965.

By *Ambassador Ramani on Page* 75 *of the Working Paper.*

In the course of his remarks Ambassador Ramani made the following comment on one of the observations that had been made by Ambassador Young in the Working Paper:

"On page 75 of the Working Paper in the middle paragraph Mr. Young sets out briefly, and quite accurately, the history of how Malaysia came into being. Then, in the last paragraph on this page 75 he says that, before the Secretary General published his findings on September 14, 1963, the Government of Malaya announced that Malaysia would come into being as a sovereign nation on September 16, 1963, and he says that the Secretary General regretted the timing of this announcement.

I want to ask you to follow me and understand what happened. Malaya did nothing illegal, nothing immoral, nothing which can be thought to be politically wrong. Indeed, if anything, it was a little too legal. The British plan for the creation of Malaysia had come into being on July 9, 1963, in London. That plan contained an Article 2 which provided:

'The Government of the Federation of Malaya will take such steps as may be appropriate and available to them to secure the enactment by the Parliament of the Federation of Malaya of an Act in the form set out in Annex A to this agreement and that it is brought into operation on 31st August 1963 (and that date on which the said Act is brought into operation is hereinafter referred to as 'Malaysia Day').'

In accordance with that provision, the Malaysian Act was passed which provided in Section 1 that it was to come into force on the 31st day of August, 1963, or on such later day as might become necessary as a result of consultations with the Heads of the States of Indonesia and the Philippines and as might be designated by Proclamation. When the Malaya Government found that these consultations with the Indonesian and Philippine Governments could not take place before the end of August and the beginning of September, they were faced with the impossibility of the Act taking effect on the 31st of August. Some other date had to be fixed, but that date had to be fixed before the 31st of August. The Secretary General at the time wrote a letter to me in which he said that he had tried to organize Work Teams with the greatest possible speed and they had been instructed to complete their work as quickly as possible. He hoped to complete the task and make his conclusions known to the three governments by the 14th of September, 1963.

This letter from the Secretary General was dated 15th August, 1963, and it was placed before Parliament when we had to fix the effective date. As we were unable to sit beyond 31st August, we fixed a date after the date indicated by the Secretary General. I should like to read what the Secretary General later said on this subject:

"I later informed the governments concerned that I would endeavour to report my conclusions to them by the 14th of September. During the course of the enquiry, the date of the 16th of September was announced by the Government of the Federation of Malaya, with the concurrence of the British Government, the Singapore Government, and the Governments of Sabah and Sarawak for the establishment of the Federation of Malaysia. This has led to some misunderstanding, confusion, and even resentment among other parties to the Manila Summit Agreement, which could have been avoided . . .
(and, ladies and gentlemen, and lawyers, please mark these words)
if the date could have been fixed after my conclusions had been given."

He did not say, and he would not say (because he knew the facts), "if the date had been fixed", but rather "if the date could have been fixed". He was aware that it could not have been fixed.

I therefore think it is a slight error to say that the Secretary General regretted the timing of the Government of Malaya's announcement . . ."

PART TWO

THE FORUM

THE FORUM:

A SUMMARY OF THE PROCEEDINGS

INTRODUCTION

In introducing Ambassador Young, the Moderator mentioned that he had not only served as United States Ambassador to Thailand but also been educated in China, as well as at the Sorbonne and Harvard, and had been a specialist in Far Eastern Affairs in the State Department's Office of Southeast Asian Affairs from 1954 to 1958. The Moderator also paid tribute to the major role played by Ambassador Young's father-in-law, the late George Maurice Morris (President of the American Bar Association in 1942-43), following World War II, in stimulating interest by American lawyers, especially the younger ones, in international law and foreign affairs.

REMARKS OF AMBASSADOR YOUNG

Let us look beyond the bomb line to a peace goal; beyond the battlefields and the burning huts, the ransacked buildings and ravaged, mutilated bodies, to hope-keeping and order-making. Not that restraint and force in pursuit of survival and peace are illegal or irrelevant. Indeed they are vital in Southeast Asia where violence unfortunately remains a creed in defiance of law, and where the fruits of transgression are whetting appetites for great power, in truth for world hegemony. And for that reason a new law—in the broad sense of a community-sanctioning process for containing many levels of conflict and regulating all sorts of relations— has a vital role to play. It is unfortunately neglected.

Yet, I venture to submit that the conflicts over Southeast Asia can be litigated some day. Although extremely complicated, a bargaining situation and a negotiating process can be foreseen. The parties at interest in this crisis can resolve the terms of the conflict by arranging a convergence of their interests, and enforcing a reciprocity of pledges, in a community of limited purposes.

139

To suggest this is not to ignore the profound divergencies and serious hostilities regarding Southeast Asia. Nor is it to minimize the almost irreconcilable confrontation between nationalist aspiration and communist expansion.

The menace of China is indeed the overriding political issue in our time. Chinese control of Southeast Asia would be an unacceptable threat to the national interests of the United States. Yet, this threat is more political and subversive than military. That makes it tricky but not impossible to handle.

It is hard to visualize Chinese soldiers swarming into New Delhi, Rangoon, Bangkok or Singapore. Nor is it likely that Peking will actually send nuclear warheads into those cities, although Peking may someday threaten leaders in these capitals with either submission or destruction. Instead Peking and its allies are aiming to destroy the underpinnings of Southeast Asia and hasten the collapse of the United States. Stripped to its core the object in the Southeast Asia conflict is to negotiate a shift in Peking policies in the direction of its accommodation with the world in a legal framework and a limitation of Peking's power to defense of China's legitimate national interests.

I am suggesting that a combination of nationalism, trans-nationalism, and internationalism could bring this about and settle Southeast Asia's principal disorders. First of all, continuation of the historical tenacity and traditional adaptivity of the Southeast Asian states is vital. The independence and solidity of Viet Nam, Thailand and Indonesia in particular, and the other countries of Southeast Asia in general, should be the first goal of diplomatic, political, legal, economic and military measures. Beyond that basic foundation of nationalistic independence, legal-sanctioning and institutional building elements such as the Association of Southeast Asian States, the United Nations, the Mekong Community, and even overhauled Geneva arrangements, have each something to contribute to a new synthesis of transnational and international order in that region.

All of this will be a supreme test for broad-scale diplomacy and patient negotiation on our part. The resolution of conflict and new approaches to regional order in Southeast Asia will require a skillful meshing of political and military actions and the use of diplomacy and force in tandem. Military containment alone never has been and never will be sufficient to bring about an acceptable settlement. Only a blend of political, social, economic and defensive measures, particularly in Viet Nam, can start us along the road toward stabilization of the conflict. A new law of community centered on transnational organization and functional cooperation and involving all the parties at interest—non-communist and communist—is the valid and practical goal in the search for peace. And that search should start on workable specific targets with short commitments in time, small requirements for resources, and low risks of political impairment. As experience and confidence grow, the targets, the commitments, the resources and the political risks can be expanded and increased.

It is time for major efforts of diplomacy to utilize the potential elements of regional equilibrium, to rework these tools and to establish a wide consensus on the goals of our efforts. But diplomacy is much too important to be left only to diplomats, even the most skillful. The United States Government is fortunate to have a first-class diplomatic service. But other talents must be brought together and trained for a new kind of American teamwork in Southeast Asia. There is more than enough room and certainly a crying need for the lawyer, the anthropologist, the political scientist, the historian, the psychiatrist, as well as the diplomat, economist, engineer, and colonel to strengthen and perfect American efforts for the long pull.

The Commission of Jurists of South and Southeast Asia, which met in Bangkok last spring, demonstrated the vast need for legal talent to help resolve conflicts there. I suggested in my Working Paper that the profession of law and the administration of justice in Southeast Asia, both in the domestic and transnational spheres, could utilize many more direct contacts with lawyers and legal research in Japan, India, the United States and Europe. Would it not be useful to develop international cooperation in providing libraries and textbooks, case studies for teaching the law, assistance in legal research on the interaction of different types of law in Southeast Asia, legal studies of regional and international aspects of means for settling conflict and transnational equilibrium? I am surprised and even startled to find how little attention legal research and legal journals pay to legal problems of sovereignty and transnational cooperation, such as those arising out of the Geneva Agreements of 1954 and 1962, and the role of the United Nations and other international institutions. Therefore I salute the Bar Association of New York for putting together the bibliography on United Nations documents concerning Southeast Asia. It is the only one available, although for reasons of space it is not exhaustive. In any event, this bibliography is a start for such research, as well as a testament to our faith in the United Nations.

We can also take heart in the recent Conference on World Peace through Law in Washington. A number of judges and lawyers came from Asia. Some of the suggestions emerging from this Conference could be put to work by, for example, taking international law out of the purely government-to-government realm and moving it closer to individuals, to exchanges among lawyers and to the ordinary courts, strengthening the World Court so that it may adjudicate more than just one Southeast Asian case in twenty years, setting up a regional tribunal for Southeast Asia, and innovating new laws of transnational relations and functional federalism.

I think we have neglected these approaches. While I was in Thailand, I was depressively impressed by the infrequent passage of American judges and lawyers through Bangkok compared to the deluge of politicians, generals, businessmen and social scientists. It seemed to me that just about every profession but the law was inundating this cultural crossroads.

To give effect to these and many other considerations, I have ventured to submit to you a five-point proposal for a policy of convergence beyond containment. I mean the bringing together of mutual, parallel and conflicting interests of contending parties for their resolution. My five points are: international insulation, a U.N. Commission for Southeast Asia, the development of a Mekong Community, a new Geneva order, and federal co-existence in Viet Nam.

There are five principles underlying these five proposals:

1. Peace and order in Asia first needs to wall out aggression. The responsibility for that must become primarily Asian. The technique would be internationalized insulation by several national armed forces of agreed-upon zones, like the 17th parallel.

2. The United Nations can play an increasing role in Southeast Asia, but it alone cannot settle transational disputes involving Communist China and Communist Viet Nam. The U.N. needs more continuity of involvement in Southeast Asia peace-keeping. The technique would be a permanent U.N. Commission for Southeast Asia if the regional states agreed.

3. Development and expansion of the Mekong Community and the Mekong River Project should be the center and keystone for building new law, new consensus, and new sanction in mainland Southeast Asia. This needs expansion of institutional scope, financial resources, and membership, again subject to the mandate of the regional states. The Mekong idea is the best one for blending the particularly Southeast Asian style of nationalism, transnationalism, and internationalism.

   and 1962 are necessary for negotiating and guaranteeing another settlement in Viet Nam, Laos and Cambodia, and for guaranteeing the Mekong Community and Mekong Project.

5. The political resurgence of South Viet Nam is the key to successful strategy in Southeast Asia. That would solidify its neighbors and shift trends in Indonesia. The war in Viet Nam can be won, but the political revolution may be lost again. 1966 is the year of decision.

These principles and proposals are so closely interrelated that they must be taken as a whole, organically. Each one alone would fall far short of helping to restore some peaceful order. The partial or fragmented approach of focussing on one or two policies—which has been the American style of approach— often backfires and causes worse results than no policy at all.

143

The subtle complexities of Southeast Asia require a total, comprehensive approach—what Alfred Whitehead called the "habit of surveying society from the standpoint of generality and the instinctive grasp of the relevant features of social currents."

These proposals attempt to reflect some characteristic and significant ways of thinking, feeling and doing in Southeast Asia. While generalizations on psychological and intellectual matters are dangerous, I do believe that several impulses, mainly instinctive, determine the style and thrust of action and reaction there. In brief, one finds an immediate respect and longing for centered authority and power from some international leadership. Now that China has again begun to throw its weight around in Asia, eyes are turned toward Washington and New York, New Delhi or Tokyo. Will the U.S. and the U.N. stick to the challenge and not go away? That is the question asked every day in Asia. Nevertheless, they prefer an internationalized approach. They are too proud to want dependence on the Americans, and a foreign protection. So these proposals stress multilateral connections.

Asians also lean toward rounded postures and indirect responses rather than rigid stance and clear-cut statement. They seem to hanker for elements of harmony and solidarity, shying away from direct confrontation when conciliation, compromise or even total circumvention will do. The formidable stresses of modern times are perhaps increasing the natural tendency of Southeast Asians to seek convergence wherever possible and avoid confrontations. If that is so, then our policy and our style should move with the mainstream of the Asian currents.

I am increasingly worried over the political and psychological impact on Asians of the American-Chinese confrontation and the simultaneous confrontation with Western technology. The effects of both Maoism and modernization may create a backlash and a boomerang of great strength and danger. Reactions in Asia may tend more and more toward what I would call rejection of both China and America, a disalignment from world politics, increasing discord and antagonism within Asia, and even a postponement of modernization. This is now just a cloud on the horizon, but it is a growing cloud, as we can see in Burma, Cambodia and Indonesia. The more American-Chinese confrontation becomes exclusively Chinese and American, the more the Asian states may one by one try to avoid any involvement or entanglement.

Some Asian reactions seek a return to the past, cutting off external relation. This is a withdrawal within the confines of the nation or the group. It is not so much the "Yankee go home" impulse as it is the "foreigner keep out" feeling. The more we stress anti-communism, containment, prosecution of war, security alliances, and the menace of China, and the longer we neglect political and psychological policies with depth of perception, the more we may drive Asian intellectuals, and particularly the younger Asians, away from us and back into an atavistic hiding place. The more the Chinese threaten, infiltrate and manipulate as they have done with India, Pakistan, Indonesia, Thailand, Cambodia, Laos and Viet Nam, the more will people in these countries turn against China. But the net result is that they will be turning against both China and America, if we are not careful. Therefore, our dilemma in Southeast Asia is a much deeper one than even trying to figure out what should be our policy in Viet Nam and elsewhere or what would be feasible courses of action to carry out any such policy.

Allow me in the words of Judge Learned Hand to
". . . ask you to go with me, not into questions which have direct relation to the law or to government, but to those which concern the mental habits of our people, since these, indirectly at any rate, in the end determine its institutions."

Let us grapple with the hard affirmative issues. Do we have the right goals and suitable values concerning Asia? How are we doing in those terms? What are our premises? Where do we want to end up? These are the basic questions, even for law.

Something is still missing in our Southeast Asian policies. President Sukarno has accused us, for example, of having forsaken the revolutionary nationalism and instant change of Asia. Who among us speaks for an ideology appealing to the farmer, the student, the housewife, the soldier, the priest, and the worker in Viet Nam or Indonesia, Thailand or Malaysia?

Prince Sihanouk once called us geniuses at technique but ostriches in politics. Have we indeed overemphasized material resources, new gimmicks and mechanical processes, and severed technology from politics and "know how" away from "know why"? Perhaps we have not paid enough attention to promoting new political action and new political leaders, or to encouraging judges and lawyers, social workers and psychiatrists, instead of just colonels and economists. If Prime Minister Lee Kwan Yew of Singapore has a point in warning us of lacking depth, judgment and vision in Asia, let us start by forming a point of view with vision and vitality. Not even the communists question our enormous power. But they and many others suspect our intentions.

Our style of communication and our method of execution must be tuned and sensitive enough to reach the understanding and responsiveness of persons and peoples in Southeast Asia. They react with values, motives and assumptions different from ours. While Westernization and modernization are altering some of their concepts and practices, the leaders and peoples there act according to inherited and traditional views of authority, time, well being, leadership, the universe, and communications. For example, they do not decide matters naturally and instinctively by the process of one man one vote, by the head count or majority rule. They prefer consensus by consultation in a time-consuming process to arrive at agreement. The leadership and elite of Southeast Asia bespeak magical and religious symbolism as well as paternalism and decision-making at the top. The lack of personal or group action in these countries on the part of the peasant or the intellectual often baffles or shocks us, because we take political self-expression and social self-reliance of the individual for granted. These are values alien to this region. Their communicative style flows from allegory, symbol and myth between the leaders and the led, by suggestion and implication, rather than by logical formula and neat equation familiar to the western mind. Their

146

concepts and practices in law and politics are very different. The pattern of authority is not like ours.

The role of the United States in Southeast Asia would have been more effectively performed during these past years if we had not lived in the dangerous vacuum of our own preconceptions and prejudices, indifferent to the limited amount of tolerance to be expected from local personalities, institutions and practices. Instead of trying to make an objective evaluation of what these shifting Southeast Asian societies could absorb, support and endure, we have expressed our interests and devised our policies as if only Washington were the touchstone and as if only Americans were the instruments of policy. It will be tragic for everyone if our efforts end up alienating Asia instead of helping to free it from a hostile ideology.

We must shift our style of operations from immediate targets to far-off goals, from instant expectation to patient persistence. Asia has been around for a long time—and will be for longer. We are newcomers. We listen too little. We have a lot to learn to blend in with Asian hopes, values and styles.

A wiser and more effective role for the United States in the conflicts of Southeast Asia will only come out of our recasting three things: our act of responsibility, our style of congeniality, and our resources of viability. If we are skillful and wise, our action, style and resources can lead to a new strategy of convergence beyond containment. We can build on confidence, the touchstone in Asia more so even than power. I believe that my five-point policy would build confidence, bring hope, and encourage peace.

We ourselves have unwittingly added to the disorders of Asia by our long-standing rejection of an authoritative commitment of landed power on the Asian mainland. For twenty years our hesitations over involvement there and our classical reliance on our overwhelming superiority of sea, air and nuclear power have served to divide the strategic problems regarding Asia into two arbitrary and unrealistic categories: ocean and space power outside the continent on the one hand, and land power within Asia on the other. This categorical division may have led Mao to call us a "paper tiger". We are of course nothing of the kind, as Mao and his associates realistically appreciate. Our power can annihilate but it cannot "settle" Asia's disorders. As long as we maintain this artificial dichotomy between land power and air power, and as long as we temporize on our pledges and actions of responsibility, we have far less, in fact all too little, political influence and viability. For this and many other reasons, I am submitting this interdependent five-point policy. It stresses power, multilateral relations, and convergence.

International Insulation

The big countries and some of the smaller in Asia have not yet shown initiative or taken cooperative responsibility for their own defense and development. And we have not successfully inspired and encouraged them to do this. Instead, we may have contributed to divisive, centrifugal tendencies, to the disunities of nationalism and communism and the maladjustments of modernization. We have taken what has seemed to us the easier path of applying unilaterally the power and policies of the United States in overwhelming and unbalanced proportions to meet particular crises: India, Viet Nam, Taiwan and Korea. We have chosen to become the counterweight to deficiencies of policy and lack of power which characterize the foreign policies of most of the independent nations of Asia at the present time. We have said that we had no choice. But our assumption of this vital commitment, while strategically correct, is politically vulnerable because it lacks and has never seriously sought to negotiate an Asian mandate.

Across Asia there is no consensus on the goals or strategy for containing communist military and nuclear power inside China or for insulating Asian nationalism. One of China's ancient books known throughout Southeast Asia, the *History of the Three Kingdoms,* begins with the following observation:

"Let us speak of the general situation in the world. What has been separated and divided for a long time must certainly rediscover its unity. And what for a long time was united must inevitably someday disintegrate again."

148

The immediate question for the United States in Southeast Asia is how to unite it.

I suggest international insulation of a suitable zone or strip across Southeast Asia. We do not know and will not know for a long time whether the outcome there will be domination, stalemate or accommodation on the part of the communists. If we were sure that any proposal would eventually lead to a satisfactory stabilization, then there would be no need for an institution of international insulation. But given the virtually irreconcilable conflict and contradictory objectives of nationalism and communism, it is safe to assume that some form of international separator is the first requirement for our long-term objectives and strategies. At least we can try to set up a political and military "fire wall", "breakwater" and "embankment" to keep out the wave of hegemony and the seepage of subversion. In turn, such a zone of insulation could assure China of security for its vulnerable and sensitive southern area.

This proposal does not require negotiation with Peking and Hanoi, although their agreement would of course serve to establish a cessation of hostilities and an armistice, political and military. A policy of insulation would probably work either with or without negotiations only if it represented an international composition and not just an American line.

It would obviously be a complicated and costly proposal to set up a zone along the 17th parallel in Viet Nam which would then dogleg northwest up through the valleys of Laos towards the international confluence where Burma, Laos and China meet on the Mekong River. The military forces required for such a zone would probably be at least half a million. I hope they would be drawn from several nations, but obviously the United States would have to provide the majority. The political complications would be even greater, because international insulation would compromise, if not contradict, the Geneva Agreement of 1962 on Laos. However, I think for reasons of policy and power we would have to proceed on the basis that the 1962 Agreement has been nullified by the communist signatories. If it were restored in working order, or replaced by an effective or enforceable international agreement, the positioning of an international force and the international arrangements for such insulation would have to remain in effect. In other words, the policy of insulation would be predicated upon an eventual settlement by convergence with the Peoples Republic of China for the independence, security and development of Southeast Asia.

The Indian President has proposed an Asian force for this. The United States has endorsed it. China has rejected it. But the idea should not be dropped. Even if American troops must temporarily help man a "hold-fast" line in Southeast Asia, it would be a valuable political goal to justify to some extent the lives and hardships of American men in Viet Nam.

We did not exercise much American power in 1954 or in 1962. We are paying for those mistakes now. Let us not make that error again. Let us put our legal talent to work to formulate new arrangements for helping to insulate Asia by Asian initiative and responsibility with American commitments and guarantees.

Asian interposition should be developed by the Asians themselves to form one of the major members in a new world structure of power and stability. A consensus and institution of Asian interposition would mean that some or all of these states would stand on their own collective feet against their Chinese neighbors, forming a barrier to China's illegal militaristic expansion on the one hand, and serving as a channel on the others to encourage and facilitate China's accommodation with Asian states, the Slavic area, the North Atlantic and Africa. If the Asians were to develop some such solidity of structure, it is probable that the Chinese would eventually be persuaded to accept rather than defy the alternative of cooperating or joining with them. In fact, China would have nowhere else to go. Despite the rabid hostility of Chinese and other Asian communist leaders toward Asian nationalists and their fanatical hatred of Americans and Europeans, Chinese leaders might decide that "if they couldn't lick us, they would have to join us". And Peking already has had a bad year. The political harvest in Indonesia, Viet Nam, Laos, Thailand, India and Africa has been disappointing.

The history of peacekeeping and conciliation in Southeast Asia shows that the United Nations has played a useful, and can continue to play an increasingly helpful, role subject to the sovereign determinations of the very independent governments there. But I am impressed by an apparent weakness in this role. It has always been *ad hoc*. Each time a particular conflict has arisen, a new resolution has had to be negotiated and approved either in the Security Council or the General Assembly. A new committee or commission of entirely different national representatives from various parts of the world has been composed and introduced into the particular conflict or matter. Outside of its able and dedicated Secretariat, the United Nations has had, so far as I can judge, little continuity of expertise regarding Southeast Asia. I wonder, then, if the time has not come to suggest consideration of either a permanent commission or a panel of distinguished men and women for counsel and conciliation with respect to the bi-lateral and transnational conflicts and disputes which exist or may arise among the states of Southeast Asia. I am specifically excluding the issue of Viet Nam and the conflict with the Peoples Republic of China and the Democratic Republic of Viet Nam. But even in that most difficult and menacing area, the Secretary General of the United Nations and any such commission or panel might well be able to play an effective role of quiet diplomacy in the search for a cease-fire, for bringing some of the parties together, and for probing the areas of negotiable or justiciable issues.

I wish to stress the value of the United Nations as an impartial agency for Southeast Asian governments, leaders and peoples. Despite the hazards and hardships which the U.N. and the United States have faced in this area since 1945, our attitude and our policy should be one of maximum but prudent promotion of the peacekeeping and nation-building capacity of the United Nations. The United States should disengage from any and every activity of its own whenever and wherever that activity can be capably assumed by a U.N. agency.* And, of course, that capability contains the desire and

---

*When I was in Thailand I transferred an economic advisory role out of the United States government to the U.N.

consent of the independent governments of Southeast Asia.

Development and Expansion of the Mekong Community

If we assume military insulation and U.N. presence in Southeast Asia, I have come to believe that the Mekong Project offers the most hopeful prospects for peace and progress in that region. I realize that this is just a dream at the moment, when pessimism and discretion are prevalent. And I understand the many qualifications one must make about this idea. Yet, hope-making and peace-building need missionary dimensions. The Mekong project has them.

I am not talking just about harnessing a giant watershed for its electricity, flood control and irrigation. A TVA on the Mekong stirs our imaginations, and well it should. But releasing the tensions of men, channeling the ambitions of governments, and subduing the feuds of nations could also be the gift of the mighty Mekong—if the wit and wisdom of mankind turn to its account soon enough. If men can get together to build dams, they can gather together for peace. This is why I would make the Mekong community the center and keystone of the search for lasting peace and real progress.

Expansion is possible in three respects: in powers and responsibilities; in financial resources; and in membership and participation. This "core concept" blends the chief elements of nationalism, transnationalism, and internationalism.

The national interest and sovereign involvement of Cambodia, Laos, Thailand and South Vienam form the bedrock of this political community and engineering project. Their individual mandates and their respective advantages are primary. Only if leaders and people in each country see tangible benefits coming to the nation, will each continue cooperating in a "Mekong Spirit". Fortunately, they all want to see the Mekong Project grow to produce benefits for each. They have subordinated acute political differences for eight years to work together in the Mekong Committee. They are now reaching the turning point in 1966 for large-scale construction, massive financing, and major reorganization.

As a transnational form of functional federalism these four Buddhist nations could now evolve for themselves a "Mekong Middle Way" of transnational cooperation in a novel kind of "riparian condominium". By joint agreements, they could establish the sanctity of their contractual rights over the water and its products for all their neighbors to respect. By national and regional masterplans, they could program their social and economic needs for international sources to help support. By treaties and compacts they could build and solidify transnational institutions for the big powers to guarantee.

A fraternal association of Cambodia, Laos, Thailand and Viet Nam, representing Buddhist ideals of peacefulness, cooperation and compassion, would somewhat discourage flagrant defiance and subversion. It would be harder than at present to defy the mandate of a Mekong Middle Way, or to subvert the solidarity of a Mekong community. However favorable the first eight years of the Mekong Project have been regionally, the next few years will be crucial, and decisive. Here we and many others have exciting, dramatic opportunities.

As this is a big idea, so we must think in big concepts, not just in costs. We want to accelerate the cumulative effect of the project so as to intensify its national and transnational impact on the political level. Dramatic economic targets might induce significant political results if Mekong development and the Mekong community could become the central theme and unifying yardstick among these four governments. It is for them to determine together the interplay of political, social, and economic growth of the region as a whole. The Project would provide many opportunities to take actions designed to remove all kinds of bottlenecks which limit the economic growth of the transnational watershed.

The evolution of the Mekong idea will depend on the willingness of the four countries together to:
  —Join in a common strategy of transnational development;
  —Formulate their national plans within a regional framework;
  —Participate in common facilities for training, research, production, marketing and transportation;

—Pool limited skills and capital and specialize in commonly agreed upon industries; and
—Operate, staff and finance a central organism and subsidiary transnational and national bodies.

To ask whether such an agenda is feasible is the key question. Its answer is partly one of faith and partly one of logic.

Many new agencies would be needed for an expanding Mekong Community as my friend Vu Van Thai, the new Vietnamese Ambassador to Washington, and a Mekong expert, has boldly suggested:

—A broad authority for planning, programming and budgeting regional development by broadening the powers of the existing Mekong Development Committee;
—Several limited-authority agencies for production and distribution of electric power, transportation and agricultural development;
—A regional university, with a common training center and research institute;
—Mixed corporations for development of common-use industries which would be costly and uneconomic for one country alone to construct and manage profitably, to be located by mutual consent in one of the four riparian countries for the production of steel, aluminum, petrochemicals, pharmaceuticals, agricultural fertilizers, other chemical products, paper products for marketing in the region and for export after the electric, water and navigable resources of the Mekong Watershed were developed; and
—A regional clearinghouse for transnational monetary transactions.

This is just a sketch of the institutional expansion of the Mekong community. It would require many legal talents to develop a "law of incorporation" and to put flesh and bones on the skeleton of a law of community. The alternative to such a scheme would be slow, uneven growth menaced by communist take-over or internal disintegration.

154

Meanwhile, an increasing number of professionally-trained young Southeast Asians are learning to work together across frontiers of time and politics. They know that a constant growth rate of 6 to 7 per cent in the whole region will accumulate over the decade a *demand* for electricity using several million kilowatts of installed capacity, a *need* for agricultural produce requiring rapidly accelerating inputs of substantial capital, and a *desire* for industrial products deriving from an expanding network of cross-border distribution and communications. The rising generation knows, too, that only regional cooperation will guarantee national benefits. One can justly conclude that the Mekong region is a natural region, with more carriers for order than barriers to peace. By itself it can be a catalyst of regional harmony and solidarity.

The serious handicap or deterrent is international—financial and political. This involves two things: the inherently international and non-political character of the Mekong Project on the one hand, and the basic need for peaceful resolution of the Viet Nam question and the participation of North Viet Nam and China on the other.

The next and second stage for the Mekong Project depends primarily on money—international money. Only public investment from the wealthy countries of the order of several billion dollars will finance construction projects. Those dollars are the cost of development. They are also premium payments to insure peace in Southeast Asia. External finance must be pledged and guaranteed over a long period. But it must also be contributed solely for the cooperation and development of the riparian states, and not for external power politics or outside national influence. The widest possible diversity of donors besides the United States would be highly desirable. Here is where Moscow could make good its pledges to co-existence. Here is where Peking could quietly replace its strategy of violence for the politics of peace. In this broad sense the task for a broad-gauged diplomacy in Southeast Asia is to work for the neutralization of the Mekong Community and its institutions and projects. This would be much more promising than proposals implying the predominance of China.

The most difficult international requirement would be either the toleration or the participation of Hanoi and Peking. Successful evolution of Mekong could offer Hanoi, as a by-product, a political and economic alternative to undesirable options of unsuccessful subjugation of the South, unthinkable capitulation to the Americans, or unavoidable satellization under the Chinese. At some stage North Viet Nam might be offered electric power, trade, and sharing of technical assistance as an outside country or as a member of the Community. If Cambodia and Laos were to take an increasingly active part in the political and institutional development of the Project, such as establishing the headquarters and staff of the Mekong Project in Phnom Penh, while committee meetings rotate among the riparian capitals, the attraction for Hanoi might increase. This may, however, be as remote as it may seem a far-fetched possibility.

In any event, Hanoi—and the leaders who will come after Ho Chi Minh—would have to weigh the real benefits of co-operation in the Mekong against the penalties of alternatives. Indeed, the really crucial political target in Southeast Asia is the "neutralization" of Hanoi and its orientation towards and into the Mekong Community. Despite strong ideological and other differences and animosities, some affinities could bring Hanoi and Saigon, Bangkok and Phnom Penh, onto the same track.

China's benevolent neutrality is probably the most that can be expected from Peking for a long time. And all of us will be hard put even to induce that. Yet 30 per cent of the Mekong is in China. Peking's participation would help regulate its immense flow of water. And China could join in the trading or common market arrangements for "off-take".

We cannot foresee all the implications of the Mekong Project and the potentialities of a Mekong Community. We can all too easily strangle it with qualifications and reservations. It is a fragile, nebulous vision, perhaps idealistic. The real question about it is not "why" but "how". Is there a way to negotiate it?

A forum outside the United Nations to secure and safeguard the Mekong Community is necessary. The fourth part of a policy of convergence beyond containment would focus on resuming other dialogues, and negotiating new agreements, among the 14 Geneva powers and perhaps adding a few qualified participants such as Japan, Indonesia, Malaysia and Australia. This "Geneva" policy is predicated on the assumption that, while the United Nations can contribute to peace-keeping in Southeast Asia, it cannot provide the auspices for any convergence with Peking and Hanoi—nor should the U.N. be expected to. I remain convinced that an enforceable settlement by convergence outside the U.N. is mandatory before either Peking or Hanoi should be considered for membership in the U.N. at all. If agreements are reached and executed under Geneva machinery, then such membership might be considered.

In the context of stalemated hostilities in Viet Nam, where Hanoi could no longer win and is losing, the Geneva machinery would of course renegotiate the standard principles for such agreements—a military cease-fire and stand fast, phased regroupment of North Vietnamese and foreign forces out of South Viet Nam, prohibitions on military strengthening, and maintenance of the demilitarized zone. However, the political provisions this time would be more significant.

Each Viet Nam would have to undertake reciprocal obligations to respect the integrity and inviolability of the other and to engage in specified forms of exchange and other relationships. All the participants would undertake reciprocal pledges to respect the Mekong Community and to demilitarize the eastern or Vietnamese side of the watershed. They might even be asked to agree to an international policing force—not under the U.N. but in liaison with it—along the eastern limits of the watershed.

The Conference would have to set up new machinery for observation and compliance. It would have to reach agreements among the big powers on guaranteeing the whole arrangement without a veto. And this time the Geneva members should make provision for periodic meetings of the Conference.

157

For the two Viet Nams and their neighbors, these associated agreements would be "a hands-off guarantee" and "let-live compacts." I would urge that a third Geneva Conference leave internal Vietnamese questions alone. Elections, unifications, forms of federated or autonomous relations, two Viet Nam states in one Viet Nam nation—these should be left to time and the Vietnamese to handle in their own way. The crux of the matter comes down to the strength and morale of South Viet Nam—is it healthy and robust enough to stand on its own feet?

Viet Nam

The real issue in Viet Nam is political, not military. It is how to win a political war while not losing a military campaign. And we can win the war only to lose the peace. This is the third time we have come in on the political ground floor. In 1954-56 and in 1963-64 we muffed our chances. Next year will be our last chance in Viet Nam, politically speaking. The Vietnamese nation—from the Chinese border to the Camau Peninsula—has lived in war, under the shadow or sound of guns, for all of the last 25 years. It has also lived in revolution and lost revolutions during those 25 years. It is ironic that the four nations of the modern world with revolutionary heritage and inspiration—America, France, Russia and China—have all been deeply involved in Viet Nam. None has yet succeeded in helping the Vietnamese fulfill their own kind of revolution.

The challenge in Viet Nam is clear. It is forceable unification by Hanoi versus self-determination and independence for Saigon. The communist regime in the north is rigidly and fanatically determined to capture and dominate South Viet Nam. To succeed, Hanoi so far has used every weapon of violence and assault in its substantial arsenal except massed invasion by Viet Nam or Chinese armies. And Hanoi has nearly had victory. Poor leadership, bad administration and growing antagonism in the cities and hamlets of the south considerably abetted Hanoi's campaign to steal the people away from local and central government. Hanoi will not concede at any conference the political power which it has been ac-

158

cumulating over the paddies and hills of the Vietnamese countryside, no matter how much we bomb the North. Hanoi will eventually retire and retreat when it begins to lose political momentum and military initiative. But if it can win all Viet Nam, it intends to control its neighbors, Laos, Cambodia and Thailand.

The resurgence of an independent South Viet Nam is the way to foil Hanoi and change the conflict in Southeast Asia. That strip of land—from the Mekong Delta to the 17th parallel with about 15,000,000 inhabitants—is the keystone for holding a nationalist Southeast Asia together. Abandon it, or let Hanoi capture the keystone, and the arch of confidence will collapse. A psychological tidal wave of defeatism and defection will engulf every capital and every elite group in Southeast Asia. Those are the stakes in the Viet Nam encounter.

Assuming the United States and Vietnamese governments succeed in stabilizing the military situation, and Hanoi and Peking come to realize the impossibility of conquering Viet Nam by force, these are the key questions:

(1) Will Washington and Saigon grasp the new political opportunity to inspire a new spirit of Vietnamese resurgency, rally the population, and reconstruct a new nationalist revolution with justice?

(2) Will ways be pursued to provide any new leadership in Hanoi with "open door" options and alternatives to Chinese hegemony and "satellization" so that Vietnamese nationalism north and south can learn to work together within one nation?

(3) Will both Viet Nams, transformed by suffering and disciplined by realities, move toward a Southeast Asian framework of association to increase the opportunities for Viet Nam's improvement?

The crux of the internal issue in Viet Nam is the encouragement of a new spirit of national solidarity and resurgency among Vietnamese students, Buddhists, soldiers, and farmers.

159

A new all-Vietnamese plebiscite is not necessarily the answer, although the goal of Vietnamese nationhood in unity is. There are many ways to develop political forms for Viet Nam. The municipal and provincial elections of May, 1965, have already developed a new free and legitimate base for responsible and responsive government. What the Vietnamese want most is a chance for their own forms of political change and social revolution to take place without violence or coercion from the outside. Whether the two Viet Nams can learn to live and let live, and associate together, will depend greatly on a much broader framework of reference than just Viet Nam itself.

A regional Mekong Community in particular is vitally necessary to bring North Viet Nam into peaceful exchange and acceptance of a non-communist South Viet Nam and non-communist Southeast Asia. Regional cooperation can provide Viet Nam nationalists and non-communists with the opportunities and resources to bring an evolving kind of nationalized Vietnamese political party in North Viet Nam into acceptable associations for all concerned.

Honoring our legal and political commitments in Viet Nam is a vital beginning for us. The President is establishing that confidence among Asians and that credibility among our adversaries which comes from a well-established act of responsibility and from a well-defined execution of commitment. The country should support him there. But the act must transcend Viet Nam, even though it is an arena of decision, to cover Asia.

Bolstering social and economic institutions in Southeast Asia is the companion piece to commitment there. The President's pledge of a billion dollars and American support for the Asian-sponsored Asian Development Bank are more than promissory notes. They will provide the wherewithal for crucial building across frontiers. More than dams, power lines and highways, international instruments in treaties, executive agreements and international structures of secretariats, commissions and boards will help knit Southeast Asia together in a new order of security without war. Americans can play their best roles as administrators, engineers, doctors, diplomats, teachers—and lawyers.

I want to discuss for a few minutes this evening the question of how, if at all, the situation in Viet Nam relates to the framework of international law. We are made keenly aware by the news reports each day of the factors of military power as they are brought to bear on the conflict in Viet Nam. We are also aware of the political factors in that struggle, where South Viet Nam's civic action program and other programs assisted by the United States are contending against Communist ideology and organization. It is far less clear what *law* has to do with the conflict.

Although some might urge that Viet Nam is simply a power struggle, being waged on military terms and with political and economic weapons as well, it would be a mistake to conclude that the element of law is absent from this whole picture. A legal background of international agreements lies behind the present armed conflict. Parties to the conflict have argued their case on a footing of legal obligations and rights. There are international legal rules to govern the military conduct of hostilities. And, in the end, any negotiated settlement of the problem will require a new set of international legal arrangements regarding Viet Nam.

In 1954 at the Geneva conference on Indo-China, a whole series of international agreements was reached—several of them relating specifically to Viet Nam. These agreements included the following elements, among others: complete cessation of hostilities; a demarcation line between North and South Viet Nam; withdrawal of military forces by each side from the zone of the opposing side; a prohibition on foreign troop reinforcements and introduction of additional war materiel.

There were also provisions for "free general elections by secret ballot" throughout Viet Nam in 1956. Consultations were to be held between the authorities of North and South Viet Nam from July 1955 onward.

One of the early legal questions that arose under these agreements was the issue of who was bound by them. The new Government of South Viet Nam, which had been formed during the conference, protested particularly against the political provisions of the agreements which had been concluded by France, without its participation; the South Vietnamese, therefore, reserved their freedom of action with respect to the agreements. It has, nevertheless, been generally assumed that South Viet Nam was bound through the signature and adherence of the French Union. And, in fact, South Viet Nam has done nothing to upset the basic arrangement created by the Geneva agreements.

The United States withheld its formal adherence. Instead, this country made a declaration taking note of the agreements and stating that it would not use force or the threat of force to disturb them. The declaration also stated that the United States would view any renewal of aggression as a matter of grave concern.

Questions of compliance with obligations laid down by the Geneva agreements were raised almost from the outset. A crescendo of violations by North Viet Nam, and the responses to those violations, underlie the current armed struggle.

Contrary to Article 15 of the Viet Nam cease-fire agreement, the North Vietnamese left military and political cadres behind in the South to organize and carry on the very acts that were prohibited under the cessation of hostilities. Armed personnel were infiltrated from North into South Viet Nam, and arms were clandestinely supplied. Large quantities of new war material were imported into North Viet Nam from other Communist Bloc countries, and—again contrary to agreement— North Viet Nam prevented the International Control Commission from discharging its functions of inspection and supervision.

During these early years, United States assistance to South Viet Nam was kept carefully within the limits imposed by the Geneva agreements. This was done both out of respect for international undertakings and out of a practical judgment that the Geneva settlement had value to the extent that it could be kept operative. Even today, long after the time when we concluded that North Vietnamese violations relieved the other side of full compliance, neither South Viet Nam nor the United States has acted to nullify or abrogate the Geneva settlement. The demarcation line at the 17th Parallel remains the basis of the separate identity of South Viet Nam.

One of the turning points in Vietnamese history of the last ten years was the issue of free elections in 1955 and 1956. North Viet Nam insisted that there be elections and that consultations be undertaken to prepare for them. South Viet Nam insisted that the elections be *free,* and that political liberties be granted in the North before any consultations could take place. Each side based its position on provisions in the 1954 Geneva settlement. The United States, United Kingdom, and France, on their own reading of the agreements, urged President Diem at least to conduct discussions with the Communist authorities, and for as long as necessary, on the conditions indispensable to *free* elections.

However, South Viet Nam continued to insist that conditions in the North were such that no honest and fair election could take place. The time for holding elections in the summer of 1956 passed with very little comment, perhaps because the North Vietnamese knew their case was weak. General Giap's speech to the Tenth Congress of the North Viet Nam Communist Party in October 1956 was very frank in its admission of terror and oppression in the North.

Toward the end of the 1950's, Hanoi apparently realized that South Viet Nam was not going to capitulate as the result of economic or social breakdown. The North then launched a campaign of infiltration and subversion against the South that was marked by widespread use of terror. Village leaders and school teachers were systematically assassinated in an attempt to undermine the political and social fabric of rural South Viet Nam.

By 1961 the Communist breaches of the Geneva agreements had created a serious threat to the independence and territorial integrity of South Viet Nam, which then found it necessary to request extensive outside help. The United States responded by sending military personnel and materiel. Both governments made it clear, in communications to the International Control Commission and otherwise, that once the North Vietnamese ceased their aggressive acts and complied with the Geneva agreements there would no longer be a need for the increased assistance to South Viet Nam. Thus, once again, actions in Viet Nam were related to outstanding international obligations.

By early 1965 the scale of the Communist "war of liberation" in the South had mounted alarmingly in intensity and extent. Elements of a North Vietnamese regular division were found in the South. The supply of arms and strategic direction of the war from the North led the United States Government to conclude that North Viet Nam had now stepped up its aggression to the level of armed attack against the South, bringing into play the right of individual and collective self-defense recognized in Article 51 of the United Nations Charter.

In taking measures of collective self-defense, the United States once more related its actions to international law, here reflected in the Charter of the United Nations. The right of self-defense is not unlimited as to the quantum of response in the event of attack. Questions of military judgment are, of course involved. But they are not the last word. I would note here that US bombing in North Viet Nam has been limited to military targets, and that it has avoided some military targets for the sake of sparing centers of civilian population. International law has something to say about keeping the defensive response proportionate to the armed attack. This has been a factor in United States actions in Viet Nam.

Upon initiating last winter measures of collective defense against the armed attack in Viet Nam, the United States proceeded to comply with the provision of Article 51 that calls for reporting measures of self-defense to the Security Council. We had also done this earlier after the August, 1964, attack on US destroyers in the Tonkin Gulf and the aerial bombing of North Vietnamese naval facilities that followed.

There have been those who question the correctness of our analysis of the 1965 situation in Viet Nam and doubt the justification for our actions. Whatever the view taken, it is worth noting that the discussion has concerned international legal obligations and rights.

As part of the discussion, strong contentions have been advanced that we were obligated to place the whole Viet Nam problem in the hands of the United Nations. In fact, the United States Government would welcome any constructive steps by the United Nations to bring about a peaceful and just settlement in Viet Nam.

The President has urged the Secretary-General to use his good offices to move the Viet Nam problem from the battle-field to the negotiating table, and he has replied that he would do so. It is in the field of quiet diplomacy that the UN is most likely to be able to play a constructive role in the near future. Formal UN involvement is more difficult, particularly if the effort were to give the UN military responsibility for the area. This, of course, could be contemplated only if such responsibility were assumed in a way so as to afford continued protection of the political independence and integrity of South Viet Nam. In present circumstances this would mean asking the UN to engage in military action against North Viet Nam. It seems quite clear that neither the Security Council nor the General Assembly is prepared to undertake such action. Even a more modest formal UN involvement is difficult to envision in view of the repeated pronouncements by Hanoi and Peking that the UN has no competence to deal with this question.

International law has a bearing on the manner in which hostilities are conducted in an armed conflict. It deals with the means used in carrying on armed conflict.

Some have criticized or attacked the use of tear gas as violating a rule of international law thought to have grown out of the Geneva Protocol of 1925 on poison gas. The United States, for its part, has answered that no rule of law forbids use of a temporarily disabling gas that has been employed for decades in countries all over the world for police purposes. Our legal defense has stressed the humane character of the controlled use of tear gas as far preferable to the conventional death-dealing weapons of war.

Four Red Cross Conventions drafted at Geneva in 1949 lay down comprehensive rules for the humanitarian treatment of prisoners of war and other war victims. The United States and South and North Viet Nam have all become parties to these conventions. The United States and South Viet Nam have both informed the International Committee of the Red Cross that

165

we consider these conventions apply to the present conflict. No satisfactory response has been obtained from Hanoi.

The United States Government is fully aware of its responsibilities under these conventions, and has acted to see that units of the American armed forces in Viet Nam are adequately informed and instructed in the requirements of the Geneva Conventions. The Government is also aware of its responsibility in respect of prisoners captured by our forces and transferred to the Government of South Viet Nam. We are continuing measures to assure that our responsibilities under the Geneva Conventions will be discharged.

Last month the Viet Cong executed two American prisoners, without trial and without even charges of specific offenses. The Viet Cong said the executions were in retaliation for executions of convicted defendants carried out earlier by the South Vietnamese Government at Danang. The United States at once denounced the Viet Cong actions as *reprisals* directly forbidden by the Geneva Conventions. Thereafter Hanoi ceased to speak of retaliation, and instead stated that it considered US pilots captured in raids on North Viet Nam as subject to trial as war criminals.

Earlier this month the International Red Cross Conference at Vienna adopted by an overwhelming majority (117 to 6) a resolution on prisoners of war sponsored by the United States delegation. The resolution recalled that the use of prisoners of war as objects of retaliation is inhumane and that reprisals are condemned. It called upon all parties to armed conflict to give prisoners the full protections of the Geneva Conventions and to enable the International Committee of the Red Cross to carry out its humanitarian functions.

International law as set forth in the United Nations Charter requires that nations seek a peaceful settlement of their disputes. The United States interprets this as a duty that does not come to an end simply because a resort to force may have been made necessary by aggressive armed attack. In the Viet Nam conflict, the United States Government through President Johnson, Secretary Rusk, and Ambassador Goldberg has repeatedly made clear its strong desire for a peaceful solution in Viet Nam that will allow the people of the South to determine their future free from external force. The United States has emphasized its readiness to engage unconditionally in negotiations on a Viet Nam settlement.

When that settlement is made it will constitute a further international legal regime reinforcing or building on the Geneva agreements of 1954.

I have tried to indicate a number of ways in which international law has a bearing on the situation in Viet Nam. Some will consider it remarkable that law has *any* relation to the politically-charged and grim military struggle for power in Southeast Asia. The element of law was not present much if at all in the two World Wars or in the armed conflicts of earlier centuries.

Modern technology being what it is, international law has been transformed from a luxury to a necessity. Its role and influence will grow in the future. Progress will be recorded as more nations become convinced that law is better than force.

REMARKS OF DR. LARSON

The first thing I would like to do is to express my profound admiration for the background book that Ambassador Young has prepared for this occasion. The highest compliment I can pay to it is that I have read every single word of it (which is more than I can say for most books), and some of it twice. If Conferences like this did nothing else than form the occasion for the writing of books of this kind, that alone would justify them. I hope every one of you will read it carefully. And I hope everybody else does. What we need in this crisis period we are going through now is more reading and less rioting.

I am going to start with an observation the obviousness of which is exceeded only by the extent to which it is ignored in practice. This is that any discussion about this kind of problem must start with the facts as they are tonight if it is going to be of any practical utility.

Whenever you hear somebody say, "My position always has been and always will be . . .", watch out. Perfect continuity and consistency is a virtue only when applied to perfectly unchanging facts. It is a vice when applied to rapidly changing facts such as those we see in the international situation. It is, in fact, one of the commonest of human failings, particularly when people act in large aggregates, such as governments.

My contribution to this discussion tonight is going to have to do mostly with the United Nations. In fact, it is the contribution I have been trying to make for the past four years. I first started proposing, both officially and unofficially, United Nations involvement in Southeast Asia a little over four years ago, in the fall of 1961. I am not going to review what might have been, or what all the arguments were then. I will only say that at that stage of the game it would have been perfectly feasible to propose the kind of involvement in South Viet Nam that we so naturally proposed in the Congo in an essentially similar situation—that is to say, a situation in which the essential ingredients were an internal uprising complicated by the involvement of outside powers.

As the years have gone by and our military involvement has increased, it has become increasingly difficult and by now impossible to imagine the United Nations taking on this military burden, especially when we have very little inclination to allow them the elbow room to deal with the political necessities that woud have to be handled at the same time. I do think that at one stage of the game and for a considerable period, as a legal matter, we were not merely privileged but obliged to refer this to the United Nations, because the Charter says that, when all other measures have failed and the parties are attempting to deal with a threat to the peace, they not only may, they shall, take the matter to the Security Council.

But we now have 140,000 men under arms, and it is going up very soon to 200,000, and I see no point in reviewing what might have been. Of all the sad words the saddest are these, "It might have been"; of all the futile and infuriating words of tongue and pen, the most infuriating and futile are: "I told you so."

Where do we go from tonight? Our war aim in South Viet Nam has been clearly stated. We are trying to bring matters to

168

the point, not where we shall have an unconditional victory and can dictate terms, but where we can produce bona fide negotiations. The suggestion, then, that I would like to make tonight is this: That the negotiations that we are talking about are certain to be of such complexity, involving so many continuing responsibilities of interpretation and administration, so many other parties of Southeast Asia, and so many side issues, that they can only be carried on within the framework of an ongoing established world organization.

Everybody is agreed on one thing: the problem we are talking about is immensely complex. Any settlement, when the time comes to make it, will involve not only such things as the five points that Ambassador Young has outlined that might be a part of any over-all arrangement for the future, but also population transfers, economic development arrangements, finely balanced and phased military withdrawals, buffer zones, all sorts of other crucial features. In short, this is the kind of job that cannot be handled by some *ad hoc* pick-up team, assembled for a one-shot conference. It is not going to be a tete-a-tete with two or three questions that can be answered yes or no.

I don't see any organization other than U.N. on the scene that meets these prescriptions of what the organization will have to be. I don't think the Geneva set-up is adequate. It hasn't done very well up until now. It wasn't really set up to do this total kind of job. It was set up to supervise what was thought to be a temporary job of supervising a cease fire, pending national elections. Of course, the South East Asia Treaty Organization isn't set up for this. This is a defensive military alliance. One might talk about creating a new international organization, but even if this were desirable, I don't think it would be done. It is hard enough to create an organization when the parties are on speaking terms. It would be impossible when they are not even talking to each other.

When we look around the world today at the explosive and dangerous spots, it becomes apparent that they have one thing in common. What are some of the threats? Of course there is Viet Nam, by far the worst. Then there is the Indo-Pakistan war, with its fragile cease-fire, in which in one day India announced eighty people were killed. Some cease-fire. There are the instability of Indonesia and their aggressions against Malaysia and, perhaps the most dangerous thing of all, the proliferation of nuclear weapons.

What is the one element all these have in common? It is that at the center of practically all of them, or at least deeply involved, is the People's Republic of China. This being so, let's see where logic draws us. If we assume that we have to have a large, ongoing, well-established organization, with facilities for dispute-settling and for the administration of treaties (because, as every lawyer knows, a treaty is only as good as its administration), if we conclude that the only organization that meets these criteria is the United Nations, and if we conclude that most of the big dispute-settling and peace-keeping jobs in the world have China at their core, it looks as though we are going to have the People's Republic of China in the United Nations.

I don't know if you are startled to hear me say that, but I am. I have been arguing against this with all the devices at my command until very recently. What got me to come to this conclusion was the fact that I was forced to think about Southeast Asia by some of the people here. I kept going around and around and around with this problem, and there was China all the time.

I am coming to this conclusion for reasons quite different from those of many other people, but I have reached the conclusion that, weighed against the necessity of dealing with all of these trouble spots within an ongoing organization, the other serious arguments against the seating of Communist China with which we are all so familiar are overbalanced.

By equal logic, we ought to seat the representatives of all of the divided countries of the world. All of these but one, divided Germany, are in this Asian area: Korea, Viet Nam and China. It is one of the paradoxes of our time that these four divided countries, which by definition, by the fact of being divided countries, obviously are having troubles, irreconcilable

170

troubles, are not in the place where troubles are supposed to be settled.

The classical arguments for or against seating China are well known. There are two principal ones on each side: one philosophical, one practical.

The philosophical argument against the seating of Communist China is that it is not a peace-loving nation. There isn't any answer to that, particularly because the Communist Chinese are at great pains to prove that they are not peace-loving, both by their conduct and by their words. The philosophical argument the other way, is that the United Nations is supposed to be a universal organization, and therefore, because Communist China in fact controls almost a fourth of the world's population, it should obviously be in the organization.

These are both very good arguments; but to my mind they are largely rhetorical and do not go to the practical national interests of the United States one way or the other.

What are the practical arguments? One is a point that I have been particularly aware of since I was with the USIA. It is that any gesture of this kind woud have a demoralizing effect on some of our friends in Southeast Asia; especially some of the overseas Chinese. I think this could be compensated for somewhat if they realized the reasons for our action. It is by no means designed to do a favor to the Communist Chinese. The practical argument for not seating Communist China that impresses me most is that, if it is put on the Security Council, it might damage this tender little shoot that we have nourished for some time of cooperation between the Soviet Union and the United States, leading to a certain amount of peace-keeping action through the Security Council, including Cyprus and the Congo and several other actions. Would we have had Security Council action either in the Congo or in the sub-continent of India, if the People's Republic of China had been a permanent member? I don't think so.

That is a serious argument. I don't mean to minimize or detract from the seriousness at all. The only thing I can say about all of the arguments is that, as of now, I think they are

171

outweighed by the even heavier necessity of providing this kind of forum within which negotiations can take place, because the most or greatest part of the world's serious quarrels involve Communist China. Tremendous technical difficulties are involved, I realize, and legal difficulties. I would like to urge lawyers in any way that they can to think about this and to contribute to it.

There are difficulties about the Security Council seat. The most serious difficulty is the proper balancing of the interests of Nationalist China. I would say without reservation that I would never agree to any solution which involved the expulsion of Nationalist China, which is what the Communists always propose. From what I have been able to find out, I do not think the generality of the United Nations members would prefer that either. Every argument that you can make for the seating of the People's Republic of China you can almost make for the retention of a place for the Nationalist Chinese. After all, if universality is the argument, you don't start by kicking out the representatives of eleven million people. We admitted one country a little while ago with a population that I think you could put into two or three of the larger office buildings in New York, one whose population doesn't even reach six figures.

So if we are going to talk universality, let's not throw out eleven million people. Somebody might say that the mainland Chinese can speak for them. But the basis for admitting Communist China is that it *de facto* controls a certain piece of territory. The Nationalist Chinese also *de facto* control a certain piece of territory. All the arguments cut both ways.

There is a broader and perhaps a more Machiavellian purpose behind what I am suggesting here. If the Communist Chinese position and attitude are as repulsive as we think they are —and I think they are—the sooner this is felt at close range by every country in the world the better. The Communist Chinese are now having the benefit of the sympathy that goes to the underdog, the outsider. Recently, the statements of the Communist Chinese have become more and more outrageous, more and more contemptuous. The humiliating demands that they have stated as conditions to their entrance to the United Nations are an insult to every member of that organization. If they can be that repellent at a distance, think of what the effect would be if members had to be closeted with them at close quarters every day of the week. To be a little more serious about this, we would learn a lot about them and they would learn a lot about us, and I think we would both profit in the process.

You might think that this is a curious moment in time to be making this proposal. This is perhaps our last chance to take the initiative to propose the seating of Communist China and get credit for it. If we just let months slip away, things may reach the point where it will be forced upon us, and we will be accused of bowing to the inevitable.

I realize that it is extremely difficult for a democracy to do anything other than the obvious in the way of foreign policy. How one yearns for the days of Metternich and Richelieu, when diplomats could do the unexpected, the bold stroke, the paradoxical stroke. It is very hard for a democracy to do this, because of the political and other inertial guidance systems that we seem to have. But—quite seriously—we have a President who is extraordinarily secure politically, and if anybody could make a stroke of this kind and get away with it politically, I think he could.

REMARKS OF AMBASSADOR RAMANI

I am exceedingly grateful for this opportunity to be with you this evening, to take part in this Forum and to be able to address this group of lawyers because, first of all, I feel very privileged to have been asked to associate myself with a Forum which bears the great name of Hammarskjold, and secondly, because of the great opportunity given to me as a member of the Bar to have an opportunity of meeting and talking to so many members of the Bar gathered here.

I should like to begin by saying that I, too, like Professor Larson, have read this remarkable Working Paper, not once but twice. All the time that I was reading it, and reading it very carefully (of course I skipped the chapter on the Mekong River Basin, which does not interest me; as Mr. Young himself says, it does not interest Malaysia), I was aware of Mr. Young's having attempted a job of large proportions. He paints a wide variety of facts and historical traditions reaching back more than three thousand years (he even quotes Kautilya's Arthasastra) and has used a large brush to take a panoramic view of world conditions.

The Working Paper has been prepared from the other side of the world. You might call it a bird's eye view of conditions in Southeast Asia. I propose to put before you something that might be called a worm's eye view of conditions in Southeast Asia, because I live there. It may be that I shall probably find myself too often in the company of trees to see the woods clearly, but, at the same time, as I have been introduced to you as one who has for over three decades been a practitioner of the law, I may claim some acquaintance with the process by which one can take objective views of things—so long, of course, as they help the case of your own client! So I will, if I may be permitted to do so, say exactly what an Asian does feel about a situation of this nature.

The Working Paper is entitled "The Southeast Asia Crisis". What are the causes of this crisis? What are its elements? What is its form? What is its substance? If you do not understand the course and present posture of this crisis, I venture to think that you would find it very difficult to think in terms of how to solve the difficulties. I therefore propose to put before you how an Asian who lives in that territory looks at these crises. And, incidentally, I do not know why the book uses the singular and not the plural. There is not just one crisis in that part of the world; there are many crises.

What are the facts? The vital facts, I think are three: First and foremost is the fact that soon after the war there was an expulsion, a violent expulsion, if you please, of every colonial authority in all of Asia. And, as a corollary, Japan was responsible for this expulsion, whatever the subsequent consequences were of her own acts. And indeed those that suffered most in the war have now made good far better than most others who created the conditions which led to their defeats, such as Germany, Italy and now Japan. But in spite of this, it was Japan who made it possible for the colonial powers, Britain, France and Holland, to rethink their attitudes toward the colonial territories that they so largely possessed in Southeast Asia. That is the thrust of the first vital fact.

The second vital fact that you should remember is the growth of nationalism in this part of the world. Nationalism is three-quarters emotionalism and probably less than one-quarter intelligence. That is something one should always bear in mind. Even at the end of the first World War, when President Wilson, not merely satisfied with the Ten Commandments, produced fourteen and introduced in one of them self-determination, Lloyd George, the Prime Minister of England at that time, was very careful to say that this matter of self-determination was not intended to apply to Asia. Later, as recently as 1941, in the Atlantic Charter, when Roosevelt made a similar declaration, Winston Churchill would not admit that it applied to him. There was thus at the end of the war an explosive situation. One hears the word "explosive" so often in the United Nations corridors that I find it very hard to find something more explosive than "explosive". But, as a result of the Atlantic Charter, all the colonial powers, Britain, France and Holland, found themselves standing in grave peril.

But it is a significant aspect of the thinking of these great powers that they felt after the war that all they needed to do for the people in their colonial territories was to come back and say, "Here I am. I left you in the lurch during the years when you needed protection. But I am now back. How about loving me?" Britain came back to Malaya in this way, Holland to Indonesia and France to Indochina. But it must be said to the credit of Britain that in India she saw the light, and in a very great way. It is significant that India was the one country which lit the torch of nationalism and held it high, after which all the little nations of Asia and Africa had to light their own torches, little as they were. As a result of liberating India and creating Pakistan, the British attitude to colonial territories became something which was capable of being negotiated.

Many of them attained their independence, Burma, Ceylon, Malaya, and so on, in addition to India and Pakistan.

In Malaya the British were unable to protect the nine constituent states when protection was needed, but they came back after the war and offered to give protection. But unfortunately for them, political negotiations took place and by 1957 a new Federation of Malaya came into being as an independent state.

France had not learned the lesson. France itself, its leadership, was bifurcated between those who were in France and those comfortably ensconced in the refugee government in London and other parts of the world. They came back to Indochina and asked that it return to the fold but they did not learn their lesson until Dien Bien Phu. In Indonesia the Dutch not only came back, but they asked, begged, the United States and the United Kingdom to keep their arms there until such time as they could come over, and did come over. As a result, on the 17th of August, 1946, there was a revolution. Attitudes came into being which made Sukarno the great hero that he is today, or rather that he was the other day.

You must bear in mind that these situations were created by the attitudes of the colonial powers. Every new state, every new independent state, in that part of the world felt that it owed its liberation, even though they are not willing to admit it, to an Asian power, Japan. It was the expulsion of the colonial powers that gave a special feeling and warmth to the nationalistic movement in Southeast Asia. This is the second fact that one should bear in mind.

The third vital fact is the growth of the monolithic state of China. Professor Larson has referred to it, so that I need not elaborate on it. It is a fact that we must reckon with the existence of China. It began to consolidate its power in 1949 and it has now entered the nuclear club. I wish I had the time to sit here and discuss this all night long. I would be happy to sit with Dr. Larson and argue about his ideas relating to Viet Nam and the U.S. position in Viet Nam. I would like to tell him as a member of the United Nations and as a member of the Security Council that we have tried hard to understand

176

how to bring back Viet Nam into the United Nations. Without divulging confidences, I should be happy to tell him that Viet Nam cannot come into the United Nations, not because China does not want it to do so, but because the existing powers in the United Nations and in the Security Council do not want Viet Nam in the United Nations. Look at all the crises in Asia. There is the conflict between India and Pakistan. Back of it you see the menacing figure of China. There is the conflict between Malaysia and Indonesia. Again you see the menacing figure of China in the back of it. And you have the notorious Viet Nam situation which is actively aided and abetted by China. Therefore the Chinese position has got to be reckoned with, but I do not feel that this must be done in the way Dr. Larson considers it should be. The only way to get China to behave is to make her see that she has got to come into this society and look after her behavior.

I do not quite know—perhaps Professor Larson would consider this—how to deal with the notion that the lawful rights of the Chinese Government in the United Nations must be restored. China is already there, is seated there, but it is not represented by the lawful Government of China. That Government is in Peking. That is the Government which should have restored to it the power and the authority and the privilege of sitting as a permanent member in the Security Council. The state is already "there". But there are two contesting governments each asking to be recognized as the legitimate representative of China.

How does one accept the legitimacy of one representative and deny the legitimacy of the other if the socalled State not only does not want to come into the United Nations but protests to high heaven that she will not come anywhere near it? How does one deal with this? Do you go on your knees and ask China that she must come and take up her position?

I have said that these are the three essential facts that one should bear in mind as a prerequisite to understanding the mental and moral condition of the people of Southeast Asia. It does not require a great deal of research to ascertain the basic attitudes of these peoples. They are brought up under

177

what one might call a sense of deference to authority, a habit of living; something to be done by the person who knows how to do it. The son is deferential to his father, even though he does not want to do what his father wants him to do. The monarch looks after the protection of his subjects. The subjects attend to their own particular activities. That has been the tradition of Asia from the dawn of history. The idea that everyone of us, wherever he is, has just as much right as anyone else has not yet seeped into the mental attitudes of Asian states. Until that happens, we will not find a desire and an anxiety on the part of these people to control their own destinies, to take them into their own hands.

I have said that nationalism is an emotional state. It is an exclusive and an elusive force. Being the main force in Southeast Asia, it is difficult to contemplate any alternative. We in Malaysia know the defects of Thailand in the north and of Indonesia in the south. Thailand knows the defects of Malaysia in the south and of Viet Nam and Cambodia to her east. The closer we look at the problems of others, the more nationalistic, the more exclusive, we feel. The idea of promoting solidarity comes to us with greater difficulty than it came to those in Europe or Latin America. Even they, one would think, are stumbling forward in their efforts to find some sort of a cohesive position to hold them together.

Moreover, there is no cohesive factor in all of Southeast Asia other than nationalism, and that is barely two decades, or twenty years, old. That being so, one finds it very difficult to promote ideas of solidarity, of integration, within these states. And let us not forget that, although colonialism has removed its dead political hand, the center of political gravity is still in the West. London holds it, Paris holds it, and The Hague holds it. Therefore there is still a tendency to look back to one's mentors, even though there is now the basis of equality. And even though they are ready to help, there is still the feeling of dependence in the minds of those who have newly attained independence.

These are some of the difficulties in the way of trying to find any basis by which Southeast Asia can live together. One tends to look at these things with Western eyes and to say, why does this not happen? It happened quite recently in Europe; why does it not happen in Southeast Asia? I suggest that the great difficulty is the basic attitude, the psychology, of the people of Southeast Asia: fear of the unknown, fear of China, a looking back to old mentors, and a desire to be protected by them.

This has happened again and again. It has happened in Africa. Whenever Kenya and Ghana have been in trouble, they have not gone to the Organization of African States; they have gone to Mother London and cried on her shoulder. This attitude must be reckoned with. Twenty years in the life of a new state is not a very long time. Until political education seeps into the mental attitudes of the people, and a new generation is born, attitudes of freedom and honesty in political life will not really exist.

Now this Forum is presented by the Committee on the Lawyer's Role in the Search for Peace. What is this role? I think that basically the lawyer is probably the essence of society. He is a kind of Hamlet having the capacity to look before and after. Our tradition and education tell each of us to look behind and ahead. It promotes a synthesis. It does not take people away from their worries. It creates new situations for them. How happy we feel if we are able to find for a proposition of law some ancient authority of the seventeenth century. I am thinking of the British attitude. Here, of course, you find the proposition in the nineteenth century.

Therefore, we lawyers as a class could be and indeed often are to an extent the cement that holds a new society together so that it is not dominated by emotionalism. Intellectualism, sobriety and conservation have their full place in it.

Of course, domestic law is quite different from international law. In domestic law there is always a possibility of having one's judgment enforced by the authorities of a government. In international law you are faced with the fact that nobody takes a case to the International Court unless he is willing to risk losing it. The International Court is in no position to enforce its own judgments. No state new to independence wants to subject itself to this international jurisdiction.

179

In his new book on Kennedy, Sorenson cites an incident which happened when Kennedy was a Senator. He went to some place and spoke in the presence of a Catholic priest on international problems. He referred to these in such terms that the priest interposed and said "But Mr. Senator, you are a Catholic. Don't you think that all law is moral and all morals come from God?" Senator Kennedy replied, "Of course, as a true Catholic I believe that all law comes from God, but then that does not apply to international law".

So, we are still very much in a growing world, where ideas have not yet been taken into the minds of men. We look forward to the future with confidence and hope, but I think that anyone attempting a solution for the crisis in Southeast Asia will have to bear in mind these psychological factors and mental processes which, let us say, afflict the thinking of society there today.

Thank you.

COMMENT BY JUDGE BONSAL
Regarding the International Commission of Jurists

My remarks will be brief. In this wonderful Working Paper that we have here, Ambassador Young says on page 65:

"The study and profession of law and the administration of justice probably could utilize many more direct contacts with their opposite numbers in Southeast Asia as well as with other like-minded countries."

The purpose of the International Commission of Jurists is to supply those contacts. The Commission seeks to have lawyers in their own countries, through meetings with lawyers in other countries, stand up and be counted as a profession and take leadership in their own countries on the basic matters which concern lawyers. By doing so, they may aid and assist in this process about which the Ambassador from Malaysia has spoken to us this evening. Thank you.

RESPONSES TO QUESTIONS

A. *The Attitude of Asians towards the Bombings*

QUESTION: Ambassador Young, you refer to style. With regard to our style, does not our bombing in North Viet Nam
serve to strengthen the quasi-religious fervor of Ho Chi
Minh and his followers, and in South Viet Nam serve to
alienate those not committed and make more difficult the
task of building loyalty to an independent regime?

Ambassador Young: That is the kind of question that is very
hard to ask an American. Ambassador Ramani has very
cogently reminded us that we are on dangerous ground. Any
American who writes about Southeast Asia or speaks about
it necessarily tends to look at a question like that from the
Western point of view; it is awfully hard to put ourselves in
the position of the Vietnamese or the Malaysians.

I do not know what the reaction in North Viet Nam has
been. I suppose that the military efforts of the United States,
including the bombing, have up to now, anyway, increased
the determination of Ho Chi Minh and the regime of the
Democratic Republic of Viet Nam to resist. What effect it
has had on the people of North Viet Nam, I do not know.

I can only say, in answer to that question, that I have
heard from Southeast Asians, officials, that the military policy
of the President, the commitment of U. S. forces and
even the bombings, however much we don't like them, have
changed the atmosphere of confidence that I spoke of.
Whether this is looking at it from a Western point of view or
not, I don't know. All I can say in answer to that question
is: No, as far as the Southern part of Viet Nam is concerned.
The total effect of the American military effort in South
Viet Nam since last February has been to create confidence
where, in the minds of many Vietnamese, there has been
considerable uncertainty. Today there is more of a commitment among South Vietnamese than there was, say, a
year ago.

QUESTION: Ambassador Ramani, would you care to comment on the effect of military action on the attitudes of the Vietnamese people?

Ambassador Ramani: I do not think I should presume to do this, even though I have claimed that there is an Asian point of view as opposed to the American or European. I do not think I can presume to know what the Vietnamese point of view is, but, if one looks at the attitude of China, one must remember the tradition of what is called "face": they will never give in until the very last moment. But then, of course, we do not know how they are reacting to the bombing; we only know what we read in the papers. I have no better way of knowing what has happened.

We in Malaysia have a selfish interest in this situation, because if South Viet Nam falls, then we would hope you would find another base. There is not the slightest doubt but that North Viet Nam recognizes that the United States' function in the area is based on treaty. Undoubtedly North Viet Nam would not want to give in, but no one knows how things are shaping up. It was said last week that the Cambodian Government has given assistance to the Viet Cong, as we have to the South Vietnamese. As a result, we may probably find that this unfortunate war is followed up sooner rather than later by other wars.

It may be that Viet Nam now finds that, having waited for the monsoon and this not having resulted in any lessening of the war, they may wish they were out of it, but it is foolish to expect North Viet Nam to admit this by words. From what has happened during the last ten days, there seems to be some indication that North Viet Nam and the Viet Cong (which is only the political arm of North Viet Nam) may be in a position to consider treating with the United States through international organizations in order to bring an end to this unfortunate situation. That seems to be the latest position in North Viet Nam, and that is about all I can say on this.

QUESTION: Ambassador Young, do you wish to add anything?

Ambassador Young: The Ambassador made a point at the end of his principal remarks which I think is of great importance and one that I did not mention, because I felt before he spoke, before I came here tonight, that it is really the kind of thing that an American should listen to and not make an assertion about. He said that the fear of the unknown and the fear of China create a tendency in his part of the world to go back to their mentors. I think that was the expression you used—to go back to the past.

One of the things that should worry us very much here is the effect in Southeast Asia and Asia of the many confrontations, the confrontation with Communist China. Another colleague of Ambassador Ramani's from Southeast Asia referred last week to the confrontation with Western technology—the two cultures, living, as an architect in Bangkok once said to me, as a Western professional architect in the day, but as a Thai in the evening, living in a very ancient tradition. Where, he asked me, could he find a psychiatrist who could help explain both the West and the East in this terminology? It is a very serious thing that is happening. It is a hard factor, a hard development to grapple with.

I don't know what the role of the lawyer or the law is in this area. This area of clashes, this confrontation with the Chinese, is something that is very profound, and it is going to do different things to different governments, to different persons, to different groups, in all of these countries as well as to us. Also, we can't appreciate the effect of this very rapid and sudden onslaught of an alien—what is essentially an alien—way of life. This is not colonialism that I am talking about, but it has a shocking effect. It is like being ground between two millstones. We must all put together our best thoughts to work out a solution.

As I have said, lawyers, psychiatrists, economists, and political scientists must all work together so that these clashes can be moderated. I am very glad that the Ambassador for Malaysia mentioned this point about going back to mentors.

183

It would have been indelicate for an American to have said that in some areas of Asia and Southeast Asia there seems to be a tendency to revert to a kind of traditionalism that somehow avoids or defers facing up to these clashes, but I think it is an extremely important basic factor in looking ahead into the future.

B. *The Effect of the Revolt in Indonesia*

QUESTION: Ambassador Young, have recent events in Indonesia affected the views expressed in your Working Paper to any degree?

Ambassador Young: A month ago or six weeks ago I do not believe the events on September 30th, October 1st and October 2nd could have been predicted by anybody in Jakarta, in Peking, or in New York or Washington. This is one of those fascinating incidents that makes anybody who writes or speaks about Southeast Asia probably wrong within at least a week or, if not, six months. However, I think it is too soon to say that the Communist Party's political strength in Indonesia has been broken. It is very hard to tell with such limited information in the press coming out of Jakarta in the last three weeks.

I would say that the chances are a little less now that the Communist Party of Indonesia will be able to count on total governmental support in Jakarta for a confrontation, its actual confrontation policy or campaign, against Malaysia. As I understand it, that involves a good deal of infiltration and a certain amount of guerilla crossing into mainland Malaya as well as in Borneo. I do not think that what is loosely—perhaps too loosely—called the Peking-Jakarta axis is quite so much of an axis today, but I do not think the last returns are in as to how the PKI as a political organization, with roots in many parts of Java and to a certain extent in Sumatra and Bulawesi, will react to this critical power momentarily.

It is also not clear to me how a modern national army, such as the Indonesian Army is, will operate as a political organization. It is one thing to control divisions. It is another

184

thing to operate day in and day out, around the clock, as a political organization. Technology and mass organization are now going to be pitted against each other.

Ambassador Ramani: As you know, Indonesia is an archipelago of some 3,000 islands, with control on the island of Java. All the Communists are on the one island of Java; none of them are on Sumatra or any other place. Therefore, to the extent that the army is able to deal with the Communist Party in Java, it is unlikely that in the other 2,999 islands other little Communist sprouts will come up. It is demonstrably true that the PKI was controlled by China. They were closer to China than to Russia, and they said so. When Khrushchev was deposed they said, "We knew this would happen to this Communist. Our real mentors are in Peking." To the extent that the army has been able, as today's cables say, to deal with the Communist Party in Java, to the extent to which the people are willing to go and burn Chinese farms and beat up Chinese diplomats (and the Government of China has presented a strongly worded protest asking for compensation, and so on), it would appear that the power of the PKI has been effectively broken. But it is undoubtedly true, as has just been stated, that the army has no political base and will have no political base until it consolidates its power.

C. *The Role of India*

QUESTION: What role do you think India can or should play in Southeast Asia?

Ambassador Ramani: I resolved some time ago that Malaysia must propogate democracy in this part of the world if she wants to stop communism. I remember having said that democracy lives by example and communism by precept. India today is the largest democracy in the world. The fact that it is a democracy alone enables it to survive the present perils and to hold up its head in the international world. Paradoxically, this also results from its recently having strengthened the Cabinet so that they should stand shoulder to shoulder with Shastri and see that India does not go down

185

the drain. As probably the greatest democracy in the world, India can be an example in that part of the world. That is one of the reasons why Malaysia has felt that, as another working democracy, she is closer to India in her general attitudes and politics, and so on, than to other countries. If India remains in the posture of a democracy, if she has the nuclear ability, though she does not propose to create a nuclear capability, that attitude should continue as an example, and I think the best service that India can delegate to Asia.

D. *The Role of Communist China*

QUESTION: Dr. Larson, is Chinese control of Southeast Asia a threat to American control of vital interests, and, if so, why?

Dr. Larson: Yes, very definitely it is. There are many reasons. I think you are familiar with one: strategic control of all Southeast Asia would cut us off from, or at least be a very serious communications impediment to, our contact with the subcontinent and with the countries in that area in which we have a very profound interest. A second interest would be our own international posture, our reliability and so on, because quite apart from the SEATO Treaty, which for various technical reasons I won't rely upon in this connection (I have written about this elsewhere), we do have binding commitments of a mutual-defense character with at least two countries in the area. Third, there is the human reason. There are millions of people in this area who, like Ambassador Ramani, do not want to have to go and live someplace else. In questions of this kind, that kind of human consideration is the most important of all.

QUESTION: Mr. Meeker, under what circumstances do you think the People's Republic of China would be prepared to negotiate on Viet Nam either multilaterally or through the United Nations?

Mr. Meeker: That is a good question and a hard one. I do not think that there is any objective evidence on which an answer

186

can be based. If you try to base an answer on what the authorities in Peking have said, perhaps you would have to reach the conclusion that there are no circumstances at all in which they would be prepared to engage in negotiations. But I think one of the things that is interesting to notice about the People's Republic of China is that the talk is apt to be very loud and very strident, but the actions are likely to be very carefully calculated. While there is very harsh talk about war being the best school for politics, and about wars of national liberation, I think that they would be as capable as other Communist regimes in the past have been capable of adjusting their viewpoint and their ideology so as to be able to engage in negotiations if they felt that the times were favorable. Obviously the fortunes of war in Viet Nam are going to have an effect on that viewpoint.

E.   Representation of Communist China in the United Nations

(Mr. Meeker:) I would add just one thought on the question of the representation of China in the United Nations.

It does seem to me that it is a rather questionable proposition for the United States or for the United Nations to invite Communist China in at a time when it has just perfected a weapons capability in nuclear bombs and at a time when its foreign policy and its conduct in world affairs is aggressive, at the very least. It does not seem to me that this is good for China and its future conduct in world affairs, and I would also think that it would not be very helpful to that competition within the Communist world where, on the one hand, the Soviets are pressing for their theme, co-existence, as against the Chinese theory which seems to be that you get your way by force.

Having that factor in mind, it seems to me we should be quite reserved about suggesting that moves be made to bring Communist China into the UN now.

Ambassador Ramani: If there is a State which is not represented in the United Nations, but should be, it is Switzerland. One could pass a resolution unanimously, or by a two-

187

thirds vote, and then tell Switzerland, "We want you so badly to come in with us—why don't you come in?" That is one situation.

In the case of China, all we need to do is to hang the proper label; we can say, "You represent Formosa, and China is not before us at all."

But the problem that is facing us today, as it did in 1962 and 1963, is this: how do we restore rights to the legitimate government of China? China is already in the United Nations, and is entitled to be there. Suppose during the war France failed to be represented. DeGaulle was in London. Was he the representative of France? Or the government under the Nazis? The same thing has happened with regard to Poland. If someone were to say to those now in the UN, "You are not the rightful, legitimate government of China, you have no control over China. We want to put the crown on the head of Peking,"—by what right do we say this? If a legitimate government, knowing that it is the proper representative of a country, is not representing it, is it not for that Government to come forward and assert its right to be the representative? Is it for the United Nations as such, in order to support the principle of universality, to go to a government and say, "Please, why don't you come and claim your legitimate rights?" That does not seem to me legally proper at all. It is always the government, the competing government which should come and say, "Here are my credentials. They come from the proper sort of sources. I should be seated."

That is the situation facing China. It is not a question of saying for the sake of universality, "Let's admit China." In the limited legal context of rights, somebody must ask for a restoration of rights before such restoration can take place. It is for the proper legitimate government of China to make the first move.

What is the move that this government has so far made? It has done everything possible to prevent such a move. How do we restore rights that are not claimed? That is the point that I am trying to make. China should be there and, with-

188

out her, so many difficulties continue to happen. But as a matter of policy, are we going to say to the bully outside the door, as he is constantly banging on the door, let's stop the noise and have him come in and make the noise inside? That is not the right way.

Dr. Larson: I want to make very briefly a response to Ambassador Ramani's observation that Communist China would not accept membership in the UN, even if it were offered. I was aware of this problem when I made the suggestion, but I did not make it for that reason entirely. Whenever one approaches a problem of this kind, the most one can take on is what one's own country should do.

If we propose this, and if Communist China does not then accept it, that is Communist China's problem, not ours. But if this does happen (and I know it will happen at least in the first instance, because they have said so and imposed such humiliating and outrageous conditions that they certainly never would be heard by the other members of the UN, who came in without special conditions) we shall not be to blame. As a matter of fact, Nationalist China has also said she wouldn't be caught dead in the same organization with Communist China, and the Communists have said the same thing about the Nationalists; that is where the matter rests. But the United States has taken practically all of the blame for a situation which has in it all these built-in blocks. The one thing we can do, and the only thing we can do, is to clarify our position, do the thing that we think should be done, make the proposals on our terms and our conditions and our reservations, and then get the discussion circulating around our proposal.

The same observation that I have just made also applies to the Ambassador's reaction to my statement about offering the UN a role in South Viet Nam four years ago, or some other time for that matter. He says that the Security Council and the UN doesn't want the job. I say that is their problem. That is what they are paid to do—peace-keeping in the world.

When this situation reached the point, I think four years ago, when it became a threat to the peace, since the Charter

189

says it shall be taken up in the United Nations, our job was to take it there. If the U.N. didn't want it, the air would be cleared. Our posture would have been transformed. Instead of appearing to conduct a unilateral, white Western involvement in an Asian situation, with a lot of hardship resulting locally, we would have done what the Charter said. We could have tried to make it an international peace-keeping operation. Then if we felt we had to go on in this unilateral way, I don't think we would have had the criticism that we have had.

APPENDICES

APPENDIX A

Committee for Co-ordination of Investigations of the Lower Mekong Basin

STATUTE

As adopted at the meeting on 17 September 1957 of the Preparatory Committee of the four governments and amended on 31 October 1957 at the first session of the Committee for Co-ordination and approved by the participating governments.

CHAPTER I

ESTABLISHMENT OF THE COMMITTEE

The Committee for Co-ordination of Investigations of the lower Mekong basin (hereinafter called the Committee) is established by the Governments of Cambodia, Laos, Thailand and the Republic of Vietnam (hereinafter called the participating governments), in response to the decision taken by the United Nations Economic Commission for Asia and the Far East (hereinafter called the Commission) at its thirteenth session. By this decision, reported in paragraph 277 of the Commission's annual report for the period 15 February 1956 to 28 March 1957, the Commission endorsed the wish of the participating governments that secretariat studies relating to the development of the lower Mekong basin, namely, the area of the drainage basin of the Mekong river situated in the territory of the participating governments, be continued jointly with the participating governments. The participating governments have set up the Committee to perform the functions contained in the present Statute.

CHAPTER II

ORGANIZATION

Article 1

1. The Committee shall be composed of four members.
2. Each participating government will appoint one member with plenipotentiary authority and such alternates, experts and advisers as it desires.

Article 2

The chairmanship of the Committee shall be held in turn by the members of the Committee, in the alphabetical order of the member countries. Each member shall hold office for one year.

CHAPTER III

CO-OPERATION WITH THE SECRETARIAT OF THE COMMISSION

Article 3

In accordance with the decision of the Commission at its thirteenth session, the secretariat of the Commission shall co-operate with the Committee in the performance of the latter's functions.

Chapter IV
FUNCTIONS

Article 4

The functions of the Committee are to promote, co-ordinate, supervise and control the planning and investigation of water resources development projects in the lower Mekong basin. To these ends the Committee may:

(a) prepare and submit to participating governments plans for carrying out co-ordinated research, study and investigation;

(b) make requests on behalf of the participating governments for special financial and technical assistance and receive and administer separately such financial and technical assistance as may be offered under the technical assistance programme of the United Nations, the specialized agencies and friendly governments;

(c) draw up and recommend to participating governments criteria for the use of the water of the main river for the purpose of water resources development.

Chapter V
SESSIONS

Article 5

1. Subject to the provisions of this Statute, the Committee shall adopt its own rules of procedure.

2. Meetings of the Committee shall be attended by all participating countries. Decisions of the Committee shall be unanimous.

3. Decisions of the Committee shall be unanimous.

4. The Executive Secretary of the Commission or his representative may at any meeting make either oral or written statements concerning any questions under consideration.

Chapter VI
GENERAL PROVISIONS

Article 6

The Committee shall submit reports to participating governments and annually to the Commission. Such reports, or summaries thereof, may be made available to other governments and international organizations on the recommendations of the Committee.

Article 7

The Committee may invite representatives of governments and of specialized agencies to attend meetings of the Committee in the capacity of observers.

Article 8

1. It is understood that, while in all technical matters which are within the competence of this Committee, the participating governments shall act through this Committee, the stipulations contained in this Statute shall not in any way affect, supersede or modify any of the agreements which are presently in force or which may be hereafter concluded between any of the interested governments relating to the Mekong river.

2. Amendments to the present Statute which may be proposed by any participating government, shall be examined by the Committee and shall take effect when approved by all participating governments.

Final Declaration of Geneva Conference, July 21, 1954

Final declaration, dated July 21, 1954, of the Geneva Conference on the problem of restoring peace in Indo-China, in which the representatives of Cambodia, the Democratic Republic of Viet-Nam, France, Laos, the People's Republic of China, the State of Viet-Nam, the Union of Soviet Socialist Republics, the United Kingdom, and the United States of America took part.

1. The Conference takes note of the agreements ending hostilities in Cambodia, Laos and Viet-Nam and organizing international control and the supervision of the execution of the provisions of these agreements.

2. The Conference expresses satisfaction at the ending of hostilities in Cambodia, Laos and Viet-Nam; the Conference expresses its conviction that the execution of the provisions set out in the present declaration and in the agreements on the cessation of hostilities will permit Cambodia, Laos and Viet-Nam henceforth to play their part, in full independence and sovereignty, in the peaceful community of nations.

3. The Conference takes note of the declarations made by the Governments of Cambodia and of Laos of their intention to adopt measures permitting all citizens to take their place in the national community, in particular by participating in the next general elections, which, in conformity with the constitution of each of these countries, shall take place in the course of the year 1955, by secret ballot and in conditions of respect for fundamental freedoms.

4. The Conference takes note of the clauses in the agreement on the cessation of hostilities in Viet-Nam prohibiting the introduction into Viet-Nam of foreign troops and military personnel as well as of all kinds of arms and munitions. The Conference also takes note of the declarations made by the Governments of Cambodia and Laos of their resolution not to request foreign aid, whether in war material, in personnel or in instructors except for the purpose of the effective defence of their territory and, in the case of Laos, to the extent defined by the agreements on the cessation of hostilities in Laos.

5. The Conference takes note of the clauses in the agreement on the cessation of hostilities in Viet-Nam to the effect that no military base under the control of a foreign State may be established in the regrouping zones of the two parties, the latter having the obligation to see that the zones allotted to them shall not constitute part of any military alliance and shall not be utilized for the resumption of hostilities or in the service of an aggressive policy. The Conference also takes note of the declarations of the Governments of Cambodia and Laos to the effect that they will not join in any agreement with other States if this agreement includes the obligation to participate in a military alliance not in conformity with the principles of the Charter of the United Nations or, in the case of Laos, with the principles of the agreement on the cessation of hostilities in Laos or, so long as their security is not threatened, the obligation to establish bases on Cambodian or Laotian territory for the military forces of foreign Powers.

6. The Conference recognizes that the essential purpose of the agreement

relating to Viet-Nam is to settle military questions with a view to ending hosilities and that the military demarcation line is provisional and should not in any way be interpreted as constituting a political or territorial boundary. The Conference expresses its conviction that the execution of the provisions set out in the present declaration and in the agreement on the cessation of hostilities creates the necessary basis for the achievement in the near future of a political settlement in Viet-Nam.

7. The Conference declares that, so far as Viet-Nam is concerned, the settlement of political problems, effected on the basis of respect for the principles of independence, unity and territorial integrity, shall permit the Viet-Namese people to enjoy the fundamental freedoms, guaranteed by democratic institutions established as a result of free general elections by secret ballot. In order to ensure that sufficient progress in the restoration of peace has been made, and that all the necessary conditions obtain for free expression of the national will, general elections shall be held in July 1956, under the supervision of an international commission composed of representatives of the Member States of the International Supervisory Commission, referred to in the agreement on the cessation of hostilities. Consultations will be held on this subject between the competent representative authorities of the two zones from 20 July 1955 onwards.

8. The provisions of the agreements on the cessation of hostilities intended to ensure the protection of individuals and of property must be most strictly applied and must, in particular, allow everyone in Viet-Nam to decide freely in which zone he wishes to live.

9. The competent representative authorities of the Northern and Southern zones of Viet-Nam, as well as the authorities of Laos and Cambodia, must not permit any individual or collective reprisals against persons who have collaborated in any way with one of the parties during the war, or against members of such persons' families.

10. The Conference takes note of the declaration of the Government of the French Republic to the effect that it is ready to withdraw its troops from the territory of Cambodia, Laos and Viet-Nam, at the request of the governments concerned and within periods which shall be fixed by agreement between the parties except in the cases where, by agreement between the two parties, a certain number of French troops shall remain at specified points and for a specified time.

11. The Conference takes note of the declaration of the French Government to the effect that for the settlement of all the problems connected with the re-establishment and consolidation of peace in Cambodia, Laos and Viet-Nam, the French Government will proceed from the principle of respect for the independence and sovereignty, unity and territorial integrity of Cambodia, Laos and Viet-Nam.

12. In their relations with Cambodia, Laos and Viet-Nam, each member of the Geneva Conference undertakes to respect the sovereignty, the independence, the unity and the territorial integrity of the above-mentioned states, and to refrain from any interference in their internal affairs.

13. The members of the Conference agree to consult one another on any question which may be referred to them by the International Supervisory Commission in order to study such measures as may prove necessary to ensure that the agreements on the cessation of hostilities in Cambodia, Laos and Viet-Nam are respected.

BIBLIOGRAPHY

Selected Bibliography on the
Southeast Asia Crisis*

BIBLIOGRAPHIES

American Institute of Pacific Relations. Books on Southeast Asia: a select bibliography. New York. 1959. 62p.

Bibliography of Laos. New Haven, HRAF. 1956. 29p.

Chulalongkorn University. Central Library. Bibliography of material about Thailand in western languages. Bangkok. 1960. 325p.

Embree, Ainslie T., ed. A guide to paperbacks on Asia. New York, Asia Society. 1964. 89p.

Fall, Bernard B. Recent publications on Indochina. March 1956. 29 Pac. Aff. 57–64.

Focus on southeast Asia. Jan. 1961. 2 Intercon 9–35.

Hanrahan, Gene Z. Recent Chinese communist publications on Indochina and Malaya. Dec. 1954. 27 Pac. Aff. 367–70.

Hart, Donn V. Southeast Asia: an introduction to the literature. 9p. (Reprint by the Asia Society for social education. Dec. 1964, vol. xxviii, no. 8) Published by the National Council for the Social Studies.

Hay, Stephen N. and Case, Margaret H. Southeast Asian history: a bibliographic guide. New York, Praeger. 1962. 138p.

Jumper, Roy. Bibliography on the political and administrative history of Vietnam, 1802–1962 . . . Saigon?, Michigan State University, Vietnam Advisory Group. 1962. 179p.

Keyes, Jane Godfrey. A bibliography of North Vietnamese publications in the Cornell university library. Ithaca, Southeast Asia Program, Dep't of Asian Studies. Cornell University. 1962. 116p.

Michigan State University. Vietnam Project. What to read on Vietnam. New York, Institute of Pacific Relations. 1959.

Parks, C. E. and Reban, M. T. Recent articles on Vietnam: an annotated bibliography. East Lansing, Michigan State University, Vietnam Project. 1958. 25p.

South Vietnam (bibliography). July 1, 1959. 38 For. Policy Bull. 157.

Thailand (bibliography). 1961. 20 J. Asian Studies 692–96.

U.S. Library of Congress. Reference Dep't. Orientalia Division. Southeast Asia; an annotated bibliography of selected reference sources in western languages. Compiled by Cecil Hobbs . . . revised and enlarged. Washington. 1964. 180p.

Unraveling the Vietnam tangle. 14 (9) Vital Issues.

Vietnam bibliography. 1963. 22 J. Asian Studies 146; 24:175.

Wilson, Patrick. Bibliographical article: a survey of bibliographies on southern Asia. May 1959. 18 J. Asian Studies 365–76.

---

* Prepared by the Reference Librarian of the Association of the Bar Library with the cooperation of Kenneth Young, Ferdinand de May and the Asia Society.

Allen, R. H. S.   The task of western diplomacy in southeast Asia. Cincinnati, Univ. of Cincinnati. 1964. 60p.

Allison, J. M.   Freedom, democracy and American policy in southeast Asia. 1962. 38 Inst. World Aff., Proc. 88–97.

American Academy of Political and Social Sciences.
   America and a new Asia, edited by James C. Charlesworth.   Philadelphia. 1954. 243p. (Its Annals, v.294)
   Asia and future world leadership, edited by James C. Charlesworth. Philadelphia. 1958. 218p. (Its Annals, v.318)

Bell, Coral.   American policy in south east Asia. 1964. 20 World Today 256–62.

Lord Birdwood.   The defence of south east Asia. 1955. 30 Int'l Aff. 17–25.

Bone, Robert C.   Contemporary southeast Asia. New York, Random House. 1962. 132p.

Brierly, James L.   The law of nations. 6th ed. New York, Oxford Univ. Press. 1963. 442p.

Britsch, J.   Le destin de la péninsule indochinoise. 1963. 19 Rev. de Défense Nationale 1823–35.

Browne, Malcolm W.   The new face of war. Indianapolis, Bobbs-Merrill. 1965. 284p.

Buehrig, Edward H.   The international pattern of authority. 1965. 17 World Politics 369–85.

Buss, Claude Albert.   Southeast Asia and the world today. Princeton, N.J., Van Nostrand. 1958. 189p.

Butwell, Richard A.   Southeast Asia today—and tomorrow: a political analysis. New York, Praeger. 1961. 182p.

Caldwell, Malcolm.   Luddites and lemmings in south-east Asia. 1965. 41 Int'l Aff. 420–40.

Chatti, Ellen.   Development of the lower Mekong basin. Oct. 1960. Looking Ahead (a monthly report of the National Planning Association)

Chauvel, J.   Le sud-est asiatique et la politique francaise. April 15, 1965. Rev. des Deux Mondes 481–93.

Claude, Inis L., jr.   Power and international relations. New York, Random House. 1962. 310p.

Cola Alberich, J.   Acontecimientos en el sudeste asíatico. Jan/Feb. 1964. Rev. de Política Internacional 155–63.

Coplin, William D.   International law and assumptions about the state system. 1965. 17 World Politics 615–34.

Corbett, Percy E.   Law in diplomacy. Princeton, Princeton Univ. Press. 1959. 278p.

Derrett, J. Duncan M.   The maintenance of peace in the Hindu world: practice and theory. 1958. 7 Indian Yb. Int'l Aff. 361–87.

Duchacek, Ivo D.   Conflict and cooperation among nations. New York, Holt, Rinehart and Winston. 1960.

Emerson, Rupert.
   Problems of representative government in southeast Asia.   1953. 26 Pac. Aff. 291–302.
   Representative government in southeast Asia.   With supplementary

chapters by William H. Elsbree and Virginia Thompson. Cambridge, Harvard Univ. Press. 1955. 197p.

Fall, Bernard B.   South-east Asia's problems. Jan/March 1962. 18 India Q. 10–27.

Falk, Richard A.
Law, morality and war in the contemporary world.   New York, Praeger. 1963. 120p. (Princeton studies in world politics no. 5)
Revolutionary nations and the quality of international legal order (in Kaplan, Morton A., ed.   The revolution in world politics. N.Y., Wiley, 1962, pp.310–31)

Fifield, Russell Hunt.
The diplomacy of southeast Asia, 1945–1958.   New York, Harper. 1958. 584p.
Southeast Asia in United States policy.   New York, Published for the Council on Foreign Relations by Praeger. 1963. 488p.

Fisher, Charles A.   Southeast Asia; a social, economic and political geography. London, Methuen. 1964.

Fisher, Roger D.   International conflict and behavioral science; the Craigville papers. New York, Basic Books. 1964. 290p.

Fleming, D. F.   What is our role in east Asia? 1965. 18 W. Pol. Q. 73–86.

Fontaine, A.   De Gaulle's politik der bewegung un süd–und Ostasien. 1964. 19 Europa-Archiv 145–66.

Gange, J.   The southeast Asian cockpit. 1964. 351 Annals 58–71.

Greene, Fred.   Dynamics of international relations—power, security and order. New York, Holt, Rinehart & Winston. 1964. 733p.

Halberstam, David.   The making of a quagmire. New York, Random House. 1965. 323p.

Hanna, Willard A.   Eight nation makers. New York, St. Martin's Press.

Hart, D. V.   Southeast Asia and the United States: a background paper. New York, Institute of Pacific Relations. 1954. 33p. (mimeo)

Henderson, William.
The development of regionalism in southeast Asia.   Nov. 1955. 9 Int'l Org. 463–76.
Southeast Asia: problems of United States policy.   Cambridge, M. I. T. Press. 1963. 273p.

Hilsman, Roger W.   The challenge to freedom in Asia. 1963. 49 Dep't State Bull. 43–50.

Ho-Chi-Minh.   Ausgewahlte reden und aufsätze. Berlin, Dietz. 1961. 445p.

Holland, William Lancelot, ed.   Asian nationalism and the west. A symposium based on documents and reports of the Eleventh conference, Institute of Pacific Relations . . . New York, Macmillan. 1953. 449p.

Indonesia, Malaya and the North Borneo crisis.   April 1963. 3 (4) Asian Survey.

Johnstone, W. C.   The United States in southeastern Asia. 1965. 48 Current Hist. 65–68, 114.

Jordan, Amos A., jr.   Foreign aid and the defense of southeast Asia. New York, Praeger. 1962. 272p.

Kahin, George McTurnan, ed.   Governments and politics of southeast Asia. 2d ed. Ithaca, Cornell Univ. Press. 1964. 796p.

Kaplan, Morton A. and Katzenbach, Nicholas deB. The political foundations of international law. New York, Wiley. 1961. 372p.

Khoman, T. Which road for southeast Asia? 1964. 42 For. Aff. 628–39.

King, John Kerry. Southeast Asia in perspective. New York, Macmillan. 1956. 309p.

Lawrence, D. Is declaration of state of war legally required? July 26, 1965. 59 U.S. News 108.

Lepawsky, Albert. International development of river resources. 1963. 39 Int'l aff. 533–50.

Low, Francis. The struggle for Asia. London, F. Muller. 1955. 239p.

Lyon, Peter H.
    Neutralism. Leicester, Eng., Leicester Univ. Press. 1963. 215p.
    Southeast Asia. London, Oxford Univ. Press. 1965. 148p. (Royal Institute of International Affairs, Chatham House Pubs.)

McDougal, Myres S. and Florentino P. Feliciano. Law and minimum world public order; the legal regulation of international coercion. New Haven, Yale Univ. Press. 1961.

Maruyama, S. A peace corridor in Indo-China—a proposal. 1963. 10 Japan Q. 166–74.

Miller, Richard S. Legal scholarship, realism and the search for minimum world order. 1965. 17 World Politics 478–94.

Mills, Lennox A. Southeast Asia: illusion and reality in politics and economics. Minneapolis, Univ. of Minnesota Press. 1964. 365p.

Oliver, A. S. B. and MacDougall, C. South and south-east Asia. 1956/58 Survey Int'l Aff. 408–28.

Pauker, Guy J.
    Political doctrines and practical politics in southeast Asia. 1962. 35 Pac. Aff. 3–10.
    Southeast Asia as a problem area in the next decade. 1959. 11 World Politics 325–45.

Peffer, Nathaniel. Transition and tension in southeast Asia. White Plains, N.Y., Fund for Adult Education. 1957. 287p.

Rose, Saul.
    Constitutions in southeast Asia. 1960. 7 St. Antony's Papers 24–36.
    Socialism in southeast Asia. London, Oxford Univ. Press. 1959. 278p.

Sandrin, C. Les regroupements dans le sud-est asiatique. 1965. 21 Rev. de Défense Nationale 276–89.

Sastri, K. A. Nilakanta. Inter-state relations in Asia. 1953. 2 Indian Yb. Int'l Aff. 133–53.

Schaaf, C. Hart and Fifield, Russell H. The lower Mekong: challenge to cooperation in southeast Asia. Princeton, N.J., Van Nostrand. 1963. 136p.

Singh, L. P. Indochina seit Dien Bien Phu—das neutralitätsproblem in Laos, Kambodscha und Vietnam. 1964. 19 Europa-Archiv 631–42.

Stebbins, Richard P. The United States in world affairs. Published for the Council on Foreign Relations by Harper (see vols. 1954–63).

Syatauw, J. J. G. Some newly established Asian states and the development of international law. The Hague, Nijhoff. 1961. 249p.

Thayer, Philip Warren, ed. Southeast Asia in the coming world. With a foreward by William O. Douglas. Baltimore, Johns Hopkins Press. 1953. 306p.

Thomson, Ian. Changing patterns in south Asia. New York, Roy Publishers. 1962. 166p.

Thornton, Thomas Perry. Foreign relations of the Asian communist satellites. 1962/63. 35 Pac. Aff. 341–52.

U.S. Department of State. Office of Media Services. Southeast Asia: fact sheet. Washington, Gov't Print. Off. 1963. 15p.

Vandenbosch, Amry and Butwell, Richard A. Southeast Asia among the world powers. Lexington, Univ. of Kentucky Press. 1957. 336p.

Walle, R. F. Asia and the far east. 1959/60. Survey Int'l Aff. 202–98.

Ward, Barbara E., ed. Women and the new Asia; the changing social roles of men and women in south and south-east Asia. Paris?, UNESCO. 1963. 529p.

Washington Foreign Law Society. Studies in the law of the far east and southeast Asia. Washington. 1956. 104p.

White, Gilbert F. Lower Mekong—a proposal for peaceful and honorable resolution of the conflict in South Vietnam. Dec. 1964. Bull. Atomic Sci. 6.

Wright, Quincy. The role of international law in the elimination of war. New York, Oceana. 1961. 119p.

HISTORICAL MATERIALS

Alexandrowicz, Charles Henry. Treaty and diplomatic relations between European and south Asian powers in the seventeenth and eighteenth centuries (in Hague Academy of international law. Recueil des Cours, 1960, v.11, pp.207–320)

Cady, John Frank.
    The roots of French imperialism in eastern Asia. Ithaca, Cornell Univ. Press. 1954.
    Southeast Asia: its historical development. New York, McGraw-Hill. 1964. 657p.

Chânakya. . . . Arthaśastra of Kautilya: a new edition by J. Jolly and Dr. R. Schmidt. Lahore, Punjab Sanskrit Book Depot. 1923–24. 2v.

Churchill, Winston S. The grand alliance. Boston, Houghton, Mifflin. 1950. 903p.

Cöedes, Georges. Les états hindouisés d'Indochine et Indonésie. 2d. ed. Paris, E. De Boccard. 1948. 466p.

Cole, Allan Burnett, ed. Conflict in Indo-China and international repercussions; a documentary history, 1945–1955. Published under the auspices of the Fletcher School of Law and Diplomacy, Cornell Univ. Press. 1956. 265p.

Conflicts in Asia. 1955/56. Survey Int'l Aff. 7–22.

Crisis in Asia. 1954. Survey Int'l Aff. 12–95.

Dennett, Tyler. Americans in eastern Asia. New York, Macmillan. 1922.

Devillers, Philippe.
    Histoire du Viet-nam de 1940 à 1952. 3d ed. Paris, Editions du Seuil. 1952. 479p.
    Vietnam and France. Paris, Comité d'études des problèmes du Pacific; distributed by International Secretariat, Institute of Pacific Relations, New York. 1950. 51p.
    Vietnamese nationalism and French politics (in Holland, William L.,

ed.   Asian nationalism and the West. N.Y., Macmillan, 1953, pp.
    197–226)
Dunn, William Brothers.   American policy and Vietnamese nationalism,
    1950–54. Unpublished thesis, University of Chicago. Chicago. 1960. 317p.
    (Microfilm 6726E)
Eisenhower, Dwight D.   Mandate for change 1953–56. Garden City, N.Y.,
    Doubleday. 1963. 650p.
Ennis, Thomas E.   French policy and development in Indochina. Chicago,
    Univ. of Chicago Press. 1936. 230p.
Fairbank, J. K. and Teng, S. Y.   On the Ch'ing tributary system. Cambridge,
    Harvard Univ. Press. 1961.
Fall, Bernard B.
    Political development of Vietnam, VJ day to the Geneva cease-fire.   Un-
        published thesis. Syracuse, Syracuse University. 1954. 3v. (University
        microfilms no. 11,867)
    Street without joy: Indochina at war 1946–54.   Harrisburg, Pa., Stack-
        pole Co. 1961. 322p.
Foreign relations of the United States (diplomatic papers), 1941, vol. 5,
    far east.   Washington, Gov't Print. Off. 1956. p.273.
Foreign relations of the United States-Japan 1931–41.   Vol. 2. Washington,
    Gov't Print. Off. 1943. pp.529, 539–40.
Griswold, A. B.   King Mongkut of Siam. New York, Asia Society. 1961.
Grousset, René.   The rise and splendor of the Chinese empire. 1959. 3
    Siam Soc'y J.
Gurney, Natalie.   History of the territorial dispute between Siam and
    French Indochina, and post war political developments in the disputed
    territories. A thesis submitted to the Walter Hines Page School of Inter-
    national Relations, Johns Hopkins University. 1950. 192p.
Hall, Daniel G. E.   A history of south east Asia. 2d ed. London, Macmil-
    lan; New York, St. Martin's Press. 1964. 955p.
Hammer, Ellen Joy.
    The emergence of Viet Nam; study of recent political developments in
        Indochina prepared as part of a larger series of reports on nationalism
        and dependencies in the far east.   New York, International Secretariat,
        Institute of Pacific Relations. 1947. 52p.
    The struggle for Indochina.   Stanford, Stanford Univ. Press. 1954. 342p.
Hughes, Emmet John.   The ordeal of power. New York, Atheneum. 1963.
    372p.
Isaacs, Harold Robert, ed.   New cycle in Asia. Selected documents on major
    international developments in the far east, 1943–47. New York, Mac-
    millan. 1947. 212p.
Lacouture, Jean and Devillers, Philippe.   La fin d'une guerre; Indo-chine
    1954. Paris, Editions du Seuil. 1960. 381p.
Lancaster, Donald.   The emancipation of French Indochina. London, Ox-
    ford Univ. Press. 1961. 445p.
Langer, William L. and Gleason, S. Everett.   The undeclared war, 1940–41.
    New York, Published for the Council on Foreign Relations by Harper.
    1953. 963p.
Le Thanh Khol.   Le Viet-Nam, histoire et civilisation. Paris, Editions de
    Minuit. 1955. 587p.

Modelski, George. Kautilya: foreign policy and international system in the ancient Hindu world. 1964. 58 Am. Pol. Sci. Rev. 549–60.

Nawaz, M. K. The law of nations in ancient India. 1957. 6 Indian Yb. Int'l Aff. 172–88.

Nguyen Van Thai and Nguyen Van Mung. A short history of Vietnam. Saigon, Published for the Vietnamese-American Association by the Times Publishing Co. 1958. 350p.

Pillay, K. K. Early Indian "imperialism" in the far east. 1954. 3 Indian Yb. Int'l Aff. 114–25.

Robert-Martignan, Leopold. La monarchie absolue Siamoise de 1350 à 1926. 1959. 3 Siam Soc'y J.

Roberts, C. M. The day we didn't go to war. Sept. 14, 1954. Reporter 31.

Ruben, W. Inter-state relations in ancient India and Kautilya's Arthaśastra. 1955. 4 Indian Yb. Int'l Aff. 137–59.

Sastry, K. K. R. A note on Udasina—neutrality in ancient India. 1954. 3 Indian Yb. Int'l Aff. 131–34.

Thailand in the light of official Chinese historiography. A chapter in the history of the Ming Dynasty. July 1961. 49 J. Siam Soc'y pt. 1, 1–20.

Thompson, Virginia. French Indochina. London, Allen & Unwin. 1937. 517p.

Tru'o'ng-Chinh. Primer for revolt; the Communist takeover in Viet-Nam. A facsim. ed. of The August revolution and The resistance will win. With an introd. and notes by Bernard B. Fall. New York, Praeger. 1963. 213p.

What should U.S. do in Indo-China. JFK vs. Knowland. May 15, 1954. 33 For. Policy Bull. 4.

DOCUMENTARY SOURCES

Aggression from the north—the record of North Viet-Nam's campaign to conquer South Viet-Nam. 1965. 52 Dep't State Bull. 404–27.

Ambekar, G. V. and Divekar, D. V., eds. Documents on China's relations with south and south-east Asia (1949–62). London, Allen & Unwin. 1964. 491p.

American policy in Asia. 1961. Docs. Am. For. Relations 280–336; 1962:273–300; 1963:273–324.

Committee for Coordination of Investigations of the Lower Mekong Basin. Annual reports to the United Nations economic commission for Asia and the far east.

Economic and social aspects of lower Mekong development: a report by Gilbert F. White, Harold B. Dunkerley, Egbert de Vries and John V. Krutilla. Jan. 1962.

Communique of the 28th session on May 10–11, 1965. (Doc. of the U.N. Economic and Social Council E/CN–11/WRD/MY G/L–149 Rev. 1)

Conlon Associates, Ltd. United States foreign policy: Asia. Studies prepared at the request of the Committee on foreign relations, U.S. Senate. No. 5. Washington, Gov't Print. Off. 1959. 157p. (Comm. print 86–1)

East and southeast Asia. 1960. Docs. Am. For. Relations 416–57.

The far east, south and southeast Asia. 1956. Am. For. Policy Current Docs. (Dep't of State pub. 6811) 744–863.

1958:1109–1251.
1959:1144–1256.
1960:653–57.

The far east and southeast Asia.   1954 Docs. For. Relations 256–372.
  1955:294–341.
  1956:384–420.
  1957:315–74.
  1958:410–90.
  1959:431–65.
France.   Treaties, etc. 1947–54. (Auriol) Accords franco-viêtnamiens du 8
  mars 1949. Conventions d'application. La présente publication est faite
  d'accord parlies entre le gouvernement du Viêtnam et le Haut Commis-
  sariat de France en Indochine. Saigon. 1950. 258p.
N. S. Khrushchev's speech at a Soviet-Vietnamese friendship meeting in Moscow June 28, 1961 (in Khrushchev, N. S., The Soviet stand on Germany.
  N.Y., 1961, pp.63–73)
U.S. Congress.   House. Comm. on Foreign Affairs.
  (83.1) Report of the special study mission to Pakistan, India, Thailand
  and Indochina.   Washington, Gov't Print. Off. 1955. 104p.
  (83.2) Special study mission to southeast Asia and the Pacific: report by
  Hon. Walter H. Judd, chairman and others.   Gov't Print. Off. 1954.
  107p.
U.S. Congress.   Senate. Comm. on Foreign Relations.
  Report on Indochina: report of Mike Mansfield on a study mission to
    Vietnam, Cambodia, Laos.   Washington, Gov't Print. Off. 1954. 48p.
  (84.1) The southeast Asia collective defense treaty: hearing, Nov. 11,
    1954–Jan. 11, 1955, on executive K (83d Cong., 2d sess.).   Gov't Print.
    Off. 1954/55. 2pts.
  (84.1) The southeast Asia collective defense treaty: report on Executive
    K (83d Cong., 2d sess.) Jan. 25, 1955.   Gov't Print. Off. 1955. 19p.
  Vietnam, Cambodia and Laos; report by Senator Mike Mansfield.   Gov't
    Print. Off. 1955. 19p.
  Situation in Vietnam.   Gov't Print. Off. 1960. 2v.
  United States aid program in Vietnam.   Gov't Print. Off. 1960. 60p.
  (89.1) Background information relating to southeast Asia and Vietnam.
    Gov't Print. Off. 1965. 138p.
U.S. Department of State.   American foreign policy; basic documents
  1950–55. Washington, Gov't Print. Off. 1957. 2v.
U.S. Department of State.   Div. of Research for Far East. Political align-
  ments of Vietnamese nationalists. Washington. 1949. 176p.
U.S. Department of State.   Office of Intelligence and Research. Outline of
  basic treaty relationships between France and the Associated States of
  Indochina. Washington. 1952. 24p.
U.S. Department of State.   Office of Public Services.
  Aggression from the north; the record of North Viet-Nam's campaign to
    conquer South Viet-Nam.   Washington. 1965. 64p. (U.S. Dep't of State.
    Far Eastern series 130)
  A threat to the peace: North Vietnam's efforts to conquer South Vietnam.
    Pts. I and II. Washington. 1961. 102p. (Dep't of State pub. 7308. Far
    Eastern series 110)
U.S. Department of State.   Office of Strategic Services. Research and Anal-
  ysis Branch. Territorial conflicts between Thailand and French Indochina.
  1945. 150p.

U.S. Treaties, etc. 1961–(Kennedy). Amity and economic relations. Treaty between the United States of America and Viet-Nam signed at Saigon April 3, 1961. Washington, Gov't Print. Off. 1962. 25p.

United Nations. Fact-Finding Mission to South Viet-Nam. Report. Subcom. to investigate the administration of the internal security act and other internal security laws of the Comm. on the judiciary of the U.S. Senate. Washington. 1964. 324p.

UNITED NATIONS DOCUMENTS
Cambodia and Viet-Nam

General Assembly

Statements in Plenary (24 to 27 September 1962, A/PV.1129 to 1134: Official Records, 17th Session).

Statements in Plenary (25 and 27 September 1963, A/PV.1215 and 1218: Official Records, 18th Session).

Security Council

Communications from Cambodia concerning aggression by U.S. and Viet-Nam (16 April and 13 May 1964, S/5666 and S/5697: Official Records, 19th Year).

Communication in reply from Viet-Nam (26 May 1964, S/5724: Official Records, 19th Year).

Meetings to discuss situation (19 May to 4 June 1964, S/PV. 1118–1126: Official Records, 19th Year).

Resolution concerning Mission to Cambodia and Viet-Nam (4 June 1964, S/5741: Official Records, 19th Year).

Report of Council Mission (S/5832 and Corr. 1: Official Records, 19th Year).

Communication from U.S. on impartial international investigation (14 August 1964, S/5894: Official Records, 19th Year).

Communication from Viet-Nam on Mission Report (27 August 1964, S/5921: Official Records, 19th Year).

Communication from Cambodia on Mission Report (9 September and 30 November 1964, S/5952 and S/6092: Official Records, 19th Year).

Communication from Cambodia transmitting Report of International Commission for Supervision and Control in Cambodia (29 September 1964, S/5996: Official Records, 19th Year).

Exchanges between Cambodia and Viet-Nam concerning aggressions (June-November 1964: Official Records, 19th Year).

Communications from Cambodia concerning attacks by Viet-Nam and U.S. (January, March, April, May, August 1965: Official Records, 20th Year (to be published)).

Communication from Cambodia concerning proposed Observer Mission (18 August 1965, S/6640: Official Records, 20th Year (to be published)).

Comunication from U.S. concerning U.S. position (30 July 1965, S/6575: Official Records, 20th year (to be published)).

Viet-Nam Situation (Complaint by U.S.)

Security Council

Communications from U.S. and Republic of Viet-Nam concerning armed attacks by Democratic Republic of Vietnam (4 and 15 August 1964, S/5849 and S/5906: Official Records, 19th Year).

Meetings to discuss situation (5 and 7 August 1964, S/PV. 1140–1141: Official Records, 19th Year).

Communications from U.S.S.R. and U.S. concerning use of gas by U.S. forces (27 March and 2 April 1965, S/6260 and S/6270: Official Records, 20th Year (to be published)).

Communications from U.S. concerning U.S. policy on Viet-Nam and South East Asia (9 April and 30 July 1965, S/6278 and S/6575 and Corr.1: Official Records, 20th Year (to be published)).

Communications from U.S.S.R. and Australia, and U.S.S.R. and New Zealand, concerning decision to send troops to South Viet-Nam (15 May and 1 June 1965 and 14 and 16 June 1965, S/6363 and S/6399, S/6435 and S/6449: Official Records, 20th Year (to be published)).

General Assembly

Statements in Plenary (22 and 25 September 1961 A/PV. 1011 and 1013: Official Records, 16th Session).

Statements in Plenary (20 September to 8 October 1962, A/PV. 1125 to 1145: Official Records, 17th Session).

Statements in Plenary (23 September to 17 October 1963, A/PV. 1211 to 1244: Official Records, 18th Session).

West New Guinea

General Assembly

Indonesian request for inclusion in agenda, with explanatory memorandum (17 August 1954, A/2694: Official Records, 9th Session).

Reports of General and 1st Committee; draft Resolution A/2733, A/2831: Official Records, 9th Session).

Discussions in Plenary (24 September to 10 December 1954, A/PV.477 to 509: Official Records, 9th Session).

Reports of General and 1st Committees; Resolution (A/2980 and A/2985, A/3093; Resolution 915; Official Records, 10th Session).

Discussions in Plenary (23 September to 16 December 1955, A/PV. 520 to 559: Official Records, 10th Session).

Reports of General and 1st Committees; draft Resolution (A/3350, A/3565: Official Records, 11th Session).

Discussions in Plenary (15 November 1956 to 28 February 1957, A/PV. 578 to 664,: Official Records, 11th Session).

Reports of General and 1st Committees; draft Resolution (A/3670, A/3757: Official Records, 12th Session).

Discussions in Plenary (20 September to 29 November 1957, A/PV. 682 to 724: Official Records, 12th Session).

Report of Secretary-General summarizing general trends in the territory (A/3807: Official Records, 13th Session).

Statements in Plenary (18 September to 7 October 1958, A/PV. 749 to 774: Official Records, 13th Session).

Statements in Plenary (26 September to 10 October 1960, A/PV. 871 to 897: Official Records, 15th Session).

Statements in Plenary (26 September to 10 October 1961, A/PV. 1016 to 1032: Official Records, 16th Session).

Documents relating to future development of the territory (7 October 1961, A/4915; 27 October 1961, A/4944; 2 November 1961, A/4954: Official Records, 16th Session).

Draft Resolutions (A/L.354 and Rev.1, Rev.1/Corr.1; A/L.367 and Add. 1–4, Rev. 1; A/L.368: Official Records, 16th Session).

Discussions in Plenary (6 to 27 November 1961, A/PV.1047 to 1066: Official Records, 16th Session).

Request for inclusion in agenda of Netherlands-Indonesia Agreement of 15 August 1962 (A/5170 and Corr. 1, Add.1: Official Records, 17th Session).

Discussions in Plenary (20 September to 14 December 1962, A/PV. 1125 to 1193: Official Records, 17th Session).

Resolution 1752 (Official Records, 17th Session).

Report by Secretary-General (A/5578: Official Records, 18th Session).

Discussions in Plenary (23 September to 6 November 1963, A/PV. 1211 to 1255: Official Records, 18th Session).

Annual Summaries of Information transmitted by Netherlands (A/2655, A/2896, A/3112/Add.2, A/3608, A/3815, A/4048/Add.12, A/4367, A/4758: Official Records, 9th to 16th Sessions).

Security Council

Exchanges between Netherlands, Indonesia and Secretary-General relating to incidents in the territory (January, May, August 1962, S/5062, S/5123, S/5124, S/5126, S/5128, S/5135, S/5155, S/5157: Official Records, 17th Year).

Text of Netherlands-Indonesia Agreement of 15 August 1962 (S/5169: Official Records, 17th Year).

Malaysia
Creation; Peace and Security

August 1963. U.N. Malaysia Mission. Report to Secretary-General and related Annexes. (Unpublished).

14 September 1963. Final Conclusions of Secretary-General. (Release).

General Assembly

Statements in Plenary (17 September to 11 October 1963, A/PV. 1206 to 1239: Official Records, 18th Session).

Letter from Philippines concerning statements on establishment (15 October 1963, A/5574: Official Records, 18th Session).

Security Council

Letter from Malaysia requesting meeting to consider situation arising out of aggression by Indonesia (3 September 1964, S/5930: Official Records, 19th Year).

Letter from Malaysia transmitting document "Indonesian involvement in Eastern Malaysia" (11 September 1964, S/5966: Official Records, 19th Year).

Various letters from Malaysia alleging attacks by Indonesian forces (September to December 1964: Official Records, 19th Year).

Meetings to discuss situation, and draft Resolution (9 to 17 September 1964, S/PV. 1144 to 1152; S/5973: Official Records, 19th Year).

Various letters from Malaysia concerning Indonesian threats and incidents (January, March, May 1965: Official Records, 20th Year (to be published)).

Thailand Situation

Security Council

Communication from Thailand requesting consideration of threatening situation (29 May 1954, S/3220: Official Records, 9th Year).
Draft Resolution (S/3229: Official Records, 9th Year).
Meetings to discuss situation (3 to 18 June 1954, S/PV. 672 to 674: Official Records, 9th Year).

Laos Situation

General Assembly

Statements in Plenary (17 September to 7 October 1959, A/PV. 797 to 824: Official Records, 14th Session).
Statements in Plenary (29 September to 17 October 1960, A/PV. 877 to 906: Official Records, 15th Session).
Statements in Plenary (22 September to 16 October 1961, A/PV. 1011 to 1037: Official Records, 16th Session).
Statements in Plenary (26 September to 4 October 1962, A/PV. 1132 to 1142: Official Records, 17th Session).
Statements in Plenary (20 September to 17 October 1963, A/PV. 1210 to 1244: Official Records, 18th Session).

Security Council

Communication from Laos referring to aggression by Democratic Republic of Viet-Nam (4 September 1959, S/4212: Official Records, 14th Year).
Meetings to consider situation and procedural questions (7 September 1959, S/PV. 847, 848: Official Records, 14th Year).
Resolution appointing subcommittee (7 September 1959, S/4214: Official Records, 14th Year).
Report of subcommittee (3 November 1959, S/4236: Official Records, 14th Year).
Report of Special Representative of Secretary-General (17 December 1959).

Cambodia-Thailand Situation

General Assembly

Statements in Plenary (24 September to 5 October 1962, A/PV. 1129 to 1144: Official Records, 17th Session).
Statements in Plenary (25 September to 8 October 1963, A/PV. 1215 to 1233: Official Records, 18th Session).

Security Council

Communications from Cambodia and Thailand concerning Thai movements (29 November and 8 December 1958, S/4121 and S/4126: Official Records, 13th Year).
Announcement of appointment of Secretary-General's Representative (Press Release, 22 December 1958).

Communications from Thailand and Cambodia concerning assistance rendered by Representative (6 and 9 February 1959, S/4158 and S/4161: Official Records, 14th Year).

Communication from Secretary-General on appointment of his Personal Representative (18 December 1962, S/5220: Official Records, 17th Year).

Communication from Secretary-General on extension of mission of Personal Representative (9 December 1963, S/5479: Official Records, 18th Year).

Communication from Secretary-General on withdrawal of Personal Representative (9 November 1964, S/6040: Official Records, 19th Year).

Communication from Cambodia alleging Thai violation of territorial waters (31 December 1964, S/6132: Official Records, 19th Year).

Exchanges between Cambodia and Thailand concerning violations of borders (January, February, June 1965: Official Records, 20th Year (to be published)).

Admission to Membership

CAMBODIA, LAOS

General Assembly

Reports of General and Ad Hoc Political Committees (A/2733 and A/2793: Official Records, 9th Session).

Discussions in Plenary (24 September to 23 November 1954, A/PV. 476 to 501: Official Records, 9th Session).

Resolution 817 (Official Records, 9th Session).

Report of Ad Hoc Political Committee (A/3079: Official Records, 10th Session).

Discussions in Plenary (8 to December 1955, A/PV. 552 to 560: Official Records, 10th Session).

Resolution 918 (Official Records, 10th Session).

Resolution 995 (Official Records, 10th Session).

Security Council

Meetings to consider Resolutions 817 (XIX) and 918 (X) and Resolution (10 to 14 December 1955, S/PV. 701 to 705 and S/3509: Official Records, 10th Year).

VIET-NAM

General Assembly

Report of Ad Hoc Political Committee (A/2793: Official Records, 9th Session).

Discussion in Plenary (23 November 1954, A/PV. 501: Official Records, 9th Session).

Resolution 817 (Official Records, 9th Session).

Report of Ad Hoc Political Committee (A/3079: Official Records, 10th Session).

Discussions in Plenary (8 to 15 December 1955, A/PV. 552 to 556: Official Records, 10th Session).

Report of Special Political Committee (A/3519: Official Records, 11th Session).

Discussion in Plenary (28 February 1957, A/PV. 663: Official Records, 11th Session).
Resolution 1017 B (Official Records, 11th Session).
Report of Special Political Committee (A/3712: Official Records, 12th Session).
Special Report—Security Council (A/3662: Official Records, 12th Session).
Discussions in Plenary (19 September to 25 October 1957, A/PV. 680 to 709: Official Records, 12th Session).
Resolution 1144 B (Official Records, 12th Session).

Security Council

Draft Resolution on admission (S/3506: Official Records, 10th Year).
Meeting to consider draft resolution (13 December 1955, S/PV. 704: Official Records, 10th Year).
Draft Resolution on admission (S/3884: Official Records, 12th Year).
Meetings to consider draft resolution (9 September 1957, S/PV. 789–790: Official Records, 12th Year).
Draft Resolution on admission (S/4130; Rev. 1: Official Records, 13th Year).
Meetings to consider draft resolution (9 December 1958, S/PV. 842–843: Official Records, 13th Year).

MALAYA
Security Council

Draft Resolution on admission (S/3876: Official Records, 12th Year).
Meeting of Security Council to consider draft resolution (5 September 1957, S/PV. 786: Official Records, 12th Year).

General Assembly

Discussion in Plenary (17 September 1957, A/PV. 678: Official Records, 12th Session).
Resolution 1134 (Official Records, 12th Session).

MALAYSIA
General Assembly

Resolution approving Report of Credentials Committee (Official Records, 18th Session).

Withdrawal from Membership

INDONESIA
General Assembly

Communication from Indonesia concerning withdrawal (20 January 1965, A/5857 and Corr. 1: Official Records, 19th Session).
Communication from Malaysia in reply (22 January 1965, A/5861: Official Records, 19th Session).
Communication from Secretary-General concerning Indonesia's withdrawal (A/5899: Official Records, 19th Session).
Communications from U.K. and Italy concerning continuing obligations (8 March and 13 May 1965, A/5910 and A/5914: Official Records, 19th Session).

Case of the Temple of Preah Vihear
International Court of Justice

Case concerning the Temple of Preah Vihear
(Cambodia v. Thailand): I.C.J. Pleadings, 1962, Vols. I and II; Order of 5
December 1959, I.C.J. Reports 1959, p. 286; Order of 10 June 1960, I.C.J.
Reports 1960, p. 180; Preliminary Objections, Judgment of 26 May 1961,
I.C.J. Reports 1961, p. 17; Merits, Judgment of 15 June 1962, I.C.J. Re-
ports 1962, p. 6.

Chinese (Kuomintang) Troops in Burma
General Assembly

Complaint by Burma (25 March 1953, A/2375: Official Records, 7th Session).
Report of 1st Committee (Official Records, 7th Session).
Discussion in Plenary (23 April 1953, A/PV. 428: Official Records, 7th Session).
Resolution 707 (Official Records, 7th Session).
Communication by Burma concerning supporting documents (29 June
1953, A/2423: Official Records, 8th Session).
Report by Burma (31 August 1953, A/2468: Official Records, 8th Session).
Communications by China and Burma concerning situation (26 and 28 Oc-
tober 1953, A/C.1/L.69 and L.70: Official Records, 8th Session).
Communication by U.S. concerning statement by Joint Military Committee
(29 October 1953, A/C.1/L.71: Official Records, 8th Session).
Report by Joint Military Committee (A/C.1/L.89: Official Records, 8th
Session).
Report of 1st Committee (A/2607: Official Records, 8th Session).
Discussion in Plenary (8 December 1953, A/PV. 470: Official Records, 8th
Session).
Resolution 717 (Official Records, 8th Session).
Communications from China and Burma (17 March and 1 April 1954,
A/2643 and A/2644: Official Records, 9th Session).
Report by Burma (27 September 1954, A/2739: Official Records, 9th Session).
Report by Joint Military Committee (28 September 1954, A/2740: Official
Records, 9th Session).
Report of Ad Hoc Political Committee (A/2762: Official Records, 9th
Session).
Discussion in Plenary (29 October 1954, A/PV. 496: Official Records, 9th
Session).
Resolution 815 (Official Records, 9th Session).

Refugees in Cambodia

Annual Report of U.N. Commissioner for Refugees (E/3506 and Corr. 1
and Add. 1: Official Records of the General Assembly, 16th Session,
Supplement No. 11).

Violation of Human Rights in South Vietnam
General Assembly

Communications by 14 countries concerning violations of human rights (4
and 13 September 1963, A/5489 and Add. 1–3: Official Records, 18th
Session).

Exchange of communications between Secretary-General and President of Republic of Vietnam (23 September 1963, A/5542: Official Records, 18th Session).

Report of U.N. Fact-Finding Mission to South Vietnam (7 December 1963, A/5630: Official Records, 18th Session).

Discussions in Plenary (7, 8 and 11 October and 13 December 1963, A/PV. 1232, 1234, 1239, 1280: Official Records, 18th Session).

CHINA AND COMMUNISM IN SOUTHEAST ASIA

Barnett, A. Doak, ed.
  Communist China and Asia. New York, Harper. 1960.
  Communist strategies in Asia; a comparative analysis of government and parties. New York, Praeger. 1963. 203p. (*see* Some comparisons between Russian and Chinese models by Donald S. Zagoria and Two revolutionary models Russian and Chinese by Robert North)
  The roots of Mao's strategy (in Pentony, De Vere Edwin, ed. China, the emerging Red giant: communist foreign policies. San Francisco, Chandler, 1962, 262p.)

Boyd, R. G. Communist China's foreign policy. New York, Praeger. 1962. 147p.

Brimmell, J. H. Communism in south east Asia: a political analysis. London, New York, Oxford Univ. Press. 1959. 415p.

Ch'ên, Jerome. Mao and the Chinese revolution. New York, Oxford Univ. Press. 1965.

Clubb, O. Edmund. The United States and the Sino-Soviet bloc in southeast Asia. Washington, Brookings Institution. 1962. 172p.

Cohen, Arthur A. The Communism of Mao Tse-tung. Chicago, Univ. of Chicago Press. 1964. 224p.

Dutt, Vidya Prakash. China's foreign policy 1958–62. New York, Asia Publishing House. 1964. 336p.

Fall, Bernard B. French communists and party line (with bibliography). 1955. 33 For. Aff. 499–510.

Fisher, C. A. The Chinese threat to south-east Asia—fact or fiction. 1964. 51 Royal Central Asian Soc'y 251–67.

Hammarskjöld Forums, Dec. 2, 1963. The international position of Communist China; background papers and proceedings of the fifth Hammarskjöld forum, by O. Edmund Clubb and Eustace Seligman. Lyman M. Tondel, jr., editor. Dobbs Ferry, N.Y., Published for The Association of the Bar of the City of New York by Oceana. 1965. 116p.

Harris, Richard. Communism and Asia; illusions and misconceptions. 1963. 39 Int'l Aff. 13–23.

Kennedy, Malcolm Duncan. A history of Communism in east Asia. New York, Praeger. 1957. 556p.

Kroef, Justus M. van der.
  Indonesian communism's expansionist role in southeast Asia. 1965. 20 Int'l J. 189–205.
  The Sino-Indonesian partnership. Summer 1964. 8 (2) Orbis.

McConaughy, John B. Communist strategy in southeast Asia. May 1962. 42 Military Rev. 39–53.

Michigan University. Survey Research Center. The American public's view of U.S. policy toward China; a report prepared for the Council on foreign relations. New York, Council on Foreign Relations. 1964. 61p.

Purcell, Victor. The Chinese in southeast Asia. 2d. ed. London, Oxford Univ. Press. 1965. 640p. (Royal Institute of International Affairs, Chatham House Pubs.)

Sacks, Milton. The strategy of communism in southeast Asia. 1950. 23 Pac. Aff. 227–47.

Schleicher, C. P. The communist push into south Asia. 1963. 39 Inst. World Aff., Proc. 194–201.

Shen-yu Dai. Peking and Indochina's destiny. Sept. 1954. 7 W. Pol. Q. 346–68.

Tang Tsou. Mao Tse-Tung and peaceful coexistence. 1964. 8 Orbis 36–51.

Townsend, James R. Communist China: the new protracted war. Jan. 1965. 5 (1) Asian Survey.

Trager, Frank Ned. Marxism in southeast Asia: a study of four countries. Stanford, Stanford Univ. Press. 1959. 381p.

U.S. Congress. House. Comm. on Foreign Affairs (89.1) Report on Sino-Soviet conflict and its implications by the subcom. on the far east and the Pacific. Washington, Gov't Print. Off. 1965. 412p.

SEATO

Ball, M. Margaret. SEATO and subversion. March 1959. 11 Pol. Sci. (N.Z.) 25–39.

Ball, W. Macmahon. A political re-examination of SEATO. Winter 1958. 12 Int'l Org. 17–25.

Braibanti, Ralph. The southeast Asia collective defense treaty. 1957. 30 Pac. Aff. 321–41.

Dulles, John Foster. Collective defense for southeast Asia. 1954. 31 Dep't State Bull. 391–96.

Fistié, P. Les relations entre membres de l'O.T.A.S.E. face aux nouveaux états du sud-est asiatique (in Duroselle, J.B. et Mayriat, J. La communauté internationale face aux jeunes états. Paris, A. Colin, 1964, pp.99–160)

Gordon, B. K. Problems of regional cooperation in southeast Asia. 1964. 16 World Pol. 222–53.

Kennedy, D. E. The scope for collective security in southeast Asia. 1964. 20 World Today 440–48.

Lerche, Charles O. The United States, Great Britain and SEATO: a case study in the *fait accompli*. 1956. 18 J. Politics 459–78.

Lockwood, Rupert. From SEATO to "Pacific community." June 1964. Int'l Aff. 37–40.

Miller, August G., jr. SEATO—segment of collective security. Feb. 1960. 86 U.S. Naval Inst. Proc. 50–62.

Modelski, J. A.
Indochina and SEATO. March 1959. 13 Austl. Outlook 27–54.
The south-east Asia treaty organization. May 1959. 5 Austl. J. Pol. & Hist. 24–40.

Modelski, G. SEATO: six studies. Melbourne, Cheshire. 1962. 302p.

Nuechterlein, D. E. Thailand and SEATO—a ten year appraisal. 1964. 4 Asian Survey 1174–81.

Oliver, A. S. B.   SEATO; the Manila treaty and western policy in south-east Asia. London, Royal Institute of International Affairs, 1956. 24p.

Padelford, Norman J.   SEATO and peace in southeast Asia. 1960. 38 Current Hist. 95–101.

Peffer, Nathaniel.   Regional security in southeast Asia. 1954. 8 Int'l Org. 311–15.

Ravenholt, Albert.   SEATO and Indonesia. March 29, 1958. Am. Univs. Field Staff. 7p.

Reinhardt, G. Frederick.   What SEATO means to the United States. 1959. 40 Dep't State Bull. 395–98.

Royal Institute of International Affairs.   Collective defense in south east Asia: the Manila treaty and its implications. London. 1956. 197p.

SEATO council of ministers meets at Manila.   1964. 50 Dep't State Bull. 690–93.

SEATO: 1954–1964.   Bangkok, South-East Asia Treaty Organization. 1964. 81p.

Second annual report of the south-east Asia treaty organization.   1957. 36 Dep't State Bull. 496–503.

Southeast Asia collective defense treaty.   Council representatives. Report 1st–March 1956–. Washington, Gov't Print. Off.

Southeast Asia Treaty Organization.   Council. SEATO; record of partnership, 1957–58. 1958. 33p.

Thomas, M. Ladd.   A critical appraisal of SEATO. 1957. 10 W. Pol. Q. 926–36.

Tran-Tam.   Le problème de l'O.T.A.S.E. 1964. 42 Rev. Droit Int'l de Sci. Diplomatiques et Politiques 134–64.

U.S. Department of State.
    The Bangkok conference and the Manila pact powers.   Feb. 23–25, 1955. Washington, Gov't Print. Off. 1955. 45p.
    Southeast Asia treaty organization: first annual report of the council representatives.   March 1956. Gov't Print. Off. 1956. 27p.

U.S. Treaties, etc. (Eisenhower).   The southeast Asia collective defense treaty and the protocol thereto: message from the President of the United States transmitting the southeast Asia collective defense treaty and the protocol thereto, signed at Manila on Sept. 8, 1954. 1954. 13p. (83d Cong., 2d sess., S. Exec. K)

GENEVA AGREEMENTS

Bolles, B.   Coexistence at stake in Geneva. May 15, 1964. 33 For. Pol. Bull. 4.

Czyzak, J. J. and Salans, C. F.   The international conference on the settlement of the Laotian question and the Geneva agreements of 1962. 1963. 57 Am. J. Int'l L. 300–17.

Declaration on the neutrality of Laos and protocol signed at Geneva July 23, 1962.   47 Dep't State Bull. 259–63.

Documents relating to the discussion of Korea and Indo-China at the Geneva conference.   London, H.M.S.O. 1954. (Cmd. 9186, misc. no. 16)

Geneva, Conference 1954.
    Conférence de Genève sur l'Indochine (8 mai-21 juillet 1954).   Procès-

216

verbaux des séances, propositions, documents finaux. Paris, Impr. Nationale. 1955. 470p.

Documents relating to the discussion of Korea and Indochina at the Geneva conference April 27-June 15, 1954. London, H.M.S.O. 1954. 168p.

The final declaration of the Geneva conference on Indochina and Chou En-lai's statement at the final session of the Geneva conference. n.p. 1954. 7p.

Further documents relating to the discussion of Indochina at the Geneva conference June 16–July 2, 1954. London, H.M.S.O. 1954. 45p. (Cmd. 9239)

Final declaration of Indo-China. Aug. 15, 1954. 20 Vital Speeches 671.

Great Britain. Foreign Office. Vietnam and the Geneva agreements; documents concerning the discussion between representatives of Her Majesty's government and the Union of Soviet Socialist Republics held in London in April and May 1956. London, H.M.S.O. 1956. 11p.

International Conference for the Settlement of the Laotian Question. Geneva, 1961–62.

Declaration on the neutrality of Laos and protocol. 1962. 2 Indian Yb. Int'l L. 135–42.

Declaration and protocol on the neutrality of Laos, Geneva, July 23, 1962. London, H.M.S.O. 1963. 163p. (Grt. Brit. treaty series 1963, no.27)

Statement by Secretary of State Rusk. May 17, 1961 (in Documents on American foreign relations 1961. New York, 1962, pp.311–17)

Kennedy, John F. Declaration on the neutrality of Laos and protocol signed at Geneva. 1962. 47 Dep't State Bull. 259–63.

Protocol to the declaration on the neutrality of Laos, July 23, 1962. 1963. 1962. Doc. Am. For. Relations 288–93.

Purcell, Victor. The Laos conference of 1962. 1963. 17 Yb. World Aff. 47–60.

Snow, Edgar. Red China at Geneva. Jan. 9, 1954. 178 Nation 21.

Text of the Geneva agreement on Laos 1962. 1962. 161 Brit. Survey.

Ton That Thien. The Geneva agreements and peace prospects in Vietnam. 1956. 12 India Q. 375–88.

War in Vietnam and the 1964 Geneva conference. Oct. 1964. 14 External Aff. (N.Z.) 3.

What all sides say about Indo-China truce . . . U.S. News, July 30, 1954, pp.85–94.

CAMBODIA

Buchanan, Keith. Cambodia between Peking and Paris. 1964. 16 Monthly Rev. 480–92.

Cambodge. Gouvernement Royal. Livre jaune sur les revendications de l'independance du Cambodge, vol. 1. Paris, Impr. Centrale Commerciale, 1953; Vol.2, Phnom Penh, Impr. du Palais Royal, 1954.

Canchy, de. Le Cambodge et la neutralité au sud-est asiatique. Oct. 1964. Rev. Militaire d'Information 62–69.

Herz, Martin. A short history of Cambodia from the days of Angkor to the present. New York, Praeger. 1958. 141p.

International Commission for Supervision and Control in Cambodia. 1st progress report, Jan. 1, 1955–. London, H.M.S.O. 1955–.

217

Leifer, Michael.
  Cambodia and her neighbors. 1961/62. 34 Pac. Aff. 361–74.
  Cambodia and SEATO. 1962. 17 Int'l J. 122–32.
  Cambodia—in search of neutrality. Jan. 1963. 3 Asian Survey 55–60.
  Cambodia looks to China. Jan. 1964. 20 World Today 26–31.
  Cambodia—the politics of accommodation. 1964. 4 Asian Survey 674–79.
Morice, J. L'organisation judiciaire du Cambodge: la renaissance d'une
  justice nationale. 1962. 72 Penant (no. 690) 7–35.
Sihanouk, Norodom.
  Cambodia neutral: the dictate of, necessity. 1958. 36 For. Aff. 582–86.
  La monarchie cambodgienne et la croisade royale pour l'independance.
    Phnom Penh, Imprimerie Rasmey. 1961. 104p.
Smith, Roger M. Cambodia's foreign policy. Ithaca, Cornell Univ. Press.
  1965. 273p.
Steinberg, David J. Cambodia; its people, its society, its culture . . . New
  Haven, HRAF Press. 1959. 351p.
Szaz, Zolton M. Cambodia's foreign policy. 1955. 24 Far E. Survey 151–58.

LAOS

Burchett, Wilfred G. The furtive war; the United States in Vietnam and
  Laos. New York, International Publishers. 1963. 224p.
Bureau of Social Science Research. Information and attitudes in Laos.
  Washington. 1959. 122p.
Champassak, Sisouk Na. Storm over Laos; a contemporary history. New
  York, Praeger. 1961. 202p.
Chicago. University. Area handbook on Laos. General editor: Norton S.
  Ginsburg. Editor, Gerald C. Hickey. Chicago, Univ. of Chicago for the
  Human Relations Area Files. 1955. 328p.
Dommen, Arthur J.
  Conflict in Laos. London, Pall Mall Press. 1965. 338p.
  Neutralization experiment in Laos. 1965. 48 Current Hist. 89–94, 115.
Fall, Bernard B. The international relations of Laos. March 1957. 30 Pac.
  Aff. 22–34.
14 Nation declaration and protocol on Laos. 1962. 43 Current Hist. 234–38.
Gross, Leo. The question of Laos and the double veto in the security coun-
  cil. 1960. 54 Am. J. Int'l L. 118–31.
Halpern, Abraham Meyer and Fredman, H. B. Communist strategy in
  Laos. Santa Monica, Calif., Rand Corp. 1960. 162p. (Rand corp. research
  memo. RM–2561)
Halpern, Joel M. Government, politics and social structure in Laos: a
  study of tradition and innovation. New Haven, Yale University, South-
  east Asia Studies. 1964. 184p.
Human Relations Area Files. Laos; its people, its society, its culture. New
  Haven, HRAF Press. 1960. 294p.
The independent state of Laos. 1957. 13 World Today 432–41.
International Commission for Supervision and Control in Laos. First in-
  terim report, Aug. 11, 1954–Dec. 31, 1954–. London, H.M.S.O.
Jonas, Anne M. and Tanham, George K. Laos: a phase in cyclic regional
  revolution. 1961. 5 Orbis 64–73.

Jones, P. H. M. Laos in Vietnam's shadow? 1964. 43 Far E. Econ. Rev. 517–21.
Karnow, S. Laos—the settlement that settled nothing. April 25, 1963. 28 Reporter 34–37.
Kumar, L. C. The crisis in Laos. 1964. 13 For. Aff. Rep. 161–64.
Laos: cold war battleground; background summary; chronology and comment: significant statements; land and people by the editors of Deadline data on world affairs. 1963. 1 (4) On Record 1–64.
Le Bar , Frank M. and Adrienne Suddard, eds. Laos: its people, its society, its culture. New Haven, HRAF Press. 1960. 294p.
Mavrakis, M. C. L'affaire du Laos 1954–62. July 23, 1963. 3011 Doc. Francaise. Notes et Etudes Docs.
Neutrality of Laos. 1962. 33 (7) Current Notes on Int'l Aff. 21–27.
Pace, Eric. Laos: continuing crisis. 1964. 43 For. Aff. 64–74.
Rusk, Dean.
  Laos and Viet-Nam—a prescription for peace. 1964. 50 Dep't State Bull. 886–91.
  Why Laos is critically important. 1964. 51 Dep't State Bull. 3–5.
Sasorith, Katay D. Le Laos; son évolution politique, sa place dans l'Union francaise. Paris, Editions Berger-Levrault. 1953. 155p.
Simmonds, E. H. S.
  Breakdown in Laos. 1964. 20 World Today 285–92.
  Laos—a renewal of crisis. 1964. 4 Asian Survey 680–85.
  Power politics in Laos. 1962. 18 World Today 514–22.
Sithibourn, Sithat. Biographies des personalités du royaume du Laos. Vientiane, Edition Lao Presse. 1960.
Text of the report of the International control commission, June 2, 1962. 1962. 12 (6) External Aff. Rev. 28–32.
Tong, A. Le parti communiste laotien. Jan. 1965. 17 Est et Ouest 19–24.
Trager, Frank N. Laos and the defense of southeast Asia. 1963. 7 Orbis 550–82.
U.S. Department of State. The situation in Laos. Washington. 1959. 23p.
Urbaniak, J. The agreement on neutrality of Laos. 1962. 15 (9) Sprawy Miedzynarodowe 48–57.
Warner, D. The catastrophic non-war in Laos. June 18, 1964. 30 Reporter 21–24.
Yegorov, M. Some results of the Laos conference. 1962. 8 (9) Int'l Aff. (Moscow) 49–55.

THAILAND

Ayal, Eliezer Ben-zvi.
  Public policies in Thailand under the constitutional regime—a case study of an underveloped country (dissertation, Cornell, 1961). 364p. (Summary in 22 Dissertation Abstracts 3015–16, March 1962)
  Some crucial issues in Thailand's economic development. 1961. 34 Pac. Aff. 157–64.
Blanchard, Wendell, ed. Thailand, its people, its society, its culture. New Haven, HRAF Press. 1958. 528p.
Chakrabongse, Chula. The political and economic background in Thailand. 1955. 42 Royal Central Asian J. 116–27.

Darling, Frank C.

American policy in Thailand. 1962. 15 W. Pol. Q. 93–110.

Thailand and the United States. Introd. by Hans J. Morgenthau. Washington, Public Affairs Press. 1965. 243p.

Indiana University. Institute of Training for Public Service. Problems of politics and administration in Thailand. Bloomington, Indiana University. 1962. 205p.

Insor, D. Thailand; a political, social and economic analysis. New York, Praeger. 1963. 188p.

International Bank for Reconstruction and Development. A public development program for Thailand: report of a mission organized for the IBRD at the request of the government of Thailand. Baltimore, Johns Hopkins Press. 1959. 301p.

Johnson, U. A. Thai-United States cooperation. 1960. 2 Dep't State Bull. 1001–06.

King, J. K. Thailand's bureaucracy and the threat of communist subversion. 1954. 23 Far E. Survey 169–73.

Kroesen, Frederick J. The precarious position of Thailand. Dec. 1964. 44 Military Rev. 60–69.

Sasidhorn, Nobondh. The United States and extraterritoriality in Thailand: some unique aspects of American-Thai relations. 1960. 332p. (Dissertation, Indiana university; Summary in 21 Dissertation Abstracts 665–66, Sept. 1960)

Singh, L. P. Thailand in der internationalen politik. 1964. 19 Europa-Archiv 283–92.

Stanton, E. F. Communist pressures in Thailand. 1960. 38 Current Hist. 102–09.

Vella, Walter Francis. The impact of the west on government in Thailand. Berkeley, Univ. of California Press; 1955. 4 (3) U. Calif. Pub. in Pol. Sci. 317–410.

Wilson, David A. Politics in Thailand. Ithaca, Cornell Univ. Press. 1962. 307p.

Wood, W. A. R. A history of Siam. 2d rev. ed. Bangkok, Barnakich Press. 1933. 300p.

VIETNAM

DEMOCRATIC REPUBLIC OF VIETNAM (North Vietnam)

Avsenev, M. M. Demokraticheskaia respublika Vyetnam. Moskva, Vneshtorgizdat. 1960. 108p.

Burchett, Wilfred G. North of the seventeenth parallel. Delhi, People's Publishing House. 1956. 258p.

Chen, K. North Vietnam in the Sino-Soviet dispute. Sept. 1964. 4 Asian Survey 1023–36.

Fall, Bernard B.

Constitution-writing in a communist state; the new constitution of North Vietnam. 1960. 6 How. L.J. 157–68.

North Viet-Nam's constitution and government. 1960. 33 Pac. Aff. 282–89.

North Viet-Nam's new draft constitution. 1959. 32 Pac. Aff. 178–86.

Le Viet-Minh: la republique démocratique du Viet-Nam, 1945–60. Paris, Armand Colin. 1960. 377p.

The Viet-Minh regime; government and administration in the Democratic
Republic of Vietnam. Ithaca, Southeast Asia Program, Dep't of Far
Eastern Studies, Cornell University. 1954. 143p. (Data paper no. 14,
issued jointly with Institute of Pacific Relations)

Guillermaz, J. and Kerblay, B. H. The question of Sino-Soviet competition over North Vietnam (in International conference on Sino-Soviet bloc
affairs, 3rd, Lake Kawaguchi, 1960. Unity and contradiction: major aspects
of Sino-Soviet relations. New York, 1962, pp.233–47)

Hoang-van-Chi.
From colonialism to communism: a case history of North Vietnam: with
an introd. by P. J. Honey. New York, Praeger. 1964. 252p.
The new class in North Vietnam. Saigon, Cong Dan. 1958.

Honey, P. J.
Communism in North Vietnam: its role in the Sino-Soviet dispute. Cam-
bridge, M.I.T Press. 1963. 207p.
North Vietnam today: profile of a Communist satellite. New York,
Praeger. 1962. 166p.

Huard, Pierre and Durand, Maurice. Connaissance du Viet-Nam. Paris,
Imprimerie Nationale; Hanoi, Ecole Francais d'Extrême-Orient. 1954.

Kux, E. Ho Chi Minh between Moscow and Peking. April 1964. 14 Swiss
Rev. World Aff. 11–14.

Limbourg, Michel. L'économie actuelle du Viet-Nam démocratique.
Hanoi, Editions en Langues Etrangères. 1956.

Nguyen Duy Trinh. Government report on the three year plan of North
Vietnam, 1958–60. New York, U.S. Joint Publications Research Service.
1959. 58p. (JPRS:632D)

North Vietnam: a special survey. Jan/March 1962. China Q. 2–111.

Pagniez, Yvonne. Le Viet Minh et la guerre psychologique. Paris, La Col-
ombe. 1955.

Podkopayev, Ivan I. Demokraticheskaya respublika Vyetnam. Moscow,
Znaniye. 1955.

Salmon, M. Focus on Indo-China. Hanoi, Foreign Languages Publishing
House. 1961. 280p.

Tanham, George K. Communist revolutionary warfare: the Vietminh in
Indochina. New York, Praeger. 1961. 166p.

United States Joint Publications Research Service.
North Vietnam's first five-year plan (1961–65). June 28, 1963. 101p.
(JPRS 19952) (Translated from Nhan Dan, Hanoi, May 3–4, 1963)
Political and military report on North Vietnam. New York—. 108/1—.
Feb. 28, 1958—.

Vietnam (Democratic Republic). Ministry of Foreign Affairs. Press and
Information Dep't. Documents to the implementation of the Geneva
agreements concerning Viet-nam. Ha-noi. 1956. 202p.

Vo Nguyen Giap. People's war, People's army: the Viet Cong insurrection
manual for underdeveloped countries. Foreward by Roger Hilsman. New
York, Praeger. 1962. 217p. (Russian History and World Communism no.
119)

REPUBLIC OF VIETNAM (South Vietnam)

American Friends of Vietnam. A symposium on America's stake in Vietnam.
New York. 1956. 110p.

American University, Washington, D.C. Foreign Areas Studies Division. Area handbook for Vietnam. Washington. 1962. 513p.

Bator, Victor. Vietnam; a diplomatic tragedy. Dobbs Ferry, N.Y., Oceana. 1965. 271p.

Bombwall, K. R. Presidential leadership in the republic of Viet-Nam. 1961. 3 Int'l Studies 147–58.

Bouscaren, Anthony T. The last of the mandarins: Diem of Vietnam. Pittsburgh, Duquesne Univ. Press. 1965. 174p.

Bundy, William P.
  American policy in South Viet-Nam and southeast Asia. Feb. 8, 1965. 52 Dep't State Bull. 168–75.
  A perspective on U.S. policy in Viet-Nam. June 21, 1965. 52 Dep't State Bull. 1001–05.

Burchett, Wilfred G. Vietnam: inside story of the guerilla war. New York, International Publishers. 1965. 253p.

Buttinger, Joseph. The smaller dragon; a political history of Vietnam. New York, Praeger. 1958. 535p.

Buu Hoan. Vietnam: economic consequences of the Geneva peace. 1958. 25 Far E. Econ. Rev. 753–57, 789–90, 839–42.

Can Vietnam be neutralized? April 1964. 4 War/Peace Rep. 3.

Carver. G. A. The real revolution in South Viet Nam. 1965. 43 For. Aff. 387–408.

Critique of United States public position. June 1965. 17 Venture 9.

Devillers, Philippe. The struggle for the unification of Vietnam. Jan/March 1962. China Q. 2–23.

Do Vang Ly. The emergence of Vietnam. Jan. 1958. 7 For. Aff. Rep. (India) 1–19.

Donnell, J. C. National renovation campaigns in Vietnam. 1959. 32 Pac. Aff. 73–88.

Dorsey, John T. Report and recommendations on the reorganization of the presidency of Vietnam. Submitted to the President of the Republic Nov. 15, 1955 by John T. Dorsey, Michigan State University Advisors Team. Saigon? 1955. 17p.

Duncanson, Dennis. Report from South Vietnam. 1964. 51 Royal Central Asian Soc'y J. 43–52.

Fall, Bernard B.
  How chaos occurred. Spring 1964. 19 Int'l J. 139.
  Our options in Vietnam. March 12, 1964. 30 Reporter 17–22.
  The political-religious sects of Viet-Nam. 1955. 28 Pac. Aff. 235–53.
  Problems of freedom in South Vietnam. 1962. 17 Int'l J. 436–40.
  The second Indochina war. 1965. 41 Int'l Aff. 59–73.
  Sociological and psychological aspects of Vietnam's partition. 1964. 18 J. Int'l Aff. 173–86.
  South Viet-Nam at the crossroads. 1964. 19 Int'l J. 139–54.
  South Viet-Nam's internal problems. 1958. 31 Pac. Aff. 241–60.
  The truth about the war U.S. is losing. Sept. 28, 1964. 57 U.S. News & World Report 58–62.
  The two Viet-Nams: a political and military analysis. New York, Praeger. 1963. 493p.

Vietnam—the agonizing reappraisal. 1965. 48 Current Hist. 95–102, 116.
Farmer. Counter-insurgency in Vietnam. Santa Monica, Calif. Dec. 1964. (bibliography)
Fishel, Wesley R.
  Free Vietnam since Geneva. 1959. 49 Yale Rev. 68–79.
  Problems of freedom: South Vietnam since independence. Glencoe, Ill. Free Press. 1961. 233p.
  Vietnam: is victory possible? New York, Foreign Policy Association. 1964. 64p.
Grant, J. A. C. The Viet Nam constitution of 1956. 1958. 52 Am. Pol. Sci. Rev. 437–62.
Hammer, Ellen J.
  Progress report on southern Viet Nam. 1957. 30 Pac. Aff. 221–35.
  South Viet Nam: the limits of political action. 1962. 35 Pac. Aff. 24–36.
Heavner, T. J. C. The Viet-Nam situation. 1963. 49 Dep't State Bull. 393–98.
Henle, H. Das Vietnam-problem. Zehn jahre verfehlter südostasien-politik der U.S.A. 1964. 35 Zeitschrift für Geopolitik 87–111.
Hilsman, Roger. A report on South Viet-Nam. 1962. 47 Dep't State Bull. 526–33.
Honey, P. J.
  The problem of democracy in Vietnam. 1960. 17 World Today 71–79.
  Vietnam. Nov. 1964. 26 (188) Brit. Survey 1–10.
Huard, Pierre and Durand, Maurice. Connaissance du Viet-Nam. Paris, Imprimerie Nationale Ecole Francaise d'Extrême-Orient. 1954. 356p.
Hutton-Williams, B. Viet Nam. 1961. 144 Brit. Survey 1–21.
L'Indochine dix ans après Genève. 16–31 Juillet 1964. Est et Ouest Supp. 1–62.
International Commission for Supervision and Control in Vietnam.
  Interim report 1st/2d—Aug. 11, 1954–Feb. 10, 1955—. London, H.M.S.O.
  Special report to the co-chairmen of the Geneva conference on Indo-China, Saigon, June 2, 1962. 23p. (Great Britain, Parliament. Cmd. 1755)
International commission for supervision and control in Vietnam. 1965. 17 External Aff. (Canada) 114–22.
Isoart, P. J. Le phenomène national Viêtnamien de l'independance unitaire à l'independance fractionnée. Paris, Pichon et Durand-Auzias. 1961. 437p.
Johnson, Harold K. The defense of freedom in Viet Nam. Feb. 8, 1965. 52 Dep't State Bull. 176–80.
Johnson, Lyndon B.
  The nation's commitment in Vietnam. Statement by the President of the United States, July 28, 1965. Washington, Gov't Print. Off. 1965. 4p. (House Doc. 256)
  Tragedy, disappointment in southeast Asia. 1965. 52 Dep't State Bull. 650–52.
  United States Vietnam policy—destroy or build. 1965. 31 Vital Speeches 386–88.
  U.S. reply to 17 nation declaration on Viet Nam conflict. April 23, 1965. 23 Cong. Q. Weekly Rep. 786.
  Viet-Nam: the third face of the war. 1965. 52 Dep't State Bull. 838–41.
  We will stand in Viet-Nam. 1965. 53 Dep't State Bull. 262–65.

Jumper, Roy.   Mandarin bureaucracy and politics in South Viet Nam. 1957.
30 Pac. Aff. 47–58.

Jumper, Roy and Thi Hue Nguyen.   Notes on the political and administrative history of Viet Nam, 1802–1962. Saigon, Michigan State University
Viet Nam Advisory Group. 1962. 227p.

Kennedy, John F.   America's stake in Vietnam (address of 6/1/56). Aug. 1,
1956. 22 Vital Speeches 617.

Kien, N.
Le Sud-Vietnam depuis Dien-Bien-Phu.   Paris, Cahiers Libres. 1963.
Le Viet-Nam depuis 1954.   1961. 34 Ann. Politique et Economique 425–47.

Kroef, Justus M. van der.   Das dilemma der amerikanischen politik in Vietnam. 1965. 20 Europa-Archiv 233–44.

Kuebler, Jeanne.   Political instability in South Viet Nam. May 26, 1965.
Editorial Research Rep. 383–400.

Lansdale, E. G.   Viet Nam: do we understand revolution? 1964. 43 For. Aff.
75–86.

Larson, Don R. and Larson, Arthur.   Vietnam and beyond. Durham, Rule
of Law Research Center, Duke University. 1965.

Le Borge, J.   Dix ans de politique américaine au Vietnam. 1964. 20 Rev. de
Défense Nationale 1614–31.

Lindholm, Richard Wadsworth, ed.   Vietnam: the first five years; an international symposium. Lansing, Michigan State Univ. Press. 1959. 365p.

McCabe.   Impossible alternatives. Feb. 3, 1964. 47 New Leader 3.

McNamara, Robert S.
Buildup of U.S. forces in Viet-Nam.   1965. 53 Dep't State Bull. 369–74.
South Viet-Nam.   1964. 35 (3) Current Notes on Int'l Aff. 57–67.
South Viet-Nam—the United States policy.   1964. 30 Vital Speeches
394–99.
United States policy in Viet-Nam.   Washington, Bureau of Public Affairs,
Dep't of State. 1964. 7p.

Markbreiter, Tuyet Nguyet.   Vietnamese dilemma . . . events of the decade
since the signing of the Geneva agreement. 1965. 47 Far. E. Econ. Rev.
552–55.

Mecklin, John.   Mission in torment; an intimate account of the U.S. role
in Vietnam. Garden City, N.Y., Doubleday. 1965. 318p.

Murti, B. S. N.   Vietnam divided: the unfinished struggle. New York, Asia
Publishing House. 1964. 228p.

Mus, Paul.   Vietnam, sociologie d'une guerre. Paris, Editions du Seuil.
1952. 375p.

Nguyen Thai Binh.   Vietnam, the problem and a solution. Paris? Vietnam
Democratic Party. 1962. 145p.

Nguyen Thal.   Is South Vietnam viable? Manila, Printed by Carmelo &
Bauerman. 1962. 314p.

Osborne, Milton E.   Strategic hamlets in South Viet-Nam; a survey and a
comparison. Ithaca, Southeast Asia Program, Dep't of Asian Studies, Cornell University. 1965. 66p.

Paillat, Claude.   Dossier secret de l'Indochine. Paris, Presses de la Cité.
1964. 408p.

Political and military aspects of U.S. policy in Viet-Nam. 1965. 53 Dep't State Bull. 342–56.

The republic of Viet Nam. 1959. 30 Current Notes on Int'l Aff. 406–15.

Rusk, Dean.
Secretary Rusk reviews efforts to reach peaceful settlement in southeast Asia. 1965. 53 Dep't State Bull. 5–12.
The stake in Viet-Nam. 1963. 48 Dep't State Bull. 727–35.

Sacks, I. Milton. Marxism In Viet Nam (in Trager, Frank N., ed. Marxism in southeast Asia, a study of four countries. Stanford, Stanford Univ. Press, 1959, pp.102–70)

Scigliano, Robert G.
Political parties in South Vietnam under the republic. 1960. 33 Pac. Aff. 327–46.
South Vietnam: nation under stress. Boston, Houghton, Mifflin. 1963. 227p.
Vietnam—politics and religion. 1964. 4 Asian Survey 666–73.

Shah Ikbal Ali Sirdar. Viet Nam. London, Octagon Press. 1960. 232p.

Shaplen, Robert. The lost revolution. New York, Harper & Row. 1965. 404p.

Simpson, H. R. A dirty, dangerous business. 1963. 40 (4) For. Serv. J. 46–50.

Stevenson, Adlai E. Southeast Asia—the threat to peace and security. 1964. 30 Vital Speeches 487.

Struggle for South Vietnam: by the editors of Deadline data on world affairs. 1963. 1 (7) On Record 1–72.

Symposium on America's stake in Vietnam, Washington, D.C. 1956. Report. New York, American Friends of Vietnam. 1956. 110p.

Tran-Van-Tung. Viet-Nam. New York, Praeger. 1959.

Tregaskis, Richard W. Vietnam diary. New York, Holt, Rinehart & Winston. 1963. 401p.

The United States and the situation in Vietnam. April 1965. 44 Cong. Dig. 99–128.

Vietnam. Communist aggression against the republic of Viet-nam. Saigon. 1964. 181p.

Vietnam.
Violations of the Geneva agreements by the Viet-Minh communists. Saigon. 1959. 158p.
Violations of the Geneva agreements by the Viet-Minh communists, from July 1959 to June 1960. Saigon. 1960. 46p.

Vietnam. Constitution. The constitution of the republic of Vietnam. Saigon, Secretariat of State for Information. 1956. 40p.

Viet Nam: documents on Communist aggression. 1962. 33 Current Notes on Int'l Aff. 27–39.

Viet Nam. Embassy. United States. Declaration of the republic of Viet Nam in relation to the proposal of the Hanoi authorities for the "establishment of normal relations" between the communist north and the free, republic of Viet Nam in the south. Washington, D.C. 1958. 8p.

Vietnam. Ministry of Information. The problem of reunification of Vietnam. Saigon. 1958. 105p.

Warner, Denis.   The last Confucian; Vietnam, south-east Asia and the west. Baltimore, Penguin Books.

Warner, Geoffrey.   Escalation in Vietnam. 1965. 41 Int'l Aff. 267–77.

Welty, P. S.   Viet-Nam today. 1962. 125 World Aff. 4–12.

Worsnop, Richard L.   Negotiations with communists (Viet-Nam). April 21, 1965. Editorial Research Rep. 283–300.

Wurfel, David.   A formula for Viet-Nam. Jan/March 1965. 21 (1) India Q.